JOURNEY
TO THE
CENTER OF THE SOUL

Dr. G Aldana

First Edition

PAGE PUBLISHING, INC.
New York, NY

First originally published by Page Publishing, Inc. 2017

ISBN 978-1-63568-266-3 (Paperback)
ISBN 978-1-63568-267-0 (Digital)

Printed in the United States of America

ACKNOWLEDGEMENTS

The modern day psalmist writes, "You Raise Me Up," in the song of the same name by Beaty Swallocks and popularized by The Celtic Woman.

The words of this song that stand out the most for me are: "I am strong, when I am on your shoulders. You raise me up, to more than I can be."

<u>GOD</u>

I recognize God, first and foremost, as the one who has raised me up to be more than I can be.

I believe that God is completely and utterly in love with Me! No matter how many mistakes I make, no matter where I am in my life, no matter what I think of myself God loves me.

God is my "Higher Power", as He is called in some recovery groups. God has stuck with me regardless of what I have said or done in the past, just like He promised He would. ☺.

I don't know much about God, even after Seminary and a lifetime of trying to think and act like a Christian, but this I have found to be true: "Jesus loves me, this I know, for the Bible tells me so". In fact, it's obvious to me now that I'm loved by God the Father, Son and Holy Spirit regardless of myself. THANK GOD!

<u>OTHER AUTHORS</u>

There are many, even more than mentioned here, that have impacted my life. Some of those authors are: God, who inspired a bunch of guys, and probably women, to write the Bible, and others who compiled the inspired works of God (i.e. different books) so that the Bible would make sense to me and us.

Other authors would include, but are not limited to, the following:

Dr. Gary R. Sweeten, Founder, Teleios Ministries, Life Way Counseling Centers, Equipping Ministries, International, Sweeten Life Systems, Inc www.sweetenlife.com
Patient Home Advantage, L3C www.patienthomeadvantage.com

Dr. Sue Johnson, Clinical Psychologist and Distinguished Professor at Allian International University, San Diego; Author of "Hold Me Tight" and "Love Sense". @littlebrown on Twitter and at Facebook.com/littlebrownandcompany

MY CHILDREN

Carol and I have two boys or maybe we should say, they have us. One of my sons, David Suboticki, who when I occasionally advise him, relentlessly confronts me with the words, "How's that working for you, Dad". Dave gives me "pause" and reminds me to practice what I preach and evaluate what I practice.

My other son, Damian Aldana, is a constant reminder of myself and how I behaved as a youth. It's like looking in a mirror to my past; I don't always enjoy that. Once I am over the Post Traumatic Stress Disorder (PTSD) from looking at myself, I am able to compose myself and love him as a father should. Damian is also good for me.

CLOSE FRIENDS

I've had many and I'm still adding to my friendship base. Since in recovery I've learned how to have friends, real friends, that aren't afraid to tell me the truth about myself or to share the truth about themselves so we can pray for each other. This is what church was really meant to be.

WIFE (I've saved the best for last.)

There are many wives (that's supposed to be funny☺). I've been married three times before. Carol, my fourth wife, is my wife of 31 years. "Volume Four", as my relatives call her, and like God, Carol has stuck with me regardless of myself.

In fact, Carol is the closest human that I have ever found (or God found for me) that has helped me feel and experience the relentless love and power of God. Don't you know, Carol must have had a "Higher power" in order to do that. I'm no picnic.

Carol is also a writer, a murder mystery writer, and has given me immeasurable help with this book. For that, I express my gratitude.

BOOK ENDORSEMENTS

"Greg Aldana and his wife Carol attended a LIFE Seminar I conducted at The First Presbyterian Church in San Mateo, California in the 80's. It was immediately apparent that this was a couple with great energy, awesome commitment to Christ and a wealth of talents and gifts. Greg has used those attributes to attain advanced degrees in theology and is a natural in care and counsel. Much of his compassion comes from personal experiences in both receiving and giving soul care and soul cure. As a result his relationships and presentations are never dull theory but Spirit enlivened sharing that comes from deep within his soul. May the same God that brought him peace and power grant you the same as you drink from the fountain of life."

By:
Dr. Gary R. Sweeten
Founder, Teleios Ministries
Life Way Counseling Centers
Equipping Ministries, International
Sweeten Life Systems, Inc www.sweetenlife.com
Patient Home Advantage, L3C www.patienthomeadvantage.com

"I have both known and worked with Greg Aldana for many years. He loves God, loves people, loves the Scriptures, and most important of all, he gives credit for his love by pointing to its true source: Jesus with His Gospel message of forgiveness and healing.

Greg's enthusiastic approach to ministry and its application of scripture are refreshing. I have seen his heart for small groups and genuine interaction as he encourages Christians to take off their masks, show themselves as they truly are, and make themselves mutually accountable to grow in the Spirit of God.

I am glad to see that Greg has finally found a venue to broaden the scope of these experiences and insights so that others can share in the benefits.

Bob Siegel
Christian apologist and radio talk show host
KCBQ, Sunday, 6 PM
Author of "I'd Like To Believe In Jesus, But…"

CONTENTS

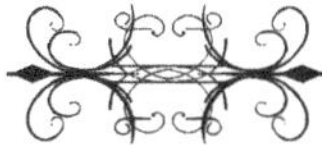

THE HISTORY

There is a new wave of the Holy Spirit taking place. This new wave began quietly about eighty years ago between a couple of men seeking God's assistance as they tried to work through their old hurts, hang-ups, bad habits, and bad addictions.

This new wave has since grown into an International Wave, attracting many people from many different nations, which you can witness every year at Alcoholic Anonymous Rallies around the world, including San Diego, California and every year at Celebrate Recovery meetings world wide as well as every August at Saddleback Church in Lake Forest, California. However, only a small portion of the entire Church has caught this new and explosive wave of the Holy Spirit. The fact that the whole Church has not caught this new wave is why God told me to write this book. We call it a bridge book, bridging groups of all kinds, including a small portion of some churches with the whole Church, the rest of the Church.

Currently, this new wave is permeating though a small portion of each different denominational and nondenominational segment of the Church, in both Christian and even non-faith-based groups. It is even moving strongly through groups of the unchurched, atheists, and agnostics, proving that God loves us all. God is not concerned whether or not individuals attend church services or not as much as he is interested in a personal relationship with each person.

This new wave of the Holy Spirit is solidly restoring, healing, and equipping all the wounded in and through a sustainable, maturing process we call journey to the center of the soul or JCS, and in the process, it's bringing unchurched people back into the Church or community groups of people in gathering places who are looking for recovery.

But when they are coming back into a church, it is becoming a new kind of church, a church that has been recovered and restored, a church on fire, with vigor, joy, forgiveness, love, and peace, ready to serve, share, and be transparent again—a replica of the first-century church. However, the majority of the Church, has not caught this new wave yet. That's what this bridge book, Journey to the Center of the Soul, is orchestrated by God to do.

This new wave of the Holy Spirit is sustainable and is equipping those who have experienced this movement by not only giving them genuine practical tools and experiences of healing and wholeness but receiving it from those who have already experienced the same.

Some of Christ's words are in bold and a few are exact quotes from the Bible, as noted. However, I do not profess to know most of the exact words Jesus said to his journeyers as they followed him. When you see most of his words in bold type, they are not his exact words I'm quoting (the Bible says I could get in much trouble if I added or changed anything). The bold type is merely for contrast, a teaching tool, and to help you expand your imagination as you navigate your way through understanding and experiencing this new wave of the Holy Spirit that comes from reading, following, and especially from doing the work as you answer the questions that are asked in this book, *Journey to the Center of the Soul.*

Remember, it only works if you work it, and it won't if you don't.

INTRODUCTION

During my recovery and while at my own Journey to the Center of the Soul international conference, God spoke to me and inspired me to write this book. For some time, I had realized the larger portion of each church was not experiencing this new wave of the Holy Spirit. The majority of the Church was missing out, not because they wanted to, but because they had developed a stigma about "those people who meet over there in that part of the church."

The majority of the Church didn't comprehend the universal spiritual offering to the whole Church or the "how-to" part of it. And so, the Lord told me to "write this book" for the rest of the Church. I was told to write this book for all the Church "small groups" that meet regularly for fellowship, learning, and service as well as for any group of two or more people anywhere.

People, including the majority of the church, often do things "as usual" because they are not aware that "if you keep doing what you keep doing, you'll keep getting what you keep getting," and what they keep getting is "church as usual"—a comfortable church. However, that's not what God ever intended the Church to be.

Because of the way the church has usually dealt with hurts, bad habits, hang-ups, and bad addictions in the past (name and claim a Scripture verse), they may be denying, ignoring, or have even forgotten what is driving them to consistently fail at overcoming their problems.

There is hope. If, like the Apostle Paul, you can't understand why you "keep doing what you keep doing" even though you know it is just wrong, then *Journey to the Center of the Soul* is written for you. You will not only be able to answer why, but you'll be able to *get set free!*

If you have any past hurts, bad habits, hang-ups, or bad addictions, and finish this *Journey to the Center of the Soul,* then you are about to experience an explosion of grace, mercy, forgiveness, empowerment, and recovery of your spirit, like never before.

This book comes with a promise: It works if you work it, and it won't if you don't.

If you do the work laid out in this book, you will come to feel a new wave of the Holy Spirit and will be empowered by God to do certain things you never tried before. Remember, this will all happen as you complete the required work on the twelve days of journey with Jesus Christ in the context of a small group (two or more).

If you are not already in a small group, then find one that is taking the journey to the center of the soul. It does not have to be a Church small group (i.e., life group, study group, etc). It can be any kind of small group where there are two or more people.

You may have to join a small group in another church, or some other kind of group, or just find a buddy and work the book *Journey to the Center of the Soul* if you can't get one started in your church.

The original biblical scriptures omitted much of what was said, taught, and shown to the journeyers by Jesus as they journeyed with him throughout his ministry.

This book is my interpretation of, not so much what Jesus might have said, but, as he was always interested in our recovery (healing) and empowerment (building up), how he might have said what he needed to communicate in order to help us recover, be built up again (empowered), and trained for ministry.

In some cases, I extrapolated (pulled out and interpreted) from the scriptures, creating my personal hermeneutic (expanded interpretation) of the scriptures. The goal was to illuminate the meaning of the scripture verses within the context of this book's primary goal which is, the recovery of our very souls (to unshackle ourselves from what is preventing us from being who God wants us to be). Let me encourage you to allow

God to mold and create within us a new character so we can really transform into the new creatures he intended us to be.

In this book, there are many assumptions. I like to call them "holy assumptions" based on my imagination of what I believe Jesus might have said to us if we were on a journey with him.

Learn more about who I am, my experiences, and my Author's Blog about my daily adventure, including PAGE PUBLISHING experiences in writing this book, JOURNEY to the Center of the Soul (JCS) at: www.gregaldana.com.

AN INVITATION

This book will enhance your spiritual insight, provide practical tools, and expand your imagination so that you can comprehend and follow the day-by-day interaction with Jesus as you journey with him.

In my humble opinion, Jesus is the author and redeemer (recoverer) of our souls and spirits and this author's motivation and guide for this book.

In the very beginning of Christianity, over two thousand years ago, Jesus began his ministry by gathering his leadership team, his journeyers. If you recall, these journeyers were not the cream of the crop nor were they among the learned and religious of the Old Testament scholarly, Pharisees, and Sadducees.

The ones who Jesus called upon for his leadership team were the least of these, should any person boast. So what did he do with them? Jesus "fit who he called." How did he do this?

We have glimpses of how he fit or equipped his early journeyers, as we read the New Testament, but we don't have the complete picture of what occurred.

However, as Jesus equipped (fit) his journeyers, we see pieces of what the "equipping" may have looked like as the Holy Spirit of God descended on them and a new wave of the Holy Spirit came over them. That specific wave has not ceased. It may have

slowed down from time to time, but it has never stopped and never will. In fact, it is gaining massive momentum and getting ready to move in a different way and in an explosive way again!

So...

Join me on a journey as we read, study, and work through this book. And walk with us as we work through one of my holy fantasies of what it may have been like to be one of Jesus's early journeyers and be equipped, restored, and recovered by the Master himself day by day, night by night. Let's walk with him together on his journey, step by step. Reimagine with me what it would have been like to walk, eat, sleep, learn, witness, and exercise your faith, all at the feet of Jesus himself.

Jesus says to you, **"Come follow me"** (Mathew 4:19).

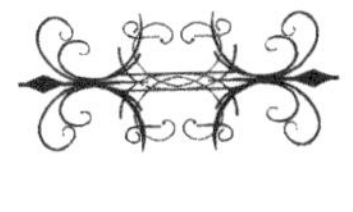

CHAPTER 1

The First Day with Jesus

On the first day as you began to follow Jesus, you observed him as you were fishing or taking in the sun in the grassy area near a big lake.

You watched him get in a boat and tell a fisherman to cast his line out in a specific area of the lake not fished before. The fisherman miraculously began to pull in one huge netful of fish after another until the boat was more than full. It was overflowing with fish!

You watched this fisherman place his arms around Jesus and hug him unceasingly because he knew this was a special man, a man who could even command the fish to get into the net.

Jesus rode in the boat as it sailed ashore where you and others came close to him as he departed from the boat onto the shore. Most who had watched this fishing miracle fell at the feet of Jesus. All seemed in awe, in shock, as we realized we were in the presence of supernatural greatness. Some seemed a little scared.

As Jesus stepped out of the boat, he said, "**Don't be afraid. For those who follow me, I will make you fishers of men**." I didn't know quite what he meant by "fishers of men." The first thing I thought, because I'm a fisherman, is what kind of bait and tackle do you use? But without hesitation, you left everything you had, including your home, and followed him—the beginning of your journey to the center of the soul with Jesus.

On the first night, you made your bedding, like the others who followed him, and then moved over, next to the fire where Jesus was.

I sat on a flat raised stone next to Jesus. I began eating what was prepared and waited anxiously for Jesus to speak.

Jesus started out by praying, almost melodically. His words, I remembered, were similar to the words from Psalm 30:11, paraphrased: ***Father, you turned my wailing and my mourning into dancing and singing. You removed my sackcloth and clothed me with Joy so that my heart may sing your praises and not be silent. Father God, I will praise you forever.***

Then, Jesus looked directly into our eyes and said, ***"Blessed are you who are spiritually poor, who are drained, spent, and have hit bottom, for yours is the kingdom of heaven."***

You felt as if he was talking directly to you and you alone. You knew you had deep hurts, bad habits, some hang-ups, and maybe some bad addictions, and that you felt you were at the end of your rope with your marriage and your finances. You have a friend who is sitting next to you who also dropped everything and is following Jesus on this journey to the core of the soul. You knew your friend has already been thrown out of his home for drinking, gambling, and abusing drugs. Yet you couldn't help but lose an awareness of your friend, or anyone else in the group of fellow journeyers, as you focused on Jesus, listening intently for his next words. You couldn't quite comprehend how you could be so blessed to have "inherited the kingdom of God," as Jesus had just said. However, you were willing to learn and understand, and then the rabbi (teacher) spoke again, saying, **"If you are feeling powerless to control some of the things you think and do, and your life seems unmanageable, then you may be at a place where you now know, without a doubt, you need help. And that awareness of needing help makes you ready and you are able to take your first steps into the kingdom of heaven. Blessed are you."**

* * *

I knew that as a result of my mistakes, risks, and hurts, I had developed anxiety that caused me to waste precious energy, thinking about my past and worrying about my future. I knew I had secrets, sick secrets (I'm only as sick as my secrets), and that kept me anxious and prevented my growth, but I was embarrassed about those secrets and didn't want to disclose them to anyone else. I knew the truth would set me free, but I didn't want to tell the truth to anyone. I was trapped, and it was a trap of my own making. I had even isolated myself from God because I knew he knew about my secrets, and I was embarrassed about that too. I was denying letting people know my real sins, my deepest hurts, hang-ups, bad habits, and bad addictions because I was embarrassed and didn't want anyone to know. My denial and alienation from others and from God only magnified my hurts and embarrassment, and soon, my secrets festered and rooted into deep shame and guilt.

Jesus said to us, **"Let me teach you an acronym. I want you to memorize and teach the acronym to others so they can be encouraged to come out of denial and come face-to-face with a past that they may have been trying to forget."** Jesus quoted Jeremiah 6:14, saying, **"You can't heal a wound by saying it is not there."** Then Jesus taught us about using the word D-E-N-I-A-L.

In the following acronym, Jesus said,

- **The *D* in the word DENIAL will help you remember the word *disables.* Denial only disables our feelings by repressing and freezing our emotions. Over time, this creates disease in our bodies and minds, affecting our spirit, especially when using artificial substances to try to suppress those feelings. I will help you face and understand your past and the associated feelings so you can work through them, pray through them, and be free of them—free from the grip your secrets have on you.**
- **The *E* in the word DENIAL will help you remember the words *energy lost.* One of the side effects of denial is anxiety, which causes you and others to waste precious energy, time, and money. Some of you run from your past while worrying about your future. I want you to teach them not to worry about their past or their**

future because it is only in the present, only today, right now, where positive change and healing occurs."

Jesus then quoted from some of the words I remembered from Psalms 146:7 saying, **"God frees the prisoners, those who are in spiritual and mental bondage. God lifts the burdens from those bent down, hunched over, beneath their loads of the past, the present, and the future. God does this in the present, your present."**

- **The *N* in the word DENIAL will help you remember that denial *negates* growth because you are only as sick as your secrets. Teach them they cannot recover until they are ready to step out of denial and conquer the truth, which will set you and them free. Are you ready? Will they be ready?**

  Remember: Only teach them these things if they are ready; otherwise, you are wasting your time and theirs. If not now, the time will come when they are ready to be healed, to learn, and to discover the ministry God has planned for them. They will be ready to enter into the kingdom of heaven, and I will call them blessed.

The Psalmist wrote, **"They cried to the Lord in their troubles, and he rescued them! He led them from their darkness and shadow(s) of death and snapped their chains."** Jesus said, **"It's important to remember that it took them 'crying out' first. Someday, just like you, they will cry out to God, and as they submit their 'wills' to God, they will soon hear those chains that kept them in bondage for so long, snap off, and they will be free at last."**

Jesus was quoting from Psalm 107:12–14, one of my favorite psalms of hope. Then Jesus went on to teach us.

- **The *I* in the word DENIAL will help you remember to teach them that their denial *isolates* them from God. God's light shines on the truth; however, our denial**

keeps God's light from shining and will keep you and others in the dark until we cry out and surrender to God.

Then I remembered the words of 1 John 1: 5–7 (OTB) paraphrased, **"God is light, in Him there is no darkness at all. [So] If we claim to have fellowship with Him, yet walk in the darkness [trying to function with our past hurts, habits, and hang-ups], we lie and do not live by the truth. But if we walk in the light, as He [God, Jesus, The Holy Spirit—The Triune God] is the light, [only then do] we have fellowship with one another [and with the Triune God] and the blood of Jesus, [God's only begotten Son] His Son, purifies us from all sin."**

Then Jesus said,

- **The *A* in the word DENIAL helps your remember to teach them that their denial will continue to *alienate* and separate them from genuine relationships.**

  Denial, like the enemy of our souls, tells you that you are getting away with it. They will think no one knows about their hurts, bad habits, hang-ups, and bad addictions, but others inherently do know because they can see what we can't. Your friends and family don't have the problem of not being able to see the forest for the trees. Your denial will even resonate with them and reminds them of their own hurts, bad habits, hang-ups and bad addictions. So those in denial end up avoiding anyone that might know the "real them." The final outcome of denial is alienation, separation from God and people we need.

Just then, I remembered the words from Ephesians 4:25 (TLB), paraphrased, **"Stop lying to each other, tell the truth for we are parts of each other, that's why we resonate, with each other and when we lie to each other we are only hurting ourselves."**

Then Jesus said,

- **The *L* in the word DENIAL helps you remember to teach them that denial just *lengthens* the amount of time they carry the hurt. They are usually under the delusion that their denial or bad addiction protects them from their hurts, bad habits, and hang-ups but all it does is reinforce their bad addiction.**

  The truth is, denial and a bad addiction just allows the hurts, bad habits, hang-ups, and bad addictions to stay longer, until they begin to fester, like gangrene to an untreated wound, until those hurts, bad habits, hang-ups, and bad addictions grow into debilitating wounds of binding shame and guilt. Whereas God and I promise that if you journey through life with us, learning and practicing what we ask, and submit to us, we will heal your wounds, your hurts and help you take away your bad habits (all of them), hang-ups, and bad addictions, and in addition, we will give you back a spirit of power, a sound mind and body and your health! God and I will replace what the locus have taken and give you more than before!

Just then, I realized that, in the context of our recovery, Jesus was quoting from Jeremiah 30:17 and Joel 2:25 (OTB) all paraphrased, when He said, **"For I will restore health to you, and your wounds I will heal, declares the Lord… I will restore to you the years that the swarming locust have eaten, because of your hurts, bad habits, hang-ups, and bad addictions."**

Then Jesus said, **"As you are taking your first steps with me on this journey, let me ask you this: What areas of your life do you think you have control over, and what areas do you feel are out of your control and unmanageable?"**

I responded first, saying;

___

___

___

___

Then Jesus said, "**Before we proceed further, let me set the following guidelines for our small group as we continue to share our answers with each other:**

- **I'd like you to keep your sharing focused on your own individual thoughts and feelings, not someone else's—some of you might have to get used to this.**
- **I'd like you to keep your sharing time to only a few minutes each. Taking too much time to share, so that someone else has less time to share, is an act of selfishness and some of you might just have to get used to a time limit.**
- **When someone is sharing, you should only listen and never comment. I call this cross talk. Each person on this journey needs to feel free to express his/her feelings without interruptions.**
- **The group is listening, *never* commenting on what someone else shares. They follow this protocol so as to support each other, *not to fix each other*. We are going to let God's Holy Spirit and each individual's guide work with each journeyer to facilitate a deeper kind of support, and any fixing or changing that might take place will be between the individual journeyer and their chosen guide and God. No one else.**
- **Anonymity and confidentiality are critical. *What is shared* within the group or individual men and women groups *must stay* in the group. Everyone, repeat: What is said here and shared here stays here and only here. Hear hear! Now everyone repeat, hear, hear! The only exception to this rule of anonymity is if someone**

threatens to harm herself or himself or another. I will have to report this behavior to the nearest Pharisee or Sadducee (police).☺

- **In our groups, we cannot tolerate offensive language because we are a Christian group. Fighting, poor or nasty stories or nasty language that may threaten another's safe journey to the center of the soul will not be tolerated."**

We all, one by one, agreed to the guidelines, then, as the day began to darken a little and someone put another log on the fire, Jesus said, **"Do you think being anxious about things has helped you?"**

I responded first again, saying;

____

____

____

____

Then Jesus asked some curious questions. I wasn't sure why he asked it, but he said, **"When you were a small child, how did you get attention? How did you protect yourself when you felt threatened?"**

Finally, someone else responded first by saying;

____

____

____

____

Jesus then said to us, **"What was your family secret that no one, outside the family, would know about?"**

Someone else responded first by say ing;

As the evening began to set and the fire, in the center of all of us, seemed to grow in intensity, we could see Jesus rubbing his hands together, and with a smile on his face, he looked at us and quoted Lamentations 3:40 (NIV), saying, **"Let us examine our ways and test them, and let us return to [God]."**

Jesus told us that as we "examine our ways," not to feel bad about our lack of control. He knows a man who will soon say he has nothing good that lives in him, just his sinful nature. Jesus knows that this man has the desire to do what is good, but he can't implement it all the time. Jesus was referencing the scriptures in Romans 7 about Paul.

Jesus gave us all hope when he said that God, a power greater than us, could restore our out of control lives to a life of joy and peace as we continue to walk and share together on this mutual journey.

As night fell and we huddled together, wrapping our jackets and blankets around our bodies, Jesus asked us a few questions before we prayed and laid ourselves down to sleep. Jesus asked, **"How have you handled emotional hurts and life's disappointments in the past?"**

We answered him. I replied first saying,

Then Jesus said something comforting that made me feel safe. He said to keep this and our answers to ourselves as we proceed to walk with each other on this journey, and as a result of our journey, we will become close friends and bond with each other. **Let's not disclose our answers to anyone else outside of our small group of**

journeyers. Later, we can decide if we wish to share our personal answers with others. We agreed.

Jesus then proceeded to ask the last couple of questions for the evening, and my eyes opened wide again. I was beginning to get drowsy, feeling warm and comforted in the presence of Jesus and others.

Jesus asked, ***"How do you anticipate addressing those things in your life, in those areas of your life, that you have been hiding? Those things you have been denying and keeping secret?"***

This time, there was a long pause from the whole group. Finally, I spoke up first and began to list the areas of my personal and professional life and the matters which I had preferred to keep hidden in the past.

I felt safe around Jesus and, strangely enough, around the people (journeyers) in our group, our fire circle, my new circle of friends. I could hardly believe I said the following, but I did, and it felt great! I said,

____

____

____

____

Then Jesus asked, **"Of those areas of your life and those secrets you just spoke of, which ones do you think you are able to face head on, working through them by talking about them, and thereby break the hold they have had on you in your past?"** I answered first saying,

____

____

____

____

Jesus said, "**Before I pray and we all go to sleep, let me ask you one more set of short questions. Do you feel closer to each other already? Do you promise to be on your honor and protect each other's secrets that we have disclosed?"**

Someone else answered first saying,

____

____

____

____

Jesus then said something we thought was odd. He said, "**I know some of you have these futuristic mobile phones so you need to realize they won't work here. However, before you get back home, I would like you to trade each other's telephone numbers, and whenever you get back home, I want you to get used to 'checking in' with each other at least twice a week. You can do the same thing manually, without phones, as we walk together on our journey together. Okay?**"

We agreed and wondered how Jesus knew about mobile phones! ☺

Summary of the First Day
What We Learned

At the end of the first day, we quit denying reality, and instead, we realized we were powerless over our bad habits, hurts, hang-ups, and bad addictions and that our lives had become unmanageable.

We were also encouraged not to fear and learned about the acronym DENIAL, as well as what our focus is and that we are *not to try and fix* anyone else but ourselves. We learned about self-examination. We promised each other to keep anonymity (secrecy, concealment), what's seen here and said here stays here. Hear hear!" And we began to bond with each other.

This reminded me of Romans 7:18–21 (OTB), paraphrased, **"For I know that I am damaged, like everyone else, and thereby evil can dwell in my flesh. For, as I grow in Christ, I have the desire to do what is good and right, but not always the ability to always carry it out. Instead, there are times when I do not do the good I want, but instead, the evil I do not want is what I keep on doing. I do this evil because of my sin, my hurts, bad habits, hang-ups, and bad addictions that still dwell within my mind and body. I know that with time and without correction, they will dwell and root in my heart and spirit. This conundrum is the law of things, my sin nature—that when I want to do right, evil, prompted by my hurts, habits, hang-ups, and bad addictions, lie close at hand within me to try and persuade me to do what is wrong again. Jesus, I really need your help!"**

Jesus then prayed to God out loud and blessed us by saying a prayer I remember from part of Luke 4:18 (NIV), paraphrased:

> ***The spirit of the lord is on me because he has anointed me to preach the good news to the poor. He has sent me to proclaim freedom for the prisoners and recovery of sight for the blind, to release the oppressed, to proclaim the year of the Lord's favor.*** **I bless you and command God's warring angels to surround you**

> **and protect you and his ministering angels to serve you. I bless you with God's Spirit to go before you wherever we travel on this journey together each day, step by step. I bless you with this and more with God's love and my love for you, forever and ever. Amen.**

We all said amen and lay down in our beds, sleeping as we never had before.

CHAPTER 2

The Second Day with Jesus

We awakened early in the morning, circled around the fire to warm up, and got ready to eat breakfast with Jesus himself! Jesus led us in a prayer of thanks for the food and drink we had, and then he recited an early morning melodic prayer to God, our Father. We watched and learned in amazement at his choice of words. Then, Jesus told us that when we head into town today, we would see what God had in store for us. But before we finished our breakfast and began our journey again, Jesus said,

> **Let me share something with you. If you don't understand it already, someday you will understand that there are very few things in life that you have under your control. It is then that you will fully understand the term *powerlessness*.**
>
> **When you admit you are powerless, you are admitting you are spiritually poor, that you couldn't do something by your own power and you are looking for help. It's humbling but foundationally and spiritually necessary for you to experience powerlessness.**
>
> **This place of realizing you are powerless puts you at a good beginning, a foundational place from which to build. It puts you at a place where you can be molded**

like clay, a place where you can be shaped into a new person, a "new creature," a place of blessedness which means you are ready to receive a full measure of God's grace, serenity, power, healing, and transformation. Congratulations!

A realization of powerlessness leads to blessedness. Let me explain to you, so you can teach it to others, in the following acronym of the word POWERLESS are the things that can rob you of this kind of state of powerlessness and forthcoming blessedness.

- The *P* in the word POWERLESS will reminds you of your *pride* and *pride* will always rob you of experiencing powerlessness and blessedness. In Proverbs, we learn that "pride ends in a fall, while humility brings honor" (Proverbs 29:23). Therefore, let go of your pride and let God.
- The *O* in the word POWERLESS will remind you that if you live a life of "only ifs," you will trap yourselves in your past and develop some stage of post-traumatic stress disorder (PTSD). You are thereby placing yourselves in bondage to something you cannot change, the past. Let it go... Let go and let God.
- The *W* in the word POWERLESS will remind you that *worrying* is not trusting God to take care of it all. Do not be anxious and worry about anything. God knows what is troubling you and will take care of it for you. Just let God take over and trust him wholeheartedly. Let go and let God.
- The *E* in the word POWERLESS will remind you that *escaping* (i.e., hurts, bad habits, hang-ups, bad addictions) and denying real-

ity only creates a fantasy world of unrealistic expectations for you and everyone else in your life.

- The *R* in the word POWERLESS will remind you that *resentments*, a "yeast of the Pharisee" yeast infection, are like an emotional cancer. If resentments fester and grow, they will negatively affect your rational decision-making and cause a multitude of physical, psychological, and spiritual diseases.
- The *L* in the word POWERLESS will remind you that choosing to be a loner is not wise. Loneliness does not free you of the hurts, bad habits, hang-ups and, certainly not the bad addictions that rob you of serenity. In fact, being a loner just makes everything worse because you are left with only yourselves and you are in a very poor state of mind, body, and spirit.
- The second *E* in the word POWERLESS will remind you of the *emptiness* you will always feel without a personal relationship with me and Father God.

You were all created with an addictive nature and a deep desire to worship. But God intended for you to be addicted to him and to worship him and, if you are lost and confused about your addictive nature or desire to worship because of your hurts, bad habits, hang-ups, and bad addictions you will worship other things (i.e. drugs, alcohol, food, sex, cars, homes, pastors, churches, etc.) because we are all "wired" to be addictive; it's in our DNA.

Therefore, God will do everything he can (even the sacrifice of his Son) to bring you back into a personal

relationship with him, but God will not override the will he created in you so you will have to, at some point in your life, swallow your pride and cry out to him. You will find that God has always been ready, with open arms, to welcome you back and begin to build you up and clear up your confusion.

Jesus took another bite of bread, swallowed it, and told us his mission is to help us to understand and live, day by day, the fullness of a real life, one which we have may not experienced before with God, our Father. He said that the kingdom of God is at hand.

Jesus also said, "Blessed are you who have been humbled and aware of your powerlessness, your spiritual poverty and need for God. You have been made ready to live a kingdom life while here, in this life, on earth."

Jesus continued with his teaching, saying,

- **The first *S* in the word POWERLESS will remind you of your human selfish nature. Until you are spiritually mature, you are like small children who only think in terms of "give me, give me, give me, it's all about me" and have not yet learned there is more blessing in giving than in receiving. You will lose your life, your soul, if you live by the immature standards of the world to have as much as you can. On the other hand, your soul will strengthen and mature as you sacrifice your time, money, and possessions to comfort others who are in need. It's this same selfish nature that has fueled all of our hurts, bad habits, hang-ups, and bad addictions.**
- **The second *S* in the word POWERLESS will remind you of the separation from God that you think you experience from time to time. Remember, it's only a feeling and not a reality. God never separates himself from you and will never abandon you. God is always there. He's always with you. You just don't always realize it. Nothing, not even hell, can separate you from**

> **God or from the love of God. Remember, you are his child, his creation, and there is not anything he wouldn't do for you. God wants to be with you and in relationship with you, forever.**

Jesus continued to say, "**Today, as you walk with me into town, I want you to mentally review the acronym POWERLESS until you have it memorized. I want you to remember this acronym POWERLESS so you can teach it to others who want to understand what is robbing them of blessedness.**"

Jesus continued, "**When we get to town, we will break for a bite to eat and something to drink, and I'll have some questions for us to discuss.**" However, just as we walked into town, we were approached by a man who came scurrying quickly toward us, and we noticed, as he fell at the feet of Jesus, you could see that the man was covered from head to toe with a debilitating skin condition. This man, however, was aware of Jesus's reputation.

The man fell with his face to the ground and looked up. While at the feet of Jesus, the man said, "Lord, if you are willing, you can make me clean." We watched and listened as Jesus said, "**I am willing, so be clean**" (Matthew 8:3, OTB, paraphrased). We were in awe again as we observed the man's skin clear up in seconds right before our eyes!

The man who was just physically healed by Jesus was dramatically joyful and bursting with praise over his healing. Jesus specifically instructed him to not disclose his healing to anyone else except for the priest. The man, however, did not obey Jesus and blabbed about his healing as he walked and danced his way over to the priests.

As Jesus suspected, the news traveled like wildfire, and within minutes, we saw huge crowds of people rushing toward us to receive healing. We were a little overwhelmed. Jesus told us to follow Him as he went inside a building and then into a room, as if he was familiar with the ins-and-outs of this town as well as the buildings and rooms.

The room we finally went into had a door that we locked behind us and also had a table with food and drink on it, waiting for us to partake. I was amazed. We reflected on the recent words of Jesus telling us to not worry about anything and to have faith in God knowing, without a doubt, that he will provide. There before us was our room and our provision.

Of course, before we ate, Jesus led us in a prayer to thank God for His provision and care. We were amazed again as he modeled for us, this matter-of-fact way he relied on God, with confidence, expecting ahead of time, and having no doubt that God would provide and care for us.

Then after the prayer, we began to eat and drink when he asked us, **"In the past, what are some of the ways your pride has hindered or stopped you from asking for the help you needed to overcome your hurts, hang-ups, and bad habits?"**

We were gaining confidence that it was okay, even beneficial to be open and honest with one another, especially with Jesus. This time, others spoke first, as I thought over my answer to his question. One of them said,

____

____

____

____

Then Jesus said, **"Remember the *O* in the word POWERLESS? It reminded you of the "if onlys" that have kept you anchored in your past instead of living step-by-step, day-by-day in the present and letting God take care of your todays and tomorrows? What memory might you be holding onto that is in your past?"**

I couldn't wait to speak. Something immediately came to my mind, and I said,

____

____

____

____

Then I realized that as we ate lunch with Jesus, he was going to have us work through our *powerlessness*. It dawned on me this was some of the healing he had in mind for us. The kind of healing that would equip us at the same time. Wow, what a rabbi, teacher, savior!

Then Jesus asked, **"Are there things you are worried about right now, in the present? What would you like to hand over to the control of God so you won't have to worry about it any longer? Also, what things about your future are you worried about?"**

Wow! There was an excitement in the air as we sensed the Spirit of God upon us again, as we shared our answers with Jesus and with one another! I couldn't help but speak up first. I was so excited to get the weight lifted off of my shoulders! I said,

____
____
____
____

Jesus asked us another question: **"In what ways have you tried to escape your past hurts, bad habits, hang ups or bad addictions?"**

Someone else answered;

____
____
____
____

As we finished our meal, Jesus asked us another question: **"Who here has experienced the Parisee-tical yeast infection of *resentment* and would like to share how this 'yeast infection,' the anger, jealously, or hate, over those resentments, has affected your life?"**

I think that this particular question was kind of a trick, investigative question, since I was certain everyone had experienced resentments of some kind over his or her lifetime. I think Jesus was wondering who was going to try and hold back the kind of transparency Jesus had in mind for us to experience. But no one in our group seemed to hold anything back. In fact, the disciple who was the quietest and shy spoke up first, saying,

____
____
____
____

Then, Jesus asked us to take some private time to pray and rest before continuing on our journey through the city. As we were all cleaning up the room, Jesus asked us to answer this question, **"If you have ever experienced *loneliness*, do you believe it was your choice or was it forced on you? Or do you believe your loneliness was your way of *escaping* from the harm you caused as a result of your hurts, bad habits, hang-ups, or bad addictions? Do you believe that being alone in your loneliness was helping you forget or deny that any harm ever happened?"**

We began to answer each of the three questions, one by one, as we continued to clean up the room. One of the participants said,

____

____

____

____

After we cleaned the room, we sat on pillows in the round while Jesus sat at the center of our circle. Jesus asked, **"Take turns describing the *feelings* associated with the loneliness you've felt. Maybe some of you are still feeling those feelings now. Now share with the group what new ways you have found to fill that place where those feelings associated with loneliness** once resided**."**

One of the other journeyers said,

____

____

____

____

Then Jesus said, **"Selfishness and unrealistic expectations usually create problems among people. In what areas of your life do you think you've been selfish and had unrealistic expectations of yourself or someone else?"**

I remembered what I read in Galatians 5:19f (NIV): "Fits of rage… selfish ambition… drunkenness… those who live like this will not inherit the Kingdom of God." Then I answered Jesus's question because no one else was speaking up. I said,

____

____

____

____

Then Jesus said, "I want you all to take a nap. The sun is out, and it is very hot, but before we nap, I want you to answer this last question. I've noticed that most of you commented earlier that you've had experiences feeling distant from God. I'm glad you realized that it was only a feeling and not a fact. In fact, God is never distant from us. So answer this: **What is it that you think you can do to feel closer to God?**"

Someone across the room answered first saying,

____

____

____

____

Then we napped.

When we awoke, about an hour later, we left the room and followed Jesus out to the outskirts of town to another home where Jesus began to teach again. He was teaching us journeyers and the crowd as well. Jesus paraphrased the prophet Jeremiah, in Jeremiah 6:14 (NIV), paraphrased, saying, **"You cannot heal a wound by saying it is not there. Time does not heal all wounds, as is a popular thought. In fact, if you avoid addressing the wound and don't try to heal it, the wound will just fester and get worse."**

Suddenly, I realized he was talking about *denial*! If I deny I have a problem (i.e., hurts, hang-ups, bad habits, bad addictions), it can't be healed, and it will, indeed, fester and get worse. On the other hand, if I confess my problem, I can pray, I can ask for prayer, I can "talk it out" with my guide and eventually be healed. It's true! Just then, I remembered the book of James 5:16 (NIV), paraphrased: "Therefore, confess your sins, hurts, bad habits, hang-ups, and bad addictions to each other and pray for each other, so that you may be healed" so that you may be healed. Okay, okay, I get it... So that you may be healed!

As Jesus kept teaching us and the crowds, and we continued to learn from his modeling how and what to teach. We sensed and could even feel the power of God which was with Jesus. We were curious to see what Jesus would do next. In the meantime, the Pharisees and teachers of the law from several neighboring cities were part of the growing crowd.

Because of the crowd, some friends of a paralytic man had to lower their paralytic friend down through a hole in the roof of the home, where we and Jesus were, in order to place the paralytic in front of Jesus. When Jesus witnessed their tenacity, their love for their friend, and their faith, Jesus was moved. Jesus spoke to the paralytic and also called him friend, saying, "**Your sins are forgiven**" (Mark 2:9, OTB). While the Pharisees and teachers of the law were jealously grumbling and feeling resentment (yeast of the Pharisee) over what Jesus had just said, Jesus addressed the paralytic again and added, "**Get up, take your mat and go home!**" (Mark 2:11, OTB). We all witnessed a miracle again, right before our eyes!

The paralytic got up on his feet, took his mat, and walked out through the crowd, shouting praises to God and Jesus. Everyone was in awe, including us journeyers. We joined in and praised God as we watched the paralytic walk home.

We finally left this home before dusk and walked toward a nearby stream with trees and set up camp near the city. Before we were finished setting up, Jesus taught us another acronym so that we could learn how to teach HOPE to others. Jesus said,

> **Let me teach you about *hope*. Simply said, without hope, we are hopeless, but there is hope in God. The following acronym of the word HOPE will help you learn how to teach about HOPE to others.**

- **The *H* in the word HOPE will remind you to teach others that God is the only legitimate *higher* power for** humanity. All "other gods pale and fail" compared to Father God who can do for you what you, or any other lesser gods, have never been able to do for yourself with any long-term consistency.

Remember that everything that is good comes from God and God alone. In addition, everything that lives owes its life to the power of God and God alone. It is the power of God that will help you recover when nothing and no one else can.

- The *O* in the word HOPE will remind you to teach others that without an *open* heart (an open attitude) to change a hurt, hang-up, bad habit, or bad addiction, they will continue to encounter strife, stress, even disease.

  Without an open heart for change, our thinking cannot change, and we will continue practicing what we have been practicing and keep getting what we have been getting. There is a saying, "If you keep thinking what you keep thinking, you'll keep doing what you keep doing, and you'll keep getting what you keep getting. Insanity is when you think you can keep thinking the same thing and get something different." So changing what you "get" happens when, first, your "stink'n' think'n' changes."

  Teach them that with an open heart, and with asking for God's help, God's power will reach you, teach you, and help you to change your thinking, even in the midst of daily trials and tribulations. How does that happen? you ask. Because of the *P*.

- The *P* in the word HOPE will remind you to teach others that with the *power* of God, and God alone, you

have the ability to eventually think and act differently. With God, all things are possible. Remind them, they will come to understand that God's power is the only power that can change their thinking and their situations. Remind them to be patient with God and especially with themselves.

- **The *E* in the word HOPE will remind you to teach other journeyers to *encourage* each other as they wait for and encounter self-change. Change is not usually fast; it's a process, and it's not always easy when it comes, but it will come. If they don't quit and tenaciously follow these guidelines, personal change will come.**

This *Journey to the Center of the Soul* workbook and guidelines work, if you work it, but won't, if you don't.

Encourage fellow journeyers to be patient because the changes, the unshackling they have longed for, is near. Encourage fellow journeyers with a reminder that hope is found through faith in God who can do all things.

At that moment, I was not only reminded of the miracles I have witnessed from Jesus, but I was aware of the change that was already occurring in my mind (my thinking) and heart. We finished setting up camp and sat together around a fire again as some of us cooked a meal over the hot coals. Jesus, sitting with us, asked us another couple of questions, **"Before you decided to follow me and learn from me, where have you tried to find hope in the past, and did you just give up looking? Why did you give up?"**

One of the other journeyers answered first, saying,

____

____

____

____

Then Jesus asked us a few questions that kind of caught us off guard. Jesus asked us, **"What are your beliefs concerning God? Who and what do you think God is? What do you think are some of God's characteristics?"**

We all thought for a while, and then, I started by giving the following answers:

____

____

____

____

By the time we finished answering the questions, the food was ready. As we were eating, Jesus asked us the following, **"Do your feelings for your heavenly Father coincide with your feelings toward your biological father, or are they different and why?"**

Another one of the journeyers spoke up first, saying,

____

____

____

____

While we ate, Jesus asked us a few more questions, **"How do you think your relationship with Father God and me will help you honestly face the hurts, hang-ups, bad habits, and bad addictions you have, and do you think God and I will help you to accept that you have problems? Do you think that facing a reality, that you, like everyone else, may have problems, is something you have not faced before? Why?"**

That was a lot to answer, but since I had already finished my meal, I spoke up first saying,

____

____

____

____

As the others finished their meals and answers, Jesus then asked us, **"If you believe that only I and God can help you change, because you've tried most everything else, then in what areas of your life are you ready to detach from, give up, in order to allow me and God to help you?"**

One of the other journeyers was brave enough to answer first. They even seemed excited while saying,

____

____

____

____

Then, before dusk and bedtime, Jesus asked us to go, two by two for a small walk and pray to our Father in heaven, as well as think and discuss what we have seen, heard, and learned so far. Then, at dusk, he asked us to return to the campfire circle for a drink and some sweetbread. He said he had more questions for us before our bedtime prayer and sleep.

We did as Jesus instructed us. The prayer time was special, more special than usual, and the time of discussion with our walk partner was also a bonding moment. We discussed how much we earnestly believe that Father God exists, that we matter to him and Jesus. Furthermore, we discussed that God and Jesus have the power to help us confront our hurts, bad habits, hang-ups, and bad addictions, to heal us and change our thinking patterns and actions. Father God and Jesus are omnipotent (everywhere at the same time), and only they are able, having the power, to restore our sanity (to recover).

While I was walking alongside a fellow journeyer, I discussed with him that I remembered Einstein once said, "Insanity is doing the same thing over and over again and expecting a different result." I was looking forward to more change, with the help of Jesus and God, so I plan to quit, thinking the same things, so I could stop doing the same things over and over again because I agree with Einstein, it's been insane so far!

I needed different results in my life, and I'm beginning to realize that only God, the Father, the Son, and the Holy Spirit, have the will and the power to help me succeed in changing the way I'm thinking (some of it stinkin'-thinkin') and thereby change some of the things I've been believing and "doing" in my life. I am ready for change, and I am ready for God and Jesus to help me change!

We returned to the campsite at dusk, some of us later than others, but eventually, we all came together again and circled up around the campfire. The campfire illumined the camp site area as it pushed against the impending darkness and kept nightfall from encroaching in on our campsite.

Jesus began to instruct us again saying, **"I have a new acronym for you to teach others. It's from the word SANITY."**

- **The *S* in the word SANITY will remind you to teach others that God will give you the *strength* to face (confront) your hurts, bad habits, hang-ups, and bad addictions, and he will pull you through.**
- **The *A* in the word SANITY will remind you to teach others that you are, no matter what, to *accept* one another just as they are. No judging or fixing! That will give others the room that they may not have ever had before, to change, if they want to!**

  Acceptance of each other is like God's grace for us, and the act of acceptance is God's starting point with all of you. To do anything less than accepting each other is to judge others and have unrealistic expectations of others.

  Judging is God's job, not yours, and "change" is between God and those who have asked him for help to change. God will not override the will he gave someone, so why should you ever try?

Someone's journey with God is no one else's business but God's and those who are asking for help to change. They might choose to share some of their personal journey later, but it is at their discretion, between them and God and none of your business.

- **The *N* in the word SANITY will remind you to teach others that you have a *new* life, a second chance, as you surrender to Father God and me. As my father has given power to me, I will give you the power to live according to your *new* life and more, without being captive (chained) to your old thinking and your old ways.**
- **The *I* in the word SANITY will remind you to teach others to develop personal *integrity* as you make your word your bond so others can trust what you say. Keep your promises to each other and "be there" for each other when they are in need.**
- **The *T* in the word SANITY will remind you to teach others to develop *trust* amongst one another, especially to develop wholehearted trust in Father God and me. This trust with God and others will build over time as you demonstrate your personal integrity and faith to God and others, and they, to you. God and I will always have your back, whether you fully trust us or not. Nevertheless, you will need to develop more and more trust in us. God and I are your best buddies. Your guides and fellow journeryers may fail you at times (they are only human). However, God and I will never fail you.**
- **The *Y* in the word SANITY will remind you to teach others that "your higher power" is God, me, and the Holy Spirit. Our arms are always open to you…**

I remembered the story of the prodigal son as Jesus continued to say, **"Regardless of what you and others have done in the past,**

God and I are ready and willing to forgive you, right now, so that you can be unshackled and continue on with the rest of your life."

I was reminded of God's word in Romans 5:8 (OTB), paraphrased: **"While we were yet sinners, Jesus will die for us, so we can have forgiveness and can recover."**

Summary of the Second Day
What We Learned

At the end of the second day, we realized that a power greater than ourselves, God and God alone, could restore us to sanity (as God had intended). We admitted that we are powerless to recover independently, and only God has the power to help us recover from our hurts, bad habits, hang-ups, and bad addictions, and restore us to sanity.

We also learned about POWERLESS through the acronym—pride and our past, resentments, loneliness, and getting close to God. We learned about the acronym HOPE and SANITY and about the power of prayer (spending time with God).

Then I remembered the words in Philippians 2:12–13 (OTB), amplified: "Therefore, my beloved… not only as in my presence but more so in my absence, work out your recovery, with fear and trembling. It's hard, but I will give you the power to do it. It is I who works in you, both to will and to work for my good pleasure."

Jesus then prayed for us and told us to get some sleep. When I climbed into my sleeping bag, I also prayed the following:

> Father God, Jesus, in the past, I have tried to fix myself by myself, and I tried to control my life's hurts, bad habits, hang-ups, and bad addictions all by myself. I now admit that I can't do it, and I now realize that I am powerless to change anything by myself. This night, I commit to you that I will trust, believe, and receive your power to help me change.
>
> *Father God, you loved me enough to send Jesus to show me, teach me, and finally to die for me, just so I could have a chance to change and recover. Help me to be open to the hope that I can only find in*

> *Jesus, your son, and in you, oh God. Please help me to start living my life for today, in the now instead of in my past, taking one day at a time and not dreading my past or worrying about my future. Someday soon, I want to celebrate my recovery with you and others, oh Lord. Thank you, Father God, for giving us your only begotten son Jesus to show us, guide us, teach us, heal us, empower and equip us, and help us recover as we discover how to live a life in you.*

That night, the other journeyers and I slept like babies.

CHAPTER 3

The Third Day with Jesus

The next morning, when we awoke, we could see the campfire was already started, food was prepared, and Jesus was praying at a short distance from the campsite near a boulder and a tree next to the river. When Jesus noticed us approaching, he came over, sat down at the fire circle, and led us in a morning prayer.

As we began to eat, Jesus asked us a couple of questions and commented, **"What specific things have you been doing repeatedly in your past and still expected a change to happen? Would you define that as *sanity*? Explain your definition of the word *sanity*."**

I couldn't wait to answer first, so I said,

____

____

____

____

We were still eating when Jesus asked us another question and commented, **"Do you think your expectations of yourself and others are unrealistic? If so, give me some past and current examples."**

Another disciple answered first, saying,

____

____

____

____

We finished eating and began to clean up our area before we continued our journey with Jesus. As we were cleaning, Jesus asked, **"How has trusting in your own feelings and emotions caused problems for you?"**

It seemed as if he was talking directly to me. It was similar to the times when the preacher gives a sermon at church and you feel as if the entire sermon is directed at you. I was aware of the habit I had been wrestling with for so long and the subsequent hurts, hang-ups, and eventual bad habits that followed. I had something I needed to share, so I said,

____
____
____
____

When we finished sharing, we cleaned our area, packed our belongings, and were ready to walk with Jesus again. We were on a main road, just outside of the main entrance into town, when we came upon the town's tax collector. He was sitting in a tax collector's booth. We later discovered his name was Levi. Jesus amazed us again as he walked up to Levi's booth and said to Levi, **"Follow me."**

To our amazement, Levi arose from his stool, came out of his booth, and left everything behind to immediately follow Jesus. It was as if Levi had been waiting for Jesus all his life and as if Jesus knew Levi would follow Him. Levi was ready to go! My utter amazement reminded me of when I was first saved. I also seemed to have been ready when someone asked me, "Would you like to know Jesus Christ as your own personal Savior?" I had already been wooed for weeks by the Holy Spirit, and I was ready to be asked.

So now Levi, the tax collector, has joined our ranks. Levi was so moved by the presence and calling of Jesus that he insisted on taking us to his home so he could prepare a delicious banquet for Jesus and us. Others from the city and countryside, other tax collectors, some of the Pharisees, of course, and other teachers of the law who seemed to be following us also came to the banquet.

The Pharisees and teachers singled some of the journeyers out and asked us, "Why do you eat and drink with tax collectors and sinners in this house of Levi?" I think Jesus was not happy that they singled us out and asked us that question instead of him. I sensed that Jesus was watching over us, like a father would make sure his children did not get picked on. Before we could give an answer, Jesus actually answered their question and said out loud for all to hear, **"It is not the healthy that need a doctor but the sick. I have not come to call** those who think they are **the righteous, but sinners to repentance" (Luke 5:32, OTB,** Paraphrased**).**

The Pharisees and the teachers did not let up, and they still don't, to this day. It seemed the Pharisees and teachers of the law had an axe to grind. They said to Jesus that his journeyers eat and drink joyfully while the journeyers of John the Baptist probably would have been fasting and praying.

Jesus seemed to have a look of despair as he asked them, **"Can you expect the guests of the bridegroom to fast while the bridegroom is with them?** [Jesus was referring to himself as the "bridegroom."] **Nevertheless, the time will come when this bridegroom will be taken from his guests** [the guest were and are those who believe, they are the children of God]**." Then Jesus said, and at that time, his guests will fast.**

The other journeyers and I remembered that the children of God were indeed sad and fasted when Jesus was taken from them, after being beaten and crucified. The church still mourns that day—Good Friday, usually a Friday in early April, right before Easter.

When I heard Jesus say what he said to the Pharisees, it became clear to me and others that we, who were currently on this journey with him, were the "guests" Jesus was talking about, and he was our bridegroom.

Sadness gripped some of us when we remembered Jesus would be taken from us. I don't think most of the Pharisees and teachers fully comprehended what Jesus was saying. Nevertheless, Jesus followed up with a parable, a great story about old versus new wine in an old versus new wineskin. I'm not sure they understood the parable either.

Regardless of the Pharisees and teachers of the law, we all had a splendid time at the banquet. When dusk came near, Jesus led us back to our old campsite and told us we would be leaving town the next day. We set up camp, created our usual campfire circle, and started cooking.

Jesus continued to teach us how to teach others by asking us, **"Regarding your decision making, as a second chance to live your life differently, how can I or Father God earn your trust, so that you will rely on us, instead of relying on your own feelings and emotions, to make decisions in the future?"**

I was a little embarrassed by the question. It was obvious to me. Jesus knew I had not fully trusted Him or God and instead had been relying on my own feelings, my own reasoning and knowledge. Look where my best thinking and decisions had gotten me, I thought. So I was compelled to be the first to answer, as I said,

____

____

____

____

Suddenly, I realized he was just not teaching us to teach others. In addition, he was in the process of reconciling us, to himself and to God! He's healing us and using us to facilitate each other's healing and equipping. Wow! I now saw what is happening! As I realized these things, I felt a wave of God come over me, a new wave of the Holy Spirit. This was a new kind of wave, a subtle but solid wave of God's spirit. I could almost touch it. I was wonderfully overwhelmed.

As we began to eat supper, Jesus asked us another question, **"What specific areas of your life are you ready to lose control of, in order to relinquish the control to me and to Father God?"**

One of the other journeyers quickly answered first, saying,

____

____

____

____

As we finished our meal and began to clean up to get ready for bed, I remembered a verse from Ephesians 2:12–13, and on this particular night, the verse went straight into my heart. The verse reads as follows:

> **Remember that in the past you were without Jesus, the Christ. You were not citizens of Israel, and you had no part in the agreements with the promise that God made to His people. You had no hope and you did not know God. But now, in Christ Jesus, you, who were far away from God are brought near.** (Ephesians 2: 12–13, OTB, paraphrased)

I did not want to remember the ending of Ephesians 2: 12–13, but I knew that now, more than ever, I was brought near to God… again through the blood of Christ Jesus at his crucifixion and death on the cross, but now I'm with him here, in the past, face-to-face, eating, sleeping, and learning from the master himself! Nevertheless, I shed a few tears as I remembered his sacrifice for us all, and I readied myself for bed.

Summary of the Third Day
What We Learned

At the end of the third day, we realized how important it was for us to always turn our personal wills over to the care and rule of God.

We also learned about our wills, the definition of *sanity*, *realistic expectations*, our *reconciliation*, and what it's like to follow Jesus.

This reminded me of the words in Romans 12:1 (OTB), amplified: **"I urge you… brothers and sisters, by the mercies of God and for the sake of others and yourselves, to present your bodies, personal wills, and spirits as a living sacrifice, holy and acceptable to God, which is your spiritual act of worship."**

Before we went to sleep, Jesus prayed over us again. I don't remember all of what he said, but I remember feeling comforted as he spoke. I felt safe, protected, even a little weightless, but above all, I felt very loved as I fell into a deep sleep.

CHAPTER 4

The Fourth Day with Jesus

When I awoke, I could see that a few journeyers had awakened even earlier and were with Jesus. Maybe they did early morning prayers with Jesus, I was envious. Now they were helping Jesus start the campfire. I pitched in to help. Some of us were also preparing the meal along with coffee. A few of the journeyers were still trying to wake up.

While the meal was being prepared, Jesus said, **"I want to commend those of you who have already committed to turn your lives, and especially your wills, over to my care and the care of God. I will keep praying for those who have not yet committed."**

I wondered who, in our group, could have possibly not turned their life or their will over yet? Then I realized, I can only pray for them because it wasn't any of my business. I remembered that what someone else does is between them and God and no one else, so I refocused my eyes on Jesus and on my own thoughts and actions alone.

As we began to eat breakfast, Jesus said,

> **Let me give you another acronym as a tool to help you teach others. This acronym is to help someone surrender their life and will over to me and God, as their higher power. Some might also refer to someone or something else as a higher power, and that's okay too. Here's the acronym tool using the word *turn* to**

help journeyers understand the process of "setting the foundation" for recovery.

- **The *T* in the word TURN is to remind you to teach others that *turning* over control of your lives to God and to me is paramount in order for you to** harness **the kind of real power that will ensure that you have a successful recovery. If you stay in control, well, you'll keep getting what you've been getting. Do you really want that?**

We all shook our heads no.

When Jesus taught us about the *T* in TURN, I was reminded of the words in Romans 10:9 (OTB), paraphrased: **"If you declare, out loud, with your mouth, that Jesus is Lord. If you confess that you are a sinner with hurts, bad habits, hang-ups, and bad addictions, just like all of humanity, and if you really believe in your heart that God raised Jesus from the dead, *you will be saved.*"**

Then Jesus said,

- **The *U* in the word TURN is to remind you to teach others that your best *understanding* got you where you are now (Oops!), and for most of you, I pray all of you, that's not a place you will want to remain. I pray you will want to rid yourself of the hurts, bad habits, hang-ups, and bad addictions that have kept you confounded and shackled to old troublesome behaviors and bad results.**

  The *U* reminds you and others not to rely on your own *understanding*, but instead, God's and my Understanding of things. Jesus quoted from Proverbs 3:5–6, paraphrased, **"Trust in the Lord with all of your heart and don't depend on your own *understanding*. In everything you do and say, acknowledge God, *and he***

***will make your paths straight*, not like the path you've been on."**

Jesus smiled at us again and continued,

- **The *R* in the word TURN will remind you to teach others about our essential need to *repent* in order to fully turn. To truly repent, said Jesus, you *must* turn 180 degrees the other way. In other words, refuse to live with your old hurts, bad habits, hang-ups, and bad addictions as you turn toward God and me instead. Repenting is turning and turning means to turn 180 degrees in the opposite direction.**
- **Finally, the *N* in the word TURN is to remind you to teach others that a *new* life is found as you *turn* and follow God and me. I promise you will no longer be bound by your old hurts, hang-ups, bad habits, and bad addictions, your old sinful nature, because, once you turn, you are *no longer*** enslaved to your past. **Therefore, the old hurts, hang-ups, bad habits, and bad addictions *no longer have a hold on you*!**

We realized that turning our lives and wills over to Jesus and God was a lifetime commitment not just for this journey. It will require a step-by-step, day- by-day (one day at a time) commitment to a lifelong, new way of life. I am ready.

We finished breakfast, and as we cleaned our area and packed to continue our journey with Jesus, I lifted my face toward heaven, and I was compelled to pray this prayer out loud:

> God, I have tried to take care of my hurts, hang-ups, bad habits, and bad addictions—all my sins—by myself, by my own knowledge and understanding, and I have consistently failed. Today, I'm going to confess my sins to myself, to God, to a sister or brother and guide. I'm going

> to ask for your forgiveness and turn my life over to your Son Jesus and to you, oh God. Forgive me, Lord, and fill me with the power of your Holy Spirit so I can have the strength to finish my Journey with Jesus and for the rest of my life as I continue to journey to the center of my soul with Jesus.
>
> I'm asking you, Jesus, to be my Lord and Savior. I need you, God, because I am convinced that it is only by your power and might that I can rid myself of these hurts, hang-ups, bad habits, and bad addictions that have plagued me for most of my life. God, help me to learn what Jesus has to teach me and to be open to his healing. Help me to focus less on me and my will and focus more on you and your will. Amen.

After I was finished, Jesus thanked me for praying out loud, then he said to the others, **"What does this prayer we just heard mean to you?"**

One of the journeyers responded first, ____

____

____

It was a Sabbath day as we continued our journey following Jesus. We were walking through some wild grain fields toward a synagogue. Some Pharisees were following us. As we picked some heads of grain and rubbed them together in our hands to eat the kernels, Jesus asked us another question while we were still walking. **"Is there anyone here who has not invited me to be in their heart as Lord**

and Savior? If so, why? If any of you have, please share where, when and what that experience was like."

One of the other journeyers shared first.

____

____

____

____

As we finished sharing, we were at the end of the grainfields, and the Pharisees who were following us walked closer to us to ask Jesus a question. They commented to Jesus saying, "Why have you and your journeyers picked grain on the Sabbath? It is unlawful!"

Jesus replied, **"Have you never read what David did when he and his companions were hungry? He entered the house of God, and taking the consecrated bread, he ate what was only lawful for priests to eat. He also gave some to his companions… The Son of Man [referring to Himself] is Lord of the harvest."**

I don't think some of the Pharisees understood what Jesus was saying, and the ones that did understand must have hated Jesus for pointing out that he (Jesus) was Lord of the harvest.

Jesus then led us away toward the road on our way to a nearby synagogue. Of course, the Pharisees were not far behind us. As we walked, Jesus asked us another question, **"What specific problems in the past have occurred in your life, as a result of your reliance on your own will and your own understanding?"**

I noticed it was getting easier to share, so I shared my thoughts first.

____

____

____

____

Then Jesus asked, **"What does the word *repent* mean to you, and what exactly do you need to repent from?"**

Someone else, who was usually slow to speak, quickly commented,

____
____
____
____

Then Jesus asked, **"When you turned your life and your will over to me and God, you were able to immediately experience new life. What does this term *new life* mean to you?"**

Someone else said,

____
____
____
____

Jesus then explained to us that when we give our life and will over to him and to God and proclaim him (Jesus) to be our Savior, as we repent of our sins, God has determined that we are "not guilty" of our sins any longer, including our hurts, hang-ups, bad habits, and bad addictions. In fact, we are immediately forgiven and unshackled so we can depend on the power of God to help us move forward freely and enjoy a new life of change and improvement with him and without the weight of sin any longer dragging us back down!

This reminded me of the Words of God in Romans 3:22 (OTB), paraphrased:

> **This righteousness from God (Jesus) comes through faith in Jesus Christ to *all* who believe. There is no difference (from one person to the other) because *all* (every single human being) have sinned and fall short of the glory of God. We are all in the same boat but are justified freely (nothing we do can earn it, therefore) by his grace (only by his Grace) do we receive this kind of forgiveness and are "freed up"**

unshackled, through the redemption that came by Christ Jesus (on the cross).

I was reminded of what God and Jesus chose to do (the cross) to redeem us, and I had mixed feelings of sadness, humility, and gratefulness all at the same time. I don't fully understand why, but I felt wonderful, I felt saved!

We finally made it to another synagogue (church) in another city, and Jesus walked in, and after doing a few things and speaking to some others, he began to teach all who were in the synagogue. It was almost as if the synagogue attendees expected him to teach, kind of like a guest teacher would come into another church of our era and teach and preach. The Pharisees, who were following us, entered the synagogue and joined the other Pharisees and teachers in the crowd.

Jesus noticed a man in the synagogue with a shriveled right hand. Jesus, of course, knew by this time that the Pharisees were just waiting to catch him doing something religiously heretical, not wrong, just heretical, as they saw it. Jesus stopped teaching for a while, knowing well what would happen and told the man with the shriveled hand, **"Get up, and stand in front of everyone!"**

That is exactly what the man did!

Then Jesus said to everyone, "**I ask you, which is more lawful on the Sabbath, to do good or to do evil, to save a life or to destroy a life? Is the law more important than a person's healing or recovery?**"

Then, after looking at everyone and not getting a response, Jesus told the man to stretch out his shriveled-up hand, and the man did as he was told and reached out for Jesus. Immediately and miraculously, the man's shriveled-up hand became unshriveled within seconds, right before our eyes, and took on a normal shape! It was like time-lapsed photography happening right in front of us, and we were awestruck.

But the Pharisees and teachers were furious that Jesus did this miracle during the Sabbath. I think the Pharisees were just furious that Jesus did the miracle, and they didn't and probably couldn't.

The Pharisees were angrily whispering amongst one another, and it was obvious they were plotting against Jesus—shame on them. That kind of talking and plotting against another still goes on in the church today, and it's just as ugly.

I remembered that the "religious," even today, believe that protocol (church rule) and their religion (church theology—their interpretation) are more important than the individual. I guess it's true that the Pharisees (those that control the church) can be the same yesterday, today, and tomorrow, just like God is the same yesterday, today, and tomorrow. I believe that's the "yeast" of the Pharisees (jealously, anger, rage, plotting, pride, corruption), that Jesus discussed with his journeyers when he warned them not to catch a yeast infection, the "yeast" of the Pharisees.

After some time passed, Jesus left the synagogue, and we followed Him, but this time, the Pharisees did not follow behind us.

Jesus led us down the road and to a meadow by a stream. We set up camp there, and as we were setting up, Jesus said,

> **Even after we've come this far together, some of you may still be stuck in a place of feeling like a failure. You may still be overwhelmed with fear or guilt or anger or even depression. Let me explain to you how to teach others how to get unstuck. Teach others to focus on the word *action.* I want you to remember another acronym to help you teach others how to take action.**

- **The *A* in the word ACTION will remind you to teach others to *accept* me and God as their Lord and Savior and as the only power that can give them a true and lasting recovery from their hurts, hang-ups, bad habits, and bad addictions. Ask those you are teaching to develop a relationship with us, as they would take the time to develop a friendship with a special friend. It takes time, mutual discussion (both talking and listening and listening and listening), and shared inter-**

ests. Think about what interests you and God have in common.

- **The *C* in the word ACTION will remind you to teach others to *commit* to a relationship with me and God, which means following our will, not their own will. The Psalmist wrote, "Teach me to do your will, for you are my God; may your good spirit lead me on level ground."**
- **The T in the word ACTION will remind you to teach others to *turn* it over. In other words, let go and let God by turning your life and its burdens over to me and God.**

Before Jesus finished teaching us about the full ACTION acronym, he suddenly asked us, "**What burdens are you carrying that you would like to turn over to me and to God?**"

One of the journeyers answered Jesus first, saying,

____

____

____

____

As we finished setting up camp, started a fire, and began cooking our meal, we moved to our usual friendship circle around the campfire and as we began to eat, Jesus finished the teaching of the acronym, saying,

- **The letter *I* in the word ACTION will remind you to teach others, *it's only the beginning* of a lifelong relationship with God and with me. We will faithfully complete the work we have begun in you.**
- **The letter *O* in the word ACTION will remind you to teach others that recovery happens *one* day at a time. Be patient with yourself and remember, if we get stuck in our yesterdays or worry about our tomorrows, we will waste the precious time of the present. The 'now'**

is precious, that's why it's called a 'Present' and then Jesus smiled at us as if to see if we 'got it. We can only address our hurts, hang-ups, and habits in the present.

This last letter *O* reminded me of the verse in Matthew 6:34 (OTB), paraphrased, **"So don't be anxious about yesterday, today, or tomorrow. God will take care of your past, present, and future. You are in good hands. Just concentrate on living one day at a time, moment by moment, only in the present."**

When we finished eating, cleaned up, and prepared for bed, Jesus proceeded to finish the acronym with the letter *N*.

- **The letter *N* in the word ACTION will remind you to teach others to take the *next* step of receiving my salvation and submitting to God and me, if they haven't already. This is a critical first step to enter into a relationship with me and God. Without this *next* step, without this spiritual BASE [see below], for some of you a first step, there can be no relationship with us and no solid assurance of recovery.**

Then Jesus taught us another acronym of the word *base* to help us remember how to teach others about the importance of having a spiritual *base* from which to work out our recovery, which is the next step;

- **The *B* in the word BASE_will remind you to teach others to *believe* that I have been sent to die on the cross for you, and I will show that I, God and the Holy Spirit become part of your life. Just believe!**

  Remember to teach them this: Seeing is not believing. Instead, believing is seeing. When I tell my other journeyers and disciples as well, 'Unless you are like one of these children, you cannot enter the kingdom of

heaven,' I'm referring to a child's innocent readiness to believe without seeing.

This reminded me of the words of the apostle Paul in 1 Corinthians 15:2–11 (OTB), paraphrased:

Now I would remind you, brothers and sisters, of the gospel I preached to you, which you received, in which you stand, and by which you are being saved, if you hold fast to the word I preached to you—unless you believed in vain (only said you believe but not really believe).

For I delivered to you as of first importance what I also received: that Jesus the Christ died for our sins in accordance with the Scriptures, that he was buried, that he was raised on the third day in accordance with the Scriptures and that he appeared to Cephas, then to the twelve.

Then Jesus appeared to more than five hundred sisters and brothers at one time, most of whom are still alive, though some have fallen past away (died). Then he appeared to James, then to all the apostles. Last of all, as to one untimely born (I wish I was born earlier), he appeared also to me. For I am the least of the apostles, unworthy to be called an apostle, because I persecuted the church of God (I murdered the people of God; this is my testimony.)

But by the grace of God, I am what I am (I've done what I've done, but it's now in the past), and his grace toward me was not in vain. On the contrary, I worked harder than any of the

other journeyers (in my opinion), though (regardless of my work) it was not I, but the grace of God that is with me (that gave me success). (The point is) We (continue to) preach, so you would believe. Believing is seeing.

Jesus continued to teach us, saying,

- **The *A* in the word BASE will remind you to teach others to *accept* God's free forgiveness of our sins. God's forgiveness is freely given to us. It's a good thing because you and others could not possibly earn forgiveness all by yourselves, even though some have tried (humanity's way).**

This reminded me of the words in Romans 3:21–26 (OTB), paraphrased:

But now the righteousness of God (Jesus Christ) has been manifested apart from the law, although the law and the prophets bear witness to (Jesus Christ, the righteousness of God)—the righteousness of God (Jesus Christ) through faith in Him for all who believe. For there is no distinction: for all have sinned and fall short of the glory of God and are justified by his grace as a gift through the redemption that is in Christ Jesus (no one deserves this grace of God or can earn or purchase it) whom God put forward as a propitiation (appeasement, conciliation) by his (Jesus's) blood, to be received by faith.

This was to show God's righteousness (to reveal Jesus), because in his (God's) divine forbearance (restraint, tolerance, mercy), he

> **(God) has passed over former sins. It was to show his righteousness (Jesus) at the present time, so that he (God) might be just and the justifier of the one (us who believe) who has faith in Jesus the Christ.**

Then Jesus continued to teach us, saying,

- **The *S* in the word BASE will remind you to teach others to *switch* from your own personal way and your own personal plans to God's way and God's plans for your lives.**

This reminded me of the words in Romans 12:2 (OTB), paraphrased, **"Do not choose your own will and be conformed to the ways of this world, but be transformed in recovery, as you journey with Jesus, which will renew your mind so that you can conform to the way and the will of God and that by testing, you may discern what is the will and the way of God, that good and acceptable and perfect will and way of God."**

Jesus continued,

- **The *E* in the word BASE will remind you to teach others the importance of *expressing* (sharing) with someone, your commitment to follow God's will and way and his plan for your life. God's ways are so much better than your ways.**

Summary of the Fourth Day
What We Learned

At the end of the fourth day we learned about surrendering our wills by turning and about the importance of repenting. We learned that believing by faith alone, and about, the "yeast of the Pharisees," and in addition, we learned about a strong BASE from which to work out our recovery. Finally, we learned that if we get stuck, how to get unstuck by taking ACTION.

This reminded me of the words in Lamentation 3:40–42 (OTB), paraphrased, **"Let us test and examine our ways by journeying to the center of our souls with Jesus and by being accountable to each other. In so doing, we will recover and get healed so we will be restored and can return to the Lord and his ways!"**

Then, as Jesus prayed a blessing over us, I tucked myself in and began to fall asleep. I prayed a reconfirmation prayer, saying,

> God, I believe you sent your son Jesus to die for my sins and the sins of others so that we can be forgiven, renewed, and recovered. I am sorry for my particular sins, and I want to be forgiven, please. I also want to assure you that I want to live the rest of my life *your* way, not *my* way. Please deposit your Holy Spirit in me to give me the power to change and believe and to direct my life. Not my will but your will, oh God. Amen.

CHAPTER 5

The Fifth Day with Jesus

I slept like a baby and awoke rested and feeling great. I had not felt this good in a long time. This time, I was one of the first to awaken, and I could see Jesus far away, sitting next to a tree. Next to him, the steam was steadily flowing. It looked like Jesus was praying.

One of the other journeyers who got up just before me told me, as we were setting up for breakfast, that he saw Jesus there an hour ago when he awakened. We learned later that Jesus started his day with a lot of communication with God (prayer) before he did anything else.

We quickly rallied around the fire as Jesus walked over to the campsite and led us in prayer. He lifted his hands toward heaven and thanked God for so many things, including those who were following him and learning from him, the food we were about to eat and the journey behind us plus the journey ahead of us. We all said amen, and then we began to eat our breakfast.

As we were eating, Jesus asked us, **"When you accepted me as your Savior and God and me as the new director of your lives, has your life been any different, and if so, how? If you just recently accepted us, then we are looking forward to your sharing that with the group of journeyers as well."**

I had already wolfed down most of my breakfast. I was really hungry, and now, I was enjoying some hot tea, so I spoke first, saying,

____

____

____

____

We finished eating and sharing, and as we cleaned up our area, preparing to continue our journey with Jesus, he asked us, **"What have you been able to turn over to God and how has that changed your definition of will power?"**

One of the other journeyers said,

____

____

____

____

Before we departed the campsite area, Jesus told us, **"You are being called out as leaders of other men and women. So I'm going to pray a special prayer for you because Father God has told me how special you are and how he has set you aside to teach you these things to help others recover as you show others that the kingdom of God is at hand."**

Then Jesus prayed for us. His words were healing and seemed to reach the core of our souls. In addition, he placed his hand on each one of our foreheads as he walked around continually praying, and we felt a special anointing (blessing, installing).

Some of us fell to our knees when he touched us; others just fell. Some began to sing and pray out loud, and one began to prophesy. When Jesus was finished, there was silence for a long time, and then, Jesus said amen, and we began to regroup slowly.

We felt very special after Jesus just prayed for us in that manner, and as we walked together, we felt a special bond. Then Jesus said to us, **"Is there any specific thing or things you fear turning over to the care and control of Our Father in heaven? If there is, what is keeping you from turning it over?"**

As Jesus walked us out of the area, I answered first,

____

____

____

____

We continued walking as Jesus asked, **"What does the phrase 'living one day at a time' mean to you?"**

Someone else answered this question,

____

____

____

____

Jesus said, "**We are getting close to a place of rest where we will quench our thirst, maybe enjoy some dates and snacks, and then continue on our journey.**"

We saw in the distance a beautiful grove of palm trees, when Jesus asked us, **"Share with us a major personal concern currently taking place in your life. Then, tell us what may be stopping you from turning it over to me and God?"**

As I was catching my breath, someone else answered,

____

____

____

____

We made it to the palm trees, and there we saw a pool of sparkling water! A large grassy area surrounded by palm trees, and the pool of water became our resting place. There was a mutual sigh of relief—an aaah—as we got some rest, drank some of the water, and ate dates under the shade of the palm trees, an oasis.

We gathered in a circle with Jesus in the middle as he quoted Proverbs 3:6 (OTB), paraphrased, **"In everything, absolutely everything you do, put God first, and he will direct your ways and crown your efforts with success."**

Jesus continued to say to us, **"I want to congratulate you all for making it this far in your journey. You've seen much, experienced a great deal, and learned tremendously, and I'm proud of you. As you learned from the acronym DENIAL, you faced the issues that you have been denying for some time. From the acronym POWERLESS, you learned to admit that you are powerless on your own, you learned to manage your hurts, hang-ups, bad habits, and bad addictions while realizing the importance of relying on God's power to help you manage these things. Congratulations!**

Just then, I recalled the words in Romans 7:18 (OTB), paraphrased, **"I know that nothing good lives in me, (because of)... my sinful nature, for I have the desire to do what is good, but I do not have the power to carry it out."**

Then Jesus said, **"As you learned from the acronyms HOPE and SANITY, you found hope in God and me to restore you to sanity. You discovered we have the power to assist you, and you realized nothing else has been able to help you in the past."**

Then I recalled the words in Philippians 2:13 (OTB), paraphrased, "**For God is at work within you, helping you to even want to obey him, and then giving you the power to help understand and do what he wants."**

Then Jesus said, **"Finally, using the acronym TURN, you turned your life over to God and my care and direction. Then, through the acronym ACTION, you took significant action and made the decision to turn your life over to God and me. Congratulations! Now, ready yourselves, I have much more to share with you."**

Suddenly, it became axiomatic to me, as I remembered a wonderful prayer I once read and memorized from Reinhold Niebuhr called the Prayer of Serenity. Now I had a clearer context to relate to the following prayer as I journeyed with Jesus. I encourage you all to memorize the Prayer of Serenity which went like this:

> God grant me the serenity to accept the things I
> cannot change,

The courage to change the things I can,
and the wisdom to know the difference.
Living one day at a time, enjoying one moment
at a time;
Accepting hardships as a pathway to peace;
Taking, as Jesus did, this sinful world as it is, not
as you would have it;
Trusting that you will make all things right, if I
surrender to Your will;
so that I may be reasonably happy in this life and
Supremely happy with You forever in the next.
Amen.

We ate and then fell asleep as Jesus prayed over us at the oasis. When we awoke, we saw Jesus off at a distance, near a large stone, praying. As we began to clean and clear the area to continue our journey, Jesus arrived in our midst and circled us up again, saying,

I want you to choose someone of the same gender to be your *guide*, so you may work together privately, one-on-one. I want you to be available to be someone else's same gender guide. A guide should never feel better than you, will not judge you, but will advise you and provide guidance if you ask them. Your guide will end up being your very special friend whom you will meet with privately, to work on your specific hurts, hang-ups, bad habits, and bad addictions, as we continue on our journey.

Keep in mind I don't want anything, not even a guide, to get in the way of your recovery so, special friend or not, your guide can always be replaced by you, no hurt feelings. If things don't work out and especially if it impedes your personal recovery in any way, do the following:

- Consider more than one person to be your guide because you don't know how someone will respond until you ask.
- Before you ask, identify the pros and cons of that person as a potential guide.
- Once you have a guide, select a few special times and places to privately discuss your Moral Inventory with your guide. I let you know more about moral inventories later.

Remember, I want you to search deeply to conduct a fearless Moral Inventory and openly examine and confess your hurts, bad habits, hang-ups, and bad addictions to yourself, to me and God, and to your guide. Later, I will give you a Moral Inventory form, a tool, so you will know what a Moral Inventory looks like and how to fill it out.

Your guide will also have guidelines separate from the group guidelines, which I will supply to the guides later. They will use these guidelines to help both you and the guide to continue your journey.

Remember this:

- You can switch guides at any time and for any reason because I don't want anything or anyone to get in the way of your personal recovery.
- Your recovery is paramount to God and me because it is foundational to equipping you for your future ministry.
- You will not be able to "love your neighbor as yourself," until you can first love yourself, and you will not be able to love yourself until you have allowed God and me to heal you and begin the recovery of your mind, body, and spirit.

> **If you do all that I ask of you on this journey, your mind, body, and spirit will recover and heal, and you will be able to truly love you neighbor. You will also be able to love God with *all* your heart, soul, and mind as well, like never before. I promise.**

At this stage of our journey, I realized, like probably so many others, that I needed to "relight" the fire that once burned bright in me (as the song goes) when I first learned that Jesus was the Son of God, that he had died for my sins and that he was my Savior, Deliverer, the Recoverer of my very soul. For years, I had been praying for the Lord to relight that fire in me. Now I knew, it was within my grasp, and I was excited!

Jesus then said to us all,

> **As we continue walking with each other on this journey via the road we were on, you might realize you are on a road to personal recovery as well as being equipped for ministry by watching me do our Father's will. Your journey to the center of your soul will enable you to teach about this and take others on their personal journey of their road to recovery, as you help others recover from their hurts, hang-ups, bad habits, and bad addictions. In order to continue to help you recover and to further equip you, I have another acronym for you to remember from the word *recovery*.**

- **The *R* in the word RECOVERY_will help you *remember* to teach others that you, or anything, or anyone else, are not God. Only God is God. Since Father God and I and God's Holy Spirit are one, only we have the power to help you recover. That is why people who try and do this on their own or they try and use a "higher power" that really has no power at all, and no interest in helping for that matter, are destined for failure. You are in a position to teach others that God is the only**

higher power that can recover their souls, and you can help them come to me for help.

- **The *E* in the word RECOVERY will help you remember to teach them to *earnestly* believe that God exists, that you and they matter to God, and that only He and I have the power to help you recover.**
- **The *C* in the word RECOVERY will help you remember to teach others that they need to *consciously* choose to commit their lives and control over to the will, way, and care of me and Father God.**
- **The *O* in the word RECOVERY will help you remember to teach others to *openly* examine and confess their hurts, hang-ups, bad habits, and bad addictions to God and me and (this is very important) to their new guide and their small group of fellow journeyers, in confidence. Therefore, they can experience our Spirit, the Holy Spirit, working with others in small groups, as they confess their hurts, hang-ups, bad habits, and bad addictions to discover the healing process.**

At this time, the words of James 5:16 (OTB, paraphrased) became so evident and real to me! This is what Jesus was saying, **"Confess [your hurts, hang-ups, bad habits, and bad addictions] to each other, and pray for each other so that you may be healed."**

That's it! That's why he wants us to confess to each other. So we can experience the Holy Spirit in each other as God heals our bodies, minds, and spirits! I got it! Then Jesus continued,

- **The *V* in the word RECOVERY will remind you to teach others that they need to *voluntarily* submit to every change God makes in their lives while humbly asking him to remove their character defects. Voluntarily submitting is the our part because God will not override the *will* he gave us, even to help us change. Therefore, we have to voluntarily submit our *wills* over to him and God will honor our submission.**

- **The other *E* in the word RECOVERY will remind you to teach others to *evaluate* their relationships so we can offer forgiveness to those who have hurt us. In addition, we can make amends—apologies, reparation, atonement, etc.—for the harm we have done to others. This matter of offering forgiveness and being forgiven will be a "major point" of your personal Moral Inventory and your work with your guides.**
- **The other *R* in the word RECOVERY will remind you to teach others to *reserve* some time with God daily for self-examination, reading Scriptures, discussion, listening, listening, listening to God to understand his will for us and to gain the power to follow his will. Some of you may have noticed during the early morning, I isolate myself with God to do exactly this.**
- **Finally, the *Y* in the word RECOVERY will remind you to teach others that they need to *yield* themselves to God. When we yield ourselves to God, he will use us to help others recover from their hurts, bad habits, hangups, and bad addictions that shackle and slow people down from serving and equipping others for ministry. By journeying with others while teaching, training, and by our words, you will demonstrate that there is healing and recovery for all, along with a plan and a purpose for all as well.**

Next to one of the towns was a gigantic lake, and we were headed to some grassy knolls next to the lake on the outskirts of town. There was a small suburb in the town, and the suburb was next to the grassy knolls. On the knolls were sheep and some shepherds. As we made our way to the grassy knolls, Jesus said to us,

> **As we continue walking, I want you to learn this next acronym to teach others. It will help you and others understand how to approach the Moral Inventory I discussed earlier. It's an acronym of the word *moral*.**

- The *M* in the word MORAL_will help you remember to teach others to *make* time by setting aside a special amount of time to begin writing out their Moral Inventory. Yes, I said *writing out.* Some of you will want to use those future computers to write it out, and that's okay. Start with just ten minutes a day and build up your writing time from there. It will take a few days, at least, and for most of you, it may take a few weeks. Hang in there and be determined to get it done because this process will be core to getting to and healing the center of your soul. It's crucial to your recovery so don't put it off and be tenacious about finishing it.

  I have placed a Moral Inventory guide and sheet on your sleeping bags for you to use. You may add sheets to it later as you need more room. You will be able to pray and work out your personal journey later, privately, with your guide.

- The *O* in the word MORAL will help you remember to teach others to *open* your minds and, in particular, to open your hearts to allow the painful feelings that will flash back as you recall the past. God and I will be with you through all this process. Talk (pray) to us as you are going through it. This process will uncover the pain at the core of your soul. This is the pain that has been blocking your spiritual growth and may have kept you in denial. Remember our first acronym DENIAL?
- The *R* in the word MORAL will help you to teach others to *rely* on God and me and on our power to give you and others the strength to make it through this journey to the center of your soul, tenaciously pursuing your recovery and equipping you and others for service at the same time. Trust us and trust this process. It will work if you work it, but remember, it won't if you

don't. You must do the work of the moral Inventory and go through this process.

Jesus then quoted from Psalms 31:23–24 (TLB), paraphrased, **"Love the Lord your God, all of you who are his people, for the Lord protects those who are his children and loyal to him, submitting to him, following him… So cheer up! Take courage as you depend on the Lord for your recovery and your continued salvation."**

Jesus continued,

- **The *A* in the word *MORAL* will help you remember to teach others to *analyze* themselves as they go through the process of stepping out of denial and as they do a fearless and honest Moral Inventory (analysis) of their past and their present. Remember to tell them that the word *moral* and the word *honest* are synonyms. Remind others that this process only works "if they work it" (a.k.a. be honest).**

Jesus quoted Proverbs 20:27–37 (GNB), paraphrased, **"The Lord God gave us a mind and conscience so that we cannot hide from ourselves or from him."**

Jesus continued to teach,

- **The *L* in the word MORAL will help you remember to teach others to *list* both the good and the bad memories in your Moral Inventory list. You will want to list the "good" with the "bad" memories in order to keep the inventory balanced. If you list just the bad things in your Moral Inventory, it will be distorted, and you will open yourself to unnecessary hurts, guilt, and shame.**

Jesus ended this teaching with the word from Lamentations 3:4 (NIV), paraphrased, **"Let us examine and list our ways and test them with our guides."**

Jesus said,

> **Examine your (list) both the pros (good) and cons (bad) of your past and your present, and go over them with your guides.**
>
> **As you complete your Moral Inventory, you will discover that you have said and done some harmful things to others and yourself. Don't be worried because you are only human and no one's Moral Inventory is flawless. All have sinned, missed the mark, at certain times of their lives and fall short of the glory of God.**
>
> **This process, this journey to the center of the soul, along with your Moral Inventory, will bring healing and an end to the hurts, hang-ups, bad habits, and bad addictions that have been at the core or your lifelong pain.**
>
> **As you continue this journey with me and continue to recover, you will teach others that doing a Moral Inventory does not make you dwell on the past but helps you to analyze (examine) and understand your past so you can offer it to God and me, allowing us to help you change. My purpose is to give life and the fullness of life. Remind others that their moral inventories will become their own unique "tool" that they will be able to use for the rest of their time here on earth.**

We now journeyed closer to the lake, and as we walked downhill toward the lake, we found a grassy plateau on top of a large grassy hill, amongst a set of hills, next to the lake.

A large number of people were already near the lake and ready to meet Jesus. Some had been following him from town to town, but there were also large crowds coming from many neighboring towns and villages to hear him speak, to be healed, and to be delivered. Jesus accommodated them, prayed and touched some of them, and let himself be touched by all who were seeking healing and deliverance. They were healed and delivered.

Just then, I remembered something Jesus had taught us earlier when he said we should only help someone recover who has shown a desire to be helped.

Then Jesus said to us, "**Teach others to always ask the person seeking help, 'How can I help you?' because it will not always be obvious to you and others why they need prayer. Don't assume anything.**"

It was clear that the people who rushed to Jesus to touch or be touched by him wanted to recover from something. Most said they wanted to be physically healed. Some wanted to be delivered and had the faith that Jesus could do it, and he did!

Now I understand that Jesus can heal, deliver, recover us, even now, if we rush toward him with the same attitude that the crowd had! I understood, like never before, that my personal attitude toward Jesus and God was at the core of everything regarding my personal recovery and my work to let Jesus and God make that recovery happen as I continued to journey to the center of my soul.

When the crowd's excitement settled down, Jesus gathered together those of us who had been on this journey with him and the ones who considered themselves to be his followers (other disciples), around him in a semicircle. Jesus sat on a small boulder to teach us all something. The other larger part of the crowd also circled around us (journeyers, followers, disciples), as the whole crowd together covered the entire hill. We listened quietly as Jesus said what I remember reading in the Gospels, Jesus said, **"Blessed are you who are poor in spirit, for yours is the Kingdom of God"** (Matthew 5:3, OTB).

When Jesus said this, I remembered that Jesus taught us earlier that it is usually in our brokenness, our point of spiritual poverty (poor in spirit), that we come to realize we need help and reach out to the kingdom of God, but it usually takes that point of brokenness to get us on the right track. Even the disciple Paul had to fall off his mule and get blinded on the road to Damascus before he was at a place where he would listen to Jesus.

It's then, at the point of our brokenness, when we are spiritually poor, that we realize we cannot control our lives because we keep doing what we keep doing and keep on getting what we keep on getting. Nevertheless, it still doesn't stop us from doing what we keep on doing. It is not until we are broken and experiencing spiritual poverty that Jesus calls us "blessed" because we finally realize we need help from God and Jesus to change our actions (our "doing") and learn how to be spiritually strong. That's when we reach out to the kingdom of God, and we realize the kingdom of God was always at hand. We are blessed.

Then Jesus said, **"Blessed are those who mourn and hunger, for you will be comforted" (Matthew 5: 4, OTB).**

We mourn and cry out to God when we are at our wit's end, and we realize we have no one and nowhere else we can go or turn to. It is usually only then that we hunger for God, and Jesus calls us blessed again because we are, finally, at a place where we realize we always needed him. We were not at the right place before we did not have the right attitude, but now, as we reach out in our pain, as we mourn and hunger for God we are blessed and God will always be there to help us, regardless of ourselves.

I remembered the Bible story of the prodigal son. Regardless of what the prodigal son did, when the son mourned and hungered for his father and coming home, his father put his arms around him, robed him, blessed him, forgave him, restored him, and that's what our Father in heaven does for us, and more. That's why Jesus calls us blessed because, when we return to God, in a similar manner, God calls us and is so happy to have us back, so happy we have finally come to our senses, he calls us blessed again.

I recalled that Jesus said to us, as we journeyed with him, we need to earnestly believe God exists and that we matter to him and we need to have faith that he (God) will help us recover.

Then Jesus said, **"Blessed are you who are meek, for you will inherit the earth"** (Matthew 5: 5, OTB).

I knew Jesus didn't mean blessed are the weak but blessed are the meek. Meekness is a synonym for submissiveness. Jesus taught us to submit to the will of God and commit our lives to God in order to recover. Jesus modeled the ultimate in meekness (submission) when he choose to be obedient to God's plan to lay his (Jesus's) life down for us when he succumbed to the cross, in payment, for all our sins, and so we could have a chance to recover. That is powerful meekness and, in our particular calling, when we demonstrate meekness (submissiveness) to God, Jesus calls us blessed.

Then Jesus said, **"Blessed are those who hunger and thirst for righteousness, a simile for justice, morality, honesty, decency, for they will be filled" (Matthew 5:6, OTB, paraphrased).**

When Jesus said this, I realized that all my life, I hungered and thirsted for righteousness (justice, morality, honesty, decency) I couldn't find from anyone or anything on the earth with consistency. I realized that I've been hungering and thirsting for a righteousness that I can only find in God and in his Son, Jesus. And as I continued to hunger and thirst for God's righteousness (Jesus) and pursue that righteousness (Jesus); He will take care of me, and he will fill me with his Spirit and with his power. My faith will increase and I will finally be filled over and over again.

Then Jesus said, **"Blessed are the merciful, for they shall be shown mercy" Matthew 5: 7, OTB).**

When Jesus said this, I recalled Matthew 6:12 (ESV), paraphrased, "And forgive us our debts, as we also have forgiven our debtors, our trespassers or those who have sinned against us," and I realized that the mercy we have been shown—Jesus sacrificing himself for our sins when we deserved death—is the mercy we need to show others. I realized, like never before, that when we take on this kind of merciful attitude, Jesus calls us blessed.

I also realized that it is in the giving of myself, by being honest and confessing my hurts, hang-ups, bad habits, and bad addictions, to another and asking for prayer that I will be humbling myself (dying of self) as Jesus did, and receiving mercy from another as they pray for me.

Wow! That's what mercy should feel like! I can be in the midst of and feel God's mercy as I show mercy by humbling myself, by giving of myself, and by practicing honesty and confessing to another and receiving prayer. At least that's one way to see, hear, and feel mercy. I may even find the courage to humble myself and give away myself in a testimony to others sometime later. God help me with that, please.

Then Jesus said, **"Blessed are the pure in heart, for they will see God" (Matthew 5:8, OTB).**

I know this is weird, but all of a sudden, I remembered the movie *The Santa Claus* with Tim Allen and the part of the movie where Tim was in Santa's room at the North Pole, and he looked out his bedroom balcony to view Santa's city where Tim saw a polar bear directing traffic.

Tim turned to the little cute pixie girl and said, with reference to the polar bear, "I see it, but I don't believe it." At which the little pixie girl retorted, "You don't understand, Santa! Seeing is not believing. Believing is seeing!" And ironically, such is our ability to "see God." In other words, in order to see God, we have to first *believe*. When we exercise our faith, we believe in the unseen, and we see God. God and Jesus call us blessed and pure in heart, like children. Jesus says, "Unless you are like one of these [children] who are 'pure in heart,' who 'see' because they first 'believe,' you cannot enter the kingdom of heaven [you cannot see God]. First believe!"

I remember that Jesus just taught us that we recover, and we also become pure in heart again by confessing our hurts, bad habits, hang-ups, and bad addictions to each other and as we pray with each other. In so doing, we submit ourselves to Jesus, God, and our guide, so that we can heal and recover. It's ironic that as we unburden ourselves by confessing, we become purified and are able to see God more clearly and believe in him with more assuredness as we are more sensitive to his Holy Spirit, as the Scriptures, the Word of God, becomes clearer to us. It's amazing.

Jesus continued, **"Blessed are the peacemakers, the go-between-ers, the arbitrators, the negotiators, those that make amends and ask and give forgiveness for their wrongs for they shall be called children of God" (Matthew 5:9, OTB, paraphrased).**

Amazing—to be called a child of God. What an honor! Like children, we are encouraged to be like God, our Father and God our Savior (Jesus) who modeled arbitration and negotiations as he placed himself on the cross for us, taking our place, and negotiating our salvation and recovery.

I knew, because of what Jesus had taught us earlier, that as we continued our journey with Jesus, submitted to him and his modeling for us, and asked for his help and power to remove our character defects, hurts, bad habits, and bad addictions, we would find and be filled with his peace, and we would be better able to be peacemakers because we would have the peace of God within us.

Then Jesus said, **"Blessed are those who are persecuted because of righteousness, for theirs is the Kingdom of Heaven" (Matthew 5: 10, OTB).**

Wow again! I'd like to have the kingdom of heaven, wouldn't you? Then I recalled again what Jesus taught us earlier when he said that as we evaluate our relationships and offer forgiveness and make amends, except when it would harm others, it may be a rough road but worth the endeavor because the kingdom of heaven is at hand.

When we seek God's will for us and struggle with the discipline required to set aside quality time for God, to read His Words, to pray and listen, it is definitely worth it. Spiritual growth, maturing in the Spirit, can be painful. When we submit to God and move, in ministry, into an upside down world that thinks it's right side up, it may result in immense trouble and hurts and, at times, sometimes more often than not, we "will be persecuted" even by the church itself (that's when it really hurts) but again, it is worth it because Jesus and God will call us "blessed" and "ours is the kingdom of heaven!"

Jesus continued talking to us as we crowded around him. Jesus taught us how to take insults and rejoice in it by seeing the big picture and praying, especially for those we consider our enemies, while remembering our battle is not against flesh and blood (people) but against powers and principalities (I call critters and their domains/ territories).

Jesus also explained to us how we are salt and light, the fullness of the law. Jesus also explained the meaning of murder, adultery, divorce, oaths, an eye for an eye, and repeated how to love those we consider our enemies as well as how to give, how to pray, fasting, what real treasures are, not worrying, the problems with judging others, and much, much more wisdom and spiritual insight. We were amazed and pleasantly overwhelmed at his teachings and especially the power behind his words.

This was a particularly long day, and we were tired. As the evening approached and some of the crowd left, Jesus asked us to set up camp on top of the large hill. Some, in the crowd, gave us fish, bread, and wine to sustain us so we added those rations to our meager provisions.

As we set up camp, Jesus asked us, **"Where, when, and at what time will you go for your quiet time with God, to begin writing down your Moral Inventory?"**

Most of us chose the end of the day or early in the morning, depending on when we slept or awakened. I committed to my quiet time with God and doing my Moral Inventory in the morning since I was an early riser. One of the others answered Jesus first, saying,

____

____

____

____

This evening, there were campfires around ours as we noticed many people stayed to camp with us, in a larger circle around us. As we began to cook our meal, break bread and drink, Jesus said, **"What fears and other feelings do you have, as you begin to do your Moral Inventory, and why do you suppose you have those fears and other feelings?"**

I answered first, saying,

____
____
____
____

Then Jesus asked, **"For those of you that have made the commitment, please share what you personally experienced when you turned your life over to God and me. Also, please explain how you plan to turn over your will to God and me on a daily basis?"**

I quickly said,

____
____
____
____

As we began to eat our fish, Jesus said, **"Describe the things you have done to try to block the hurts of your past and what you have done recently to stop denying and running from your past."**

As we continued to finish our meal, there was an awkward silence until someone else said,

____
____
____
____

Then, as we were cleaning and preparing for bed, I and some others were so very tired; nevertheless, Jesus asked us all, **"After I am no longer with you, what are some new ways you can stop running from your past and start changing, moving from denial into confessing?"**

I finished eating, and as I continued cleaning up, I answered first, saying,

____
____
____
____

Then as we climbed into our bedding, Jesus asked us yet another question, saying, **"Why do you suppose it is important for you to do a written Moral Inventory?"**

Someone else answered first, saying,

____
____
____
____

Then, Jesus said that before he prayed us to sleep, he had a couple more questions to ask. "**It's important for you to keep *balance* as you proceed to do you Moral Inventory and work with a guide. You're not just with me to recover** on your personal journey to the center of your soul, but **to receive healing, and find your ministry, but to also maintain a sense of pride that you did some positive things and will continue to do so. What are some of the positive and some of the negative things you have done in your past?"**

I replied first, saying,

____
____
____
____

Then Jesus said,

> **If you have not yet gone to someone in our circle of friends and asked them, "Would you be my guide to help me with my Moral Inventory, to guide me, and help me to keep my recovery**

balanced as we proceed on this journey with Jesus?" Then I would like you to do that by tomorrow morning please.

For those who have chosen a guide already, please raise your hands so that others can see your hands and be encouraged. Remember, it's male-to-male guides and female-to-female guides. You can be a guide to more than one person, but you can't share any information. In other words, anonymity is essential to the security and bonding capability of the group of journeyers. Also, you don't want to be a guide to more than one or two individuals for now until you have gained more experience.

Most of the group had raised their hands smiling, but I didn't. I felt a little embarrassed. But I had selected a couple of people as my potential guides whom I was going to ask in the morning if one of them could be my guide for the rest of my journey to the center of my soul.

Summary of the Fifth Day
What We Learned

At the end of the fifth day, we learned how important it was to admit to God, to yourselves, to your guides, and/or a trusted friend, the exact nature of your wrongs. Then we learned to ask for our guide's or friend's guidance and to pray for us.

We learned to make a fearless, honest, and soul-baring Moral Inventory of ourselves and that we can revise our Moral Inventory list as often as needed.

We also learned about living one day at a time, about the anointing, our guides and guidelines, our moral inventories, and the be-attitudes.

I remembered one of my most favorite scriptures in James 5:15-16 (OTB, paraphrased:

> **And the prayer of faith will help you recover… and the Lord will raise you up. And if you have any hurts, bad habits, hang-ups, or addictions, you will be forgiven and set free of these things that you struggle over. Therefore, just confess your hurts, bad habits, hang-ups, and addictions to one another and pray for one another so that you may recover, be healed, and be set free.**

Jesus then prayed us to sleep, saying,

> **Father, we already know their entire past and love them regardless. We always will. Father, give these that are journeying with me the strength and courage they will need to do their Moral Inventory lists and come clean, strengthening their spirits and bringing their spirits into wholeness as they realize the truth that will surely set them free.**

Father, help them reach out to others in their circle of friends to be available to guide others as they all work on their personal recovery and discovery of their personal missions, while on this journey with me. Help them to learn well, so they can teach others to do the same.

Father, place your warring angels around them to guard and protect them and your ministering angels with them to serve them and help them sleep. Place your spirit before them wherever their journey takes them so that people will find favor with them wherever they go. Father, I bless them all with my love and your Love for them, forever and ever, Amen.

We, including those on the camp site perimeter, who heard his prayer, fell fast and hard asleep.

CHAPTER 6

The Sixth Day with Jesus

I slept like a baby again, awoke rested, and felt fantastic. I had not slept that well for a long time. The campfire had already been started, so I slipped out of my bedding and went to a water pail on the perimeter of the campsite area to wash up.

As I headed back to the campfire to get some coffee, I saw Jesus walking toward us from the distance. I think he was off praying again. As he walked through the sparse crowd, occasionally touching them or shaking their hands, we routinely half-circled around the campfire knowing he would want to talk to us while we were eating breakfast and getting ready to walk on our journey with him.

As Jesus sat in the middle of us and the morning food and drinks we prepared, he led us in a prayer to God for thanks. He thanked God for many things: the crowd that was present, those who were following him and learning from him, the food we were about eat, and the journey ahead of us. Then, as we began to eat our breakfast, Jesus handed out a form to us labeled Moral Inventory worksheet. Jesus explained the worksheet to us, addressing us saying,

> **Good morning, the worksheet that is being distributed is what you'll complete and work on with only your guide. Let's go through this together.**

> **In column 1, "The Person." In this column; List the person or object you are bitter about, angry with, resent (unexpressed anger), feel rage or fear, or one whom you have slandered. Go back as far as you can.**

I remembered the verse in Ephesians 4:31, **"Get rid of all bitterness, rage and anger, brawling, slander, alone with every form of malice."**

Then Jesus continued,

> **In column 2, "The Cause." Remember, hurt people will hurt others. In this column, list the specific actions someone did that hurt you and, as a result, you felt bitterness, anger, resentment, rage, or fear and have slandered them, even if it was done mentally (verbally) and not physically.**

Jesus quoted Isaiah 41:10 (OTB), paraphrased, saying, **"Fear not for I am with you. Do not be dismayed or afraid. I am your God and I will continue to strengthen you; I will help you; I will uphold you in all things, including your Moral Inventory, with my victorious right hand."**

> **In column 3, "The Effect." In this column, write down *how* that specific hurtful action affected your life. List *how* it has affected your past and present.**
>
> **In column 4, "The Damage." List which of your basic needs were injured?**
>
> **A. social—from broken relationships, slander.**
> **B. security—from physical safety, financial loss.**
> **C. sexual—from abusive relationships, damaged intimacy.**

> **Remember, no matter how bad you have been hurt, or have been damaged, God and I have the will, the desire, and the power to heal you, help you recover, restore you to fullness, and discover the glorious life we have planned for you.**

Some of us began to tear up. Then Jesus said,

> **In column 5, the "My Part." Ask yourselves, what part of this hurt, bitterness, resentment, anger, or fear is my responsibility. Ask God to show you, your part in a broken or damaged marriage or relationship, even a broken or damaged relationship with a distant child or parent, or with a loss of a job or a position. List the people whom you believe you have hurt and how you may have hurt them.**

Then Jesus quoted from Psalm 139:23–24 (OTB), paraphrased, saying to us all, "**I would like you to remember this prayer: 'Examine me, oh God, you know my mind, my heart, my spirit so test me and discover… if there is any evil hurts, bad habits, hung-ups, or bad addictions in me and guide me on this journey to the center of my soul.'"**

Then Jesus quoted Ezekiel 34:16 (OTB), paraphrased, **"I will seek the lost, and I will bring back the strayed, and I will bind up the injured, and I will strengthen the weak… I will [restore them and recover their spirits and] feed them… justice."**

Then Jesus said to us,

> **It's no coincidence that you are on this journey with me. In fact, you are here because you have been found. Our Father has set you aside for his glory. Some of you have been in an abusive relationship; some were also children while**

in an abusive relationship. Your spirits need to hear and feel the following very important fact: You had no part, no responsibility for the hurt perpetrated against you. The perpetrator is guilty and responsible, not you.

As you work with your guides, you may reenact the feeling of the healing of the aforementioned words I just spoke over you and will remember the freedom of any false shame or false guilt that you have been carrying. You will be able to renounce the lies that the abuse was, in any part, your fault. That's the lie.

Remember the words of Ezekiel 11 about God: I will seek the lost, and I will bring back as I recover the strayed, and I will bind up the injured, I will heal the hurts, bad habits, hang ups, and I will strengthen the weak… I will restore them and recover their spirits and feed them… justice.

Then Jesus said,

On the rest of your journey with me, you will be meeting privately with your guides, to review and conduct a fearless personal Moral Inventory. In your Moral Inventory, you will be writing down your findings as you journey to the center of your soul. The more you do this, the more you will get used to openly confessing your hurts, bad habits, hang-ups, and bad addictions to yourself, to God, in your personal prayer time with God, and to your personal guide.

> **This will end up being a very special time for you. A time of cleansing and healing at the very center—core—of your soul as well as a special time of bonding with your guide and other journeyers and bonding with God and me, like never before. Get ready, be excited. The kingdom of God is at hand!**

When Jesus just said, **"To God, in your personal prayer time with God,"** I thought this may have been some of what he was praying to God when we saw him praying in the distance. Maybe Jesus was praying a kind of personal confession, cleansing, and searching out God's will for him and us, during his alone time with God. I don't know for sure, but I just wondered.

Then Jesus quoted Lamentations 3:40 (paraphrased) and Ecclesiastes 4:9 (paraphrased) saying,

> **Let us examine our ways (our hurts, bad habits, hang-ups, and bad addictions) and test them (writing them down and reviewing them with a guide) and let us (then) return to the Lord (by confessing our hurts, bad habits, hang ups and bad addictions to ourselves, to God and to our Guide (each other).**

> **Remember, two are better than one, because together (both) can work more effectively (for recovery). If one of them falls down (back slides), the other can help (him/her back) up, but if someone is alone, there is no one to help them (back) up. Two (of them) can resist (a compromising) attack (of the spirit and recovery) that would defeat one (person) alone.**

Then Jesus said,

As we continue to journey together, please remember four key elements to reaching your mission goal for my sake and yours:

1. **Maintain an honest attitude as you work with your guide.**
2. **Commit to following me daily and meeting at the campfire.**
3. **Learn to read God's Words daily and have a private prayer time with God.**
4. **Teach the lessons learned on this journey, to others, and be available as a guide to others. Continue serving wherever you can. Freely you have received, freely give.**

Remember, you are accountable to the rest of the group you are journeying with and you can meet with any one of them, separately, from time to time for discussion, but they are not your guides. Your guide is there to guide you through this daily journey and to be transparent too, so you can make any confession that comes to mind.

I want you to put your names and telephone numbers on a list and circulate that list to each person in your circle of friends. This way, you can stay in touch and be accountable wherever you are after our journey is over. Your guide will work deeper with you, compared to those other journeyers whom you have chosen to make friends with and accountable too.

Remember, your guide is different than your other journeyers. Your guide will hear your confessions, guide you, review your Moral Inventory, give you feedback, and help you stay on track. Your guide can spot your hurts, bad habits, hang-ups, and bad addictions if they try to return, and you begin to repeat them. Your guide is responsible to confront you with the truth, with loving kindness, without shaming you or condemning you.

Good advice, based on experience, is a guide's commitment to you. The guide will demonstrate listening skills; be strong enough to confront your denial of the truth or your procrastination; offer suggestions; disclose their personal hurts, bad habits, hang-ups, and bad addictions; and show compassion, care, and hope to you, the Journeyer. The guide will get used to asking God and me, from time to time, what to say or do for you.

When you decide to take on a guides role, I want you to do the following:

1. **Make sure you are of the same gender as the journeyer.**
2. **When asked to be a guide, you can commit to be either a short-term or long-term guide with the journeyer, or you can say no. It's okay to say no, but encourage the journeyer to keep on searching for a guide to help them.**
3. **Guides will discuss with the journeyer the personal issues divulged in our twelve-day journey to the center of the**

soul as well as issues listed on the journeyer's Moral Inventory. These issues are usually too personal and would take too much time to discuss in the larger group, when they answer my questions to them during the twelve-day journey to the center of the soul, but they can be discussed, in more detail, in the journeyer's private meetings with their guides.

4. Guides are to be available to a journeyer for regular check-in meetings and especially available when the journeyer is having a time of crisis, illness, fears, or is having a relapse.
5. Guides are to be a "sounding board" most of the time, just listening (not speaking much), so the journeyer can hear themselves talk it out. Good listening skills are a necessary talent that a guide will attain with experience and by reading books on listening skills.

   On occasion, a guide may offer an objective point of view. If you are new and inexperienced, this may take some private prayer time with God first before you offer any kind of objective point of view to the journeyer, or since another guide is bound by the same oath of confidentiality, you can call a more experienced guide and ask them what they would say or do after reminding the other guide of the importance of confidentiality.
6. The guide needs to be an encourager, giving the journeyer hope and confidence as well as guidance. The journeyer is on this journey for him/herself, but she/he

will bless you on their way, if you permit them.

7. The journeyer will be watching you. As a guide, you will want to model for them on how to be a guide. So lean on God and me as you do this and model what you are learning from God and me. Also rely on your experience as well as other guides so the journeyer can learn well.
8. A guide may always resign as a guide if they feel inadequate, or if there is too much tension between a guide and a particular journeyer or if they are having personal problems that are too overwhelming.

Talk this over with the journeyer before you resign so they can start looking for a replacement for you. You might end up changing your mind as time passes. Also, the journeyer can stop sharing with you for any personal reason that would interfere with their own personal recovery and choose another guide from the group or another similar group, and that's okay too.

The journeyer can choose a guide who has done this journey to the center of the soul with me before or from another similar group, and it's okay.

Journeyers should always be encouraged to fight tenaciously for their personal recovery with any guide who will work with them and not let them be discouraged by any particular

> **guide or other journeyer so that the journeyer will find their own personal recovery and their God-given ministry.**

Now I'm thinking what Jesus taught us about guides might just be part of what else Jesus was asking God about from time to time when he was alone with God in prayer!

As we finished eating, we began to clean up and prepare for our continued journey. Jesus asked, **"Why do you think being accountable to the entire group, your whole circle of journeying friends, is important? Also, what qualities have you been looking for in a guide to help you on this journey?"**

I answered first saying,

____

____

____

____

Then Jesus said,

> **Now we are ready to continue our journey to the center of the soul, but before we come down off this hill, let me help you understand a few things. So far, on your journey with me, you have begun the following:**
>
> 1. **a fearless examination of your past and have begun identifying the positives and negatives in your Moral Inventory,**
> 2. **connecting with your accountability circle of friends, and**
> 3. **connecting with your guide to help you achieve your goals toward recovery.**

Congratulations! As we continue our journey, remember to do the following

1. **Meditate the following from Isaiah 1:18 (TLB), paraphrased, "Come, let's talk this over! Says the Lord God; no matter how deep the stain of your sin [hurts, bad habits, hang-ups or bad addictions], I *can take it out and make you clean* as freshly fallen snow. Even if you are stained as red as crimson, I can make [your past, present and future] as white as wool!" I can *make you clean*!**
2. **Keep your Moral Inventory balanced with the positive things in your past, as well as the hurts, bad habits, hang-ups, and bad addictions, negative things. I have put a "Positive/Negative Balance of Scale" in your backpacks to review later as an encouragement because it's important for you to maintain a balance perspective of yourselves in your moral inventories.**
3. **Continue to be accountable to your group, and, for any future JCS (Journey to the Center of the Soul) groups you from, remember you can grow the group over time (not recommended after the third or fourth day of your particular future JCS group), but as your current group bonds together, remember to keep accountable to a guide so you can stay clean, sober, and recover, even long after our journey together.**

4. **Develop a prayer time with God. We, Father, Son, and Holy Spirit, are, and always will be, the greatest and closest friends you will ever have, and we long to spend time with you and develop a deeper relationship with you.**

Jesus stood up and led us down the grassy knoll and many followed behind. Some of them got as close to us as they possibly could because they wanted to hear the teachings of Jesus and our comments. Then Jesus said,

As we walk, I want you to think about, and write down, some things that you want to discuss and work on with your guide. Think about the following:

1. **Your past relationships with others.**
    a. **Who has hurt you?**
    b. **Against whom have you been holding a grudge?**
    c. **Against whom would you like to seek revenge?**
    d. **Are you jealous of someone?**
    e. **Who have you hurt?**
    f. **Have you slandered, criticized or gossiped about someone?**
    g. **Have you justified your bad attitude toward someone by assuming and/or saying it is his or her fault?**

2. **Your priorities in life.**
    a. **After accepting me as your Lord and Savior, what areas of your life have you tried to hide from God and not give them over to our control?**

b. **What have you been doing that is interfering with God's will for you, (i.e., hobbies, hurts, bad habits, hang-ups, bad addictions, money, friendships, personal goals, etc.)?**

3. **Your attitude.**
    a. **Are you a complainer?**
    b. **Are you ungrateful?**
    c. **Have you lost your temper, and what did you do?**
    d. **Are you sarcastic?**
    e. **What is it that is causing you any fear or anxiety?**

4. **Your integrity.**
    a. **Have you ever been dishonest?**
    b. **Have you ever stolen?**
    c. **Have you ever exaggerated to make yourself look better?**
    d. **Have you ever used false humility?**
    e. **Have you lived one way in your workplace, a different way with Christian friends, and another way in the privacy of your home?**

When Jesus finished informing us what to think about, write about, and review with our guide, we went to a flat, cleared out area of the road on the way to another city. We noticed a large crowd behind us, and suddenly a man who was obviously a leper came and knelt before Jesus, asking the Lord if He (The Lord) was willing to make him (the leper) clean.

Jesus reached out his hand, touching the leper, and said to the leper, **"I am willing, be clean."** And immediately, like quick time-lapsed photography, right before our eyes, the leper was cleansed from leprosy! Then Jesus gave the leper some instructions and bid him to go. The crowd was in awe, and we were all amazed. The journeyer's belief system increased and now they came to expect nothing less than the miraculous from Jesus as we journeyed with him. Our belief and faith strengthened hour by hour, step by step, day by day.

We continued walking on the road to the next town and the crowd followed. Then, Jesus asked us to verbally summarize some answers that we would be reviewing with our Guides later. Jesus asked us, **"Who has hurt you before and what did they specifically do or say to hurt you?"**

I started answering first, saying,

____
____
____
____

Then Jesus asked us, **"Are you jealous or holding a grudge against anyone and if so, why?"**

Someone else answered first, saying,

____
____
____
____

Then Jesus asked, **"Have you hurt anyone? What did you do?"**

Someone else answered first again, saying;

____
____
____
____

In the distance, I could see the vague outline of the next town ahead of us. Just then, Jesus asked us another question as we sat down to take a break and get some rest. Jesus asked us, **"Have you been critical of or gossiped about anyone?"**

Again, someone else answered first, saying,

____
____
____
____

Jesus found a place for us to rest near some fig trees for shade and for the consumption of figs, and while we were circling around eating figs and drinking water, Jesus was at the center of us. A large crowd followed. They also took a break, staying close to us and eating figs while resting in the shade as well.

Jesus asked us who were on this journey with him, **"Who specifically have you been critical of, and why did you gossip about them?"**

This time I answered, saying,

____
____
____
____

Then Jesus asked, **"Have you ever blamed someone else for your hurts, bad habits, or hang-ups?"**

I had someone in mind, so I answered,

____
____
____
____

Since I was rather tired, I asked Jesus if I could take a nap, and he gave us all permission to take a short nap before we continued to the next town. The crowd also took time to nap before we continued on. As we all awoke from our naps, we noticed that Jesus was already awake and had built a small campfire in our midst. Jesus then asked us journeyers, **"What new relationships do you see developing in the near future?"**

Someone else answered first, saying,

____

____

____

____

Then Jesus said to us, **"What areas of your life have you been able to turn over to me and God, and which areas have you not yet been able to turn over? What is stopping you?"**

Someone else answered first, saying,

____

____

____

____

As we moved down the road again, Jesus said, **"I want you to list and prioritize your personal goals for the next ninety days and then share those with us, in priority."**

I replied first, saying,

____

____

____

____

We approached the next city, Capernaum, and Jesus asked, **"In the past, what have you been ungrateful for, maybe taken for granted, and what have you been grateful for?"**

I felt compelled to answer first again, saying,

____

____

____

____

When we neared the entrance to Capernaum, Jesus asked us, **"What causes you to lose your temper, and what do you do as a result?"**

Someone else answered first, saying,

____

____

____

____

As we entered the city of Capernaum, suddenly, a Roman Centurion approached Jesus and asked for help because the centurion's servant was paralyzed and suffering. Jesus offered to go to the centurion's home to heal his servant. But the centurion, feeling embarrassed to have Jesus come into his home and because the centurion understood how "authority" worked, said to Jesus, "All you have to do is give the word and I know it will be done, even from a distance." The Centurion knew this because the Centurion knew how authority and a chain of command works, even in the spiritual world.

Jesus admired the centurion's faith and understanding of authority and how it works, so Jesus immediately proclaimed healing for the centurion's servant. We heard later, that when the centurion returned home, he found his servant was fully healed and was healed right at the time Jesus had proclaimed the healing, just as the centurion believed!

Jesus then led us across town to Peter's home which was close to a large lake. The crowd began to thin out and as us journeyers were walking along the way, Jesus asked us suddenly and with no apparent context, **"To whom have you been sarcastic to in the past?"**

Someone else answered, saying,

____

____

____

____

We continued walking and Jesus then asked, **"What from your past still concerns you?"**

I answered, saying,

____

Then Jesus asked, **"Have you noticed a change in your attitude lately?"**

Again, I answered first, saying,

Jesus told us we were getting closer to Peter's home. He then asked us, **"In the past, how have you exaggerated to make yourself look better?"**

Someone else answered, saying,

Then Jesus asked, **"Does your walk and talk as a Christian match your walk and talk at home, work, and church?**

Someone answered first by giving a personal confession as well, which took some people back. He said,

We approached Peter's home, which was by a large lake. When we entered, Jesus could see Peter's mother-in-law lying in bed with an obvious fever as she was perspiring. Jesus went to her bedside, touched her hand, and her fever immediately vanished. Almost immediately afterward, she began to wait on Jesus and us, as if she had been well for days instead of only for seconds. We were again amazed at the speed and completeness of the physical healing. We ate and drank as Peter's mother-in-law and others served us.

As Jesus healed people, in and around the home of Peter, their bodies were responding to the power of Jesus, which, as Jesus taught us later, came from God, not from him. This teaching empowered me because I realized I could facilitate that same power, the same power from God that Jesus relied on, and I didn't have to be God or Jesus to do it! I was empowered!

The Scriptures say Jesus was with God at the creation of everything, including humankind. When people received healing at the words or by the touch of Jesus, it was as if people's bodies inherently knew and responded appropriately to their creator, God, and his power. It is important for us to know and wrap our faith around this fact that we impart that same authority and power from God when we lay hands on people or pray over them, as we see Jesus doing. Jesus said we were supposed to be doing the things he did, and more!

We understood that Jesus wanted us to learn from him, to not be afraid and have faith to do what he does. The Scriptures, in Philippians 2:5–8 say he gave up all his godliness (the power of God) and instead was born a man, a human being, for us. He was doing all he did as a human but relying on the power of God so that we would know we could do the same, just as he did and more, even though we were only human like he was at the time.

Still, Jesus is the only begotten Son of God and forever the Christ, but for a short time, he was fully human! Now that's empowering! That means we can do this stuff that Jesus did too and more! Jesus consistently told us we could accomplish this and greater things. If Jesus did all these miracles relying on his own Godly power, it would have been a cruel trick to tell us that we could do the same and even more.

God is not cruel. In fact, he is always empowering. So now I realize what Jesus meant was that we also, as he (Jesus) did, could rely on the power of God as we facilitate the miracles of God as well! Jesus did all his miracles as a human being only, relying only on God as God had intended for humanity, and we can do the same as well. That's what Jesus was showing us!

As evening came over Capernaum, many who were sick and demon possessed were brought to Jesus. He healed the sick, and sometimes only with a word spoken, Jesus cast out the demons. We carefully watched and learned what and how we could do this.

The crowd quieted down and dispersed a little as we got ready for bed. We went out to Peter's courtyard and started a fire at an existing firepit as most of us spread out our beddings and circled around Jesus to listen to his next teachings. This had become our protocol.

As we found a place to sit or lie down, Jesus asked us, **"In what areas of your past have you used false humility to impress someone?"**

A friend next to me began answering,

____

____

____

____

Then Jesus asked, **"Have any of your past business or personal dealings been dishonest or have you ever stolen anything?"**

I answered first, saying,

____

____

____

____

Then Jesus said, **"Describe how you have been able to get out of your personal denial and out of any distorted or dishonest thinking."**

Someone else spoke up first, saying,

____

____

____

____

Then Jesus said, "**Before I pray over all of you so we can go to sleep, I want you to think about some things.**"

Then he said to us,

> **You have openly faced, examined and confessed your hurts, bad habits, hang-ups, and bad addictions to yourself, to God, to your guide, and sometimes to others in this circle of friends with whom you are on this journey to the center of the soul with, and I'm proud of you, because of this you will have much to teach others.**
>
> **Now, as you sleep, I want you to think about the areas of your lives where you have experienced difficulties because of your hurts, bad habits, hang-ups, and bad addictions, and where you have not allowed God to work effectively in your lives. Such areas might be in your minds, your bodies, your spirit, your families, your church, your profession, and other areas of your lives.**

Then Jesus quoted from Psalm 139: 23f (paraphrased): **Now I will pray a prayer over you that I want you to remember**

> **Search me, O God, I give you permission. Search and test my heart and my thoughts. Point out anything in me, O God, that is not right and makes you sad for me. As I exercise my will, that you have given me, oh God, and as I choose to give those things over to you, please heal me, change me, and lead me along another path than the one I have chosen in the past. Lead me on your path of everlasting life.**

Summary of the Sixth Day
What We Learned

At the end of the sixth day, we were reminded to always ask God to remove all of our character defects and be ready to have God remove our hurts, bad habits, hang-ups, and bad addictions.

We also learned about how to complete a Moral Inventory form, being accountable and creating a check-in list—how to be a guide, also four important things to remember with your guides. We also experienced another miracle! We also processed some personal stuff, did some personal goals, processed more personal stuff, and experienced more miracles and deliverances! We processed more personal stuff again, and Jesus taught us a prayer to remember.

All this reminded me of the words in James 4:10 (OTB), paraphrased: **"Humble yourselves before the Lord; confess your hurts, hang ups, bad habits, and bad addictions; and receive prayer and the Lord will unshackle you from these things. The Lord will heal you, he will set you free, and he will lift you up. He will get you back on your feet and make you a new person, a different (more mature, at peace, knowledgeable) kind of person than you were before."**

Then Jesus said,

> **Let me pray you to sleep now.**
>
> **Father, help them reach out to others in their circle of friends and to be available to work with their guides as they are working on their own recovery. Father, help them to discover their personal mission assignment from you while on this journey with me. Help them to learn well, the things I am teaching them, so they can teach others to do the same.**
>
> **Father, I place your warring angels around them to guard and protect them, and I place**

your ministering angels with them to serve them and help them sleep. Father, please place your spirit before them to "make a way" wherever their journey takes them and so people will find favor with them wherever they go. Father, I bless them all with the fullness and greatness of who you are. I speak into them the fullness of your Holy Spirit and all the gifts and fruit of your Spirit to fill them to overflowing so that they and others will be blessed. I bless them with all this and more, with my love and your love for them, forever and ever. Amen.

And we fell asleep.

CHAPTER 7

The Seventh Day with Jesus

We all had a deep sleep and awoke refreshed. Jesus must have started the fire in the courtyard pit early because it was already robustly burning as we awakened. However, Jesus was nowhere to be found until we looked far away toward the lake and saw him walking toward us. We could see his big bright smile, as usual, as he waved at us from a distance.

We all washed up as Peter's mother-in-law, and some other people were preparing breakfast for us. We gathered in a three quarter circle with a place for Jesus to sit in the middle, as others served us breakfast and beverages.

As usual, Jesus came by and made it a point to greet each and every one of us with a hug and a kiss. In the same manner, he greeted Peter and all those who were helping.

Then Jesus raised his hands in the air, looking skyward he gave thanks for our food and drink. He also prayed thanks for us journeryers and for all those at Peter's home as well as those who had been following us. As Jesus sat down and ate and drank, he began to teach and ask questions. As he asked us the first question, I remembered the words from Romans 12:2, paraphrased:

> **Do not conform any longer to the patterns, the values, the thinking of this world but be healed from your hurts, bad habits, hang-ups, and**

> **bad addictions as you are transformed by the renewing of your mind that only God can do.**

Then Jesus asked us, as Peter's household listened, **"How have you guarded your mind and your thoughts in the past? Did you just use *denial*, or did you use some other means?**

I spoke up first, saying,

____

____

____

____

Then Jesus asked us, **"Have you filled your mind with hurtful and unhealthy pictures, movies, television programs, Internet sites, magazines, or books? If you have, then how have you failed to fill your mind instead on the positive truths of the Bible?"**

I am certain I was not the only one who was amazed that he was so well-informed about electronic devices and things of the future. Then it dawned on me, *Oh, He and God are one! Duh!*

While I was still pondering his questions, someone else answered his questions first, saying,

____

____

____

____

Then as Jesus was asking us the next questions, I recalled those convicting words in 1 Corinthians 6:19f, paraphrased:

> **Haven't you learned that your body and your spirit, given to you by God, is also, since your personal salvation, the home of the Holy Spirit and so now the Holy Spirit of God resides within you? Therefore, your body and spirit no longer belong to you because your body and spirit have been bought at a great price**

> **when Jesus died for you. So use every part of you, your body, your mind, and your spirit to give glory back to God as a thank you for what God has done for you. Rejoice that God's Spirit resides in you and that God now owns you (body, mind and spirit) as you are now a child of the living God.**

As these words of God were running through my mind, Jesus asked us, **"What hurts, bad habits, hang-ups, and bad addictions have you used to mistreat or harm your body, mind, and spirit in the past? Was it food, sex, alcohol, legal or illegal drugs, purging, bulimia?"**

Someone else answered first, saying,

____

____

____

____

Then, as Jesus quoted Joshua 24:15 (paraphrased) and asked us another question saying, **"Decide today whom you will obey… and as for you and your family, will you serve the Lord God this day and all your following days? In the past, have you mistreated or have you resented anyone in your family? Do you owe them amends? Do you need to reconcile with them?"**

I had a deep need to answer this first, saying,

____

____

____

____

Then Jesus asked, **"What is your family secret? In other words, what have you have been living with and denying its existence of this entire time?"**

I wanted to share a secret. I didn't want to be "as sick as my secrets" anymore, and I really didn't care if the whole group knew my secret, not just my guide. In fact, I had already shared this secret with my guide so the "sting" (embarrassment) was no longer as intense. Yeah, God! So I answered first, saying,

____

____

____

____

As we finished eating, drinking, and cleaning, Jesus asked us a few more questions which reminded me of the words in Hebrews 10:25 (paraphrased), **"Let us not neglect going to church and small groups as we may be inclined to do from time to time. Instead, let us participate in these things and more so that we may have opportunity to disclose to each other, our hurts, bad habits, hang-ups, and bad addictions to each other and also hear and sing the Word of God to encourage each other. Remember, we need each other in all things but especially when times get tough."**

Then Jesus said, **"Have you been thankful back to God for what he has already done for you and given you, giving of your time and resources, actively volunteering at your church and small groups in the past? While volunteering, were you ever critical or judgmental of others, even in your mind?"**

Someone else answered first, saying,

____

____

____

____

Then Jesus asked, **"Have you ever discouraged any member of your family from going to church or small groups? If so, then why? Do you think you need to make amends to them?"**

I answered first, saying,

____

____

____

____

We had cleaned up the area and said our good-byes to Peter, his family, and guests, and then Jesus led us to a few sail boats docked at the large lake nearby and told us we were going to cross to the other side of the lake. Before we sailed away, a couple of men asked Jesus if they could follow him and Jesus told them what they must do, the attitude they must have, to follow. It didn't work out for them, and they never followed.

We got into the sailboats, and as we were sailing toward the middle of this large lake, a storm suddenly kicked up without warning. The waves were so large, they swept over the boats, filling the boats up with water seemingly faster than we could bail the water out!

I was in the boat Jesus was in, and we noticed that Jesus did not seem too concerned about the waves, and this seemed odd to us. In fact, at times, Jesus seemed to be nodding off. We were afraid that all our boats would capsize, and we would all drown, so we woke Jesus up and got his attention as we shouted that we were afraid. He smiled at us, saying we lacked faith, and then he stood up holding the mast with one hand and with the other reaching toward the darkest part of the storm and shouted, **"STOP!"** toward the wind and waves, and almost instantly, the waves and the wind died down.

How could this be? we all asked. How can a man control nature itself? But Jesus was obviously showing us again what we could do, with a little faith, believing in and depending on the power of God to even do, what we considered, the unimaginable. Wow. We were, once again, amazed. I had mixed feelings about whether or not I could really do that. I guess I still had little faith, so I planned to ask God, during my private prayer time with Him, to please strengthen my faith. I also planned to talk this over with my guide.

While we were still in the boats and after the sea had calmed, Jesus asked loudly, so the other journeyers in the other boats could hear: **"What worldly standards have you detached from or have just decided to give up?"**

Someone from another boat shouted out first, saying,

____

____

____

____

As we could just see the shoreline, Jesus asked us another question, saying, **"What have you already done, or what is it you plan to do to restore God's temple, which is your body, your mind, and your spirit? Remember, you are God's creation, and he did deposit his Spirit within you when you were saved, and when he did this, God did not give you a Spirit of fear but a Spirit of power, a Spirit of love, and a sound mind. So what do you plan to do with what God has given you?"**

I had something in mind, so I answered first, saying,

____

____

____

____

As we approached the shore of the lake, Jesus asked us, **"Have your relationships with others and yourself improved since you have been on this journey with me and the journey group?"**

I answered first, saying,

____

____

____

____

Soon after we had all finished answering Jesus, we arrived at the shoreline. We were met by two men who were shouting and screeching and appeared to be demon possessed. It sounded like more than two persons were shouting out when they said, "What do you want with us, Son of God? Have you come here to torture us before the appointed time?"

It was interesting that the demons could readily see what most people could not. The demons immediately knew that Jesus is the Son of God, and the words of the demons gave way to their future, that there was already an appointed time that they would be sent permanently away and tortured!

So the demons, who were afraid of an immediate exile and torture, begged Jesus that if he was going to cast them out of these two men, could he please cast them into the pigs that were nearby on the cliff overhanging the lake. I sensed that Jesus, if he desired, could have cast them into the pits of hell where they came from or have done something even worse with them. However, Jesus said to the demons a single word, "**Go!**" and they were immediately cast out of the two men and driven into the pigs on the cliff, and ironically, the herd of pigs ran off the cliff into the lake and drowned. My guess is the demons then had nowhere to reside and had to return to where they came from, into the pits of hell, anyway. Too bad!

The odd part was that the news of this miracle quickly got to the nearby town and the townspeople, instead of rejoicing that two of their own were delivered from demons, instead, because they were concerned about the loss of their pigs, asked Jesus and us to leave town. Can you imagine that? They seemed more concerned about their pigs, equated to money for them, than the two men that were delivered from demons. I wonder if it would be any different today? Today, would a community, a country, even a church, be more interested in the monetary impact of an event rather than someone's personal healing and/or deliverance?

But before we moved on, as the townspeople demanded, Jesus turned to us and asked, **"Have you ever put more value on a thing, an object, a job, a bad habit, or a bad addiction, rather than valuing yourself or the persons it affected?"**

Some things came to my mind, so I couldn't help but speak first, saying,

____

____

____

____

As we were answering, Jesus led us back to our boats, and we sailed to a nearby familiar town where Jesus was born and raised. We arrived on to the shoreline, and Jesus congratulated us again for staying with him on this journey and for being good students, good journeyers. He also commended us for our patience with each other and for our diligence (thoroughness). Jesus told us that when our journey ends, we will make good teachers, rabbis, and effective guides for others.

I have to admit, I was a little sad thinking that our Journey with Jesus, the Son of God, my Master, Savior, and King, would eventually end. As I thought about an end to this journey, my eyes teared up, but there were happy tears as well. Happy tears because of the great memories and experiences with Jesus and other journeyers. My head was lowered as I thought on these things, but when I looked up again, Jesus had his hand on my shoulder, and he was smiling at me saying, "I sure love you." I realized then, that this experience was just a new beginning and that everything would be okay.

At the distance, we could see the town we were headed for, but before we entered it, Jesus led us to an oasis at the outskirts of town to set up camp, eat, drink, enjoy the dates from the palm trees, and sleep there for the evening.

As we walked to the oasis, Jesus said, **"I know it was tough for most of you to write out a Moral Inventory. Now, with your inventory in hand, it's time to confess your hurts, bad habits, hang-ups, and bad addictions out loud, to yourself, to God and especially to your guide so you can receive the guide's prayers and guidance.**

Just then, I remembered one of my most favorite Bible verses from James 5:16, (paraphrased): **"Therefore, confess your sins, your hurts, bad habits, hang-ups, and bad addictions to one another and pray for one another, that you may be healed."**

Then Jesus said,

> **When we arrive at the oasis, we will set aside some time for this Moral Inventory task of confession and work until completion. We can always stay here an extra day**

or two if needed until completion. And as you complete this, remember the acronym CONFESS that was taught earlier. In summary:

- **The *C* in the word CONFESS is for the importance of *confessing* your hurts, bad habits, hang-ups, and bad addictions.**
- **The *O* in the word CONFESS is for *obeying* God's direction.**
- **The *N* in the word CONFESS is for doing this so you would have *no* more guilt.**
- **The *F* in the word CONFESS is for having the courage to *face* the truth.**
- **The *E* in the word CONFESS is for doing this so you could *ease* your pain (remember, we are only as sick as our secrets).**
- **The *S* in the word CONFESS is to remind us to *stop* blaming others or other things and accept personal responsibility.**
- **The other *S* in the word CONFESS is to remind us to *start* accepting God's forgiveness, so the weight would lift off our shoulders.**

This CONFESS acronym caused me to remember the words of 1 John 1:9 (NCV), paraphrased: **"But if we confess our hurts, bad habits, hang-ups, and bad addictions, he will forgive us because we can trust God to do what is in his nature and God just naturally loves us, his creation. By forgiving us, God will empower us to clean ourselves from all our hurts, bad habits, hang-ups, bad addictions, and all the wrongs we did because of them, through his sacrifice on the cross, his grace, our confession, prayer, and making amends where and whenever possible!"**

We cannot do this without God. We are aware of our need for God because of our personal histories have convinced us and proven to us, we are powerless to do this on our own.

Then Jesus asked, **"What hurts, bad habits, hang-ups, and bad addictions or secrets have been interfering with your sleep? Would you like to be free of such barriers?"**

Someone else started answering the question, saying,

____

____

____

____

As we finished answering Jesus's questions, we made it to the beautiful oasis and began to pick dates and set up camp. It was late afternoon, and there was still plenty of time to work on our moral inventories with our guides.

We circled around to hear what Jesus had to say as he spoke saying,

> **I want you to find some private places around the oasis and meet with your guides for two or three hours, to review your moral inventories and be prayed for. Make sure to do the following:**

- **Begin your meeting with prayer and seeking courage, humility, and honesty. Remember that if you say you have no hurts, bad habits, hang-ups, bad addictions or secrets, struggles, and failures, you are only deceiving yourselves.**
- **Choose a guide who is the same gender.**
- **Choose someone who has already completed this journey with me, if possible.**
- **Remember to keep your Moral Inventory well-balanced, identifying both weaknesses and strengths.**

By the time we finished meeting with our guides and began returning to our central camp area, the fire was fully enflamed so we prepared our meals and beverages. Then Jesus asked us, **"What value do you see in reviewing your Moral Inventory with your**

Guide and coming clean of your past hurts, bad habits, hang-ups, and bad addictions? As you obeyed God's direction to confess and pray for each other, was the result what you expected?

I couldn't wait to respond, so I spoke first, as we continued preparing our meals and taking a seat close to Jesus. I said,

____

____

____

____

As we ate our meals, Jesus asked, **"As you worked through your Moral Inventory with your guide, did you feel condemned or judged, or did you feel a sense of freedom? Please describe your feelings."**

Someone else responded first, saying,

____

____

____

____

Then Jesus said, **"As you have learned to teach others how to face the truth, stop the blame, ease the pain, and start accepting God's forgiveness, how have you experienced changes in the following areas: truth, blame, pain, and forgiveness?"**

Someone else responded first by addressing all four areas, saying,

____

____

____

____

We had finished eating, and the evening's darkness was upon us. The campfire flame was bright and crackling. Some of us where still cleaning up when Jesus commented, saying,

> **There are three main reasons why we need to confess our hurts, bad habits, hang-ups, and bad addictions,**

first to ourselves and to God, then to another person like our guide. Those three main reasons are as follows:

- ***You realize your personal need for healing*: Sharing with a guide and others your hurts, bad habits, hang-ups and bad addictions, your secrets, your struggles, and your failures is part of your obedience to God, God's plan for you, and part of your personal healing process. This healing process addresses your need for healing, and like this journey with me, it is your personal road to your recovery. Remember, this journey is not meant to be taken alone but with a guide and in the company of others.**

Just then, I again recalled one of my favorite verses in James 5:16 (NIV), paraphrased, **"Confess your hurts, habits, hang-ups, bad addictions, secrets, struggles, and failures [sin] to each other and then pray for each other's forgiveness and remind each other of God's plan and promises so that you may be healed."**

Yes, healing of hurts, habits, hang-ups, bad addictions, secrets, struggles, and failures (sin) seems to be a process. The miracle of our healing was instant **"by His stripes, we are healed"** (Isaiah 53:5, OTB), while yet the full actualization, the feeling, the full comprehension and understanding of our healing's completion, the freedom that comes with our healing, is sometimes realized as we work through a process, a journey, for most. It is for me.

I knew Isaiah, in verse 53, was talking about the scourge, beating, the cross, and the death of Jesus's body and that Jesus would bear for our sins. Jesus then said to us,

Another reason God wants you to confess is

- ***You realize you want your freedom*: Your secrets have kept you sick, bound up in chains, unable to function well in all of your relationships with God, self, and others. God's promise is that your chains will snap off**

and your freedom gained back when you confess your sins to yourself, to God, and to another.

Then Jesus quoted the Psalms 107:13f, (paraphrased): **"They cried out to God because of the troubles they were chained to, and he rescued them! He led them from the darkness of their hurts, bad habits, hang-ups, bad addictions, secrets, struggles, and failures, and the shadow of death that follows those things, and then, in his rescue of them, God snapped off their chains and set them free!"**

Jesus continued as he told us of another reason we need to confess:

- ***You realize your need for support*: This is one of the most wonderful experiences of confession. You will experience a flood of compassion, grace, and forgiveness instead of condemnation and judgment, as the chains break off and the burdens (hurts, bad habits, hang ups, bad addictions, etc.) lift from your shoulders.**

Jesus reminded us,

> **My yoke is easy, not only because I have unlimited power in Father God but because I use the family of God (you all), the children of God to help each other in healing all your hurts, bad habits, hang-ups, and bad addictions. Because of this, my yoke, I will give you rest, the rest you have long needed, that's my promise and the family of God's promise to you.**
>
> **Your guide will be able to help you focus and provide feedback for you, as you continue to work on your Moral Inventory sheets. Your guide can also challenge you and hold you accountable if they see you slipping back into**

> **denial. Most importantly, your guide will listen to you. This is your guide's primary mission.**

Then Jesus quoted Psalms 32:3f (TLB), paraphrased, saying,

> **Be encouraged by the words of the Psalmist who wrote, "There was a time when I wouldn't admit what a sinner I was. But my dishonesty and denial made me miserable and filled my days with frustration. All day and all night, your hand, Lord, was heavy on me as you confronted me. And because of my denial and stubbornness, my strength evaporated like water on a hot sunny day until I finally came out of denial and stopped trying to hide my hurts, bad habits, hang-ups, bad addictions, secrets, struggles, and failures from you. Instead, I said to myself, 'I will confess them to myself, to you, oh God, and to another,' and I finally felt forgiven, my guilt was broken and snapped as if was taken from me, and my burden was gone."**

I remembered the words in Romans 8:1 (TLB), paraphrased, **"So there is now no condemnation, no judgment, no chains, no burden awaiting for those who are in Christ Jesus."**

I realized that I fully comprehended this "already healed, already forgiven fact" as I worked my Moral Inventory, confessed, and prayed, so I could fully realize it!

Then Jesus said, **"Most of you will have found it a little difficult to confess your hurts, bad habits, hang-ups, and bad addictions to yourselves or to God, to your guide or to someone else. Which one was most difficult for you to confess to, and why?"**

Someone else started out answering first, saying,

____

____

____

____

We finished eating and were cleaning up while also getting ready for bed as Jesus said,

> **I want to ask you a question and teach you one more thing before I pray you to sleep. Are you entirely *ready* to have God remove all your hurts, bad habits, hang-ups, and bad addictions? As you learn to teach, let me share another acronym with you that will help you remember what it takes to be ready to have God help you to be healed and recover. It's another acronym using the word ready:**

- **The *R* in the word READY will remind you to teach others to remember to *release* control of your will over to God. You need not fear God. It's not in God's interests or nature to force his will on you, his creation. He did not force his will on Adam and Eve, or they would not have fallen. Instead, God wants his creations to develop character and strength, so he patiently waits for your spiritual development and maturity. God is excited about your recovery! You are becoming the kind of being God wants to spend eternity with!**

> **Your willingness to release control over to God is the key that goes into the lock that opens the door to God's kingdom, allowing God to come into the depths of your soul and release the chains and the burdens that come from our hurts, bad habits, hang-ups, and bad addictions. As a result of releasing control over to God, we recover our spirits and feel true freedom a price**

already paid for us. We become what God intended for us to be—children and friends of God, with reflections of his character, spiritual maturity, and strength.

Then Jesus quoted, for our purposes, from Psalms 143:10 (TLB), paraphrased:

> **The Psalmist wrote, "God, help me to do your will, not mine, for I have released control over to you because you are my God and I am your child and friend. Please set me free and heal my spirit. Please have your Spirit lead me in your good paths because I've been down my paths, and they haven't worked well for me. Help me and guide me, oh God, be my personal forever guide."**

Then Jesus continued with the acronym for READY, saying,

- **The *E* in the word READY will remind you to teach others that *easy* does it. Don't be in a hurry and don't push the** journeryer **that you happen to be guiding. Keep them on schedule and focused but don't push them. It is very important that you remember; You can lead a mule to water, but you can't make them drink it. They have to want to all on their own.**

  This process of recovery is not a quick fix because by the time they have come to you and me, as you may have come to me, they are thirsty, just as you may have been. They will have amassed a lifetime of hurts, bad habits, hang-ups, and bad addictions that, only with God's power and this journey, will they be able to even *see*, let alone *untangle* and *recover* from a life time of problems. Be patient with them, as I am with you.

Jesus continued with the acronym for READY, saying,

- **The *A* in the word READY will remind you to teach others to *accept* the changes that will take place in us. Put your will to one side and prepare yourself to accept God's will and God's help continuously throughout your full spiritual recovery and healing.**

Then I remembered the words of 1 Peter 1:13f, paraphrased:

> **Be obedient to God and do not allow yourselves to be governed by your will and shaped by those hurts, bad habits, hang-ups, and bad addictions that you had when you were still in denial and couldn't see your problem or even how to get help."**

Then Jesus continued with the acronym for READY, saying,

- **The *D* in the word READY will remind you to teach others that, as God helps you to remove old character defects (hurts, bad habits, hang-ups, and bad addictions), the importance of *doing* your part to replace your old character defects with positive ones is important. The *doing* would include working the program/journey (doing the Moral Inventory and what the guide suggests), giving of your time and money as you volunteer in your small groups, volunteering at your church, and partaking in other healthy activities that honor God. It is also important to practice hobbies that help you spiritually grow.**

I remembered that I replaced my addictions to golf and alcohol with new addictions like playing the guitar and volunteering to lead worship in my small group. I was also reminded of a verse in Matthew 12:43f, paraphrased:

When an evil spirit, nurtured and rooted into a person's spirit by hurts, bad habits, hang-ups, and bad addictions, goes out of a person, it will come back and reenter, if the house is empty and not filled with new positive habits. These new positive habits would be like volunteering in your small group, your church, other healthy activities that honor God or hobbies like daily Bible reading or just doing things that help you grow spiritually. All these new positive habits will ensure the evil spirits, and their buddies, do not have an empty room for them to reenter."

Jesus continued with the acronym for READY saying;

- **The *Y* in the word READY will remind you to teach others to *yield* to the growth of your new character and new nature that God will surely bring to you, as you continue on this journey of recovery with me. It may be a little scary and uncomfortable at first, all things that are new are usually a little scary and uncomfortable at first, but hang in there, and you will be glad you did. I promise you.**

  Your old nature, coupled with self-doubts and low self-esteem, may claim you are not worthy of the growth and the progress you are experiencing on this journey with me, but you are worth it and you are ready. You are loved and you are worthy. Let yourself yield to the growth that comes when you yield to the will of God as God's Holy Spirit works within you.

I was reminded of the verse in 1 John 3:9f (TLB), paraphrased:

> **This person, who is now a part of God's family, should not continue to be ruled by their old nature which was filled with old hurts, bad habits, hang-ups, and bad addictions, because, as they journey with God, God's new life is now in them, teaching them, through recovery, new things so that they can become a new creation.**

Summary of the Seventh Day
What We Learned

At the end of the seventh day, we are reminded to be humble (modest, meek) and always be willing to ask God to help us remove any of our shortcomings (weaknesses, flaws, inadequacies) any of our future hurts, bad habits, hang-ups, and bad addictions, which we may encounter in the future.

It's important for us to remember that God wants us to have good addictions such as time with him, time in his Word, servanthood volunteer, and being addicted to the fellowship of his church (the people of God).

We also learned about our minds, we did more processing, we learned about giving back and we sailed with Jesus!

We also experienced more miracles, processed more stuff, witnessed deliverance and healing, and processed more stuff again; we learned about CONFESS; we chose a guide; we faced the truth, stopped the blame and eased the pain; we learned why we need to confess, and that we are already healed; and then we learned to be READY.

I was reminded of the words in 1 John 1:9–10 (OTB), paraphrased:

> **If we confess our hurts, bad habits, hang-ups, and bad addictions, God is faithful and just to forgive us, our hurts, bad habits, hang-ups, and bad addictions, and God will cleanse us from all of these things.**
>
> **But remember this, if we say we have no sins, no hurts, bad habits, hang-ups, and bad addictions, we make God a liar for all have sinned and come short of the glory of God, and if we say we have no sins (no hurts, bad habits, hang-ups, or bad addictions), God's Word is not in us, and we cannot have fellowship with God.**

Then Jesus said, **"Everyone in God's Church has, at least, some hurts, bad habits, and hang-ups they need to recover from. All they have to do is ask their 'honest' friends or 'significant others' and they will find out what they are."** ☺

At our campsite, Jesus added wood to the fire and poked the coals and the wood so the flames would catch more air and increase; You could tell he was deep in thought as he stared into the campfire. We could see his smile as the glow from the fire lit his face. Then Jesus said to us, **"Now, I'll pray you all to sleep. Thank you, Father God, for taking these journeyers this far on their journey to the core of their souls and in their personal recoveries and thereby teaching them to help others on their personal journeys as well. I pray that these journeyers continue to ask you to help them to be ready to have their hurts, bad habits, hang-ups, and bad addictions healed so they can experience empowering and illuminating change.**

Jesus continued praying, saying, **"Give them the strength, oh God, to help them and their guides deal with all they reveal and turn over to you. Help them to become the glorious, gift-filled, strong persons you want them to be, with spirits of power, strength, and sound minds. Continue to protect them, oh God, in their sleep, in their dreams, and continue to fill them with the fullness of your Holy Spirit. Above all, oh God, teach them what love really is and how to love themselves and each other. I pray this for all of you, as you sleep, blessing you with God's love, my love, and the love of the Holy Spirit for you, forever and ever. Amen.**

We slept a deep sleep again.

CHAPTER 8

The Eighth Day with Jesus

As we awakened, we noticed Jesus was waiting for us in the middle of the circle around the campfire. We cleaned up and prepared breakfast as Jesus asked us, **"Did you all sleep well?"**

We all smiled at Jesus, we seemed to mumble the same contented combination of words meaning yes, we slept very well". Then Jesus said **"Good"** and asked us the following, as we were preparing our meals, **"What areas of your lives have you been able to surrender and turn over to the control of God, and what areas of your lives have you not turned over to God?"**

I answered first, saying,

____

____

____

____

As we ate, Jesus asked, **"What does the term 'easy does it' mean to you? Are there areas of your recovery you would like to have quickly fixed?**

Someone else answered first, saying,

____

____

____

____

As we finished our meals and prepared for travel, Jesus asked us, **"What do you think the difference is between 'seeing' a need for change versus 'being ready' for change, thereby, being willing to accept and incorporate a change while on your journey to the center of the soul? God has said, 'Be holy, for I am holy." Which one of you can be holy without change?"**

I recalled the words in Romans 12:2, paraphrased: **"Be transformed, changed, by the renewal of your minds and your spirits,"** and I knew that this was what Jesus was talking about. Jesus was talking about journeying to the core of our souls to disclose, pray into, heal, and discover how we can renew, transform our minds and our spirits, and by so doing, with God's help, we can discover the holiness in us, the holiness God intended for us!

I was charged up! It was like I had just discovered gold! Eureka! I knew, without a doubt, that in order for me to hear God clearer, to fully receive all of the gifting he intended for me to receive, to have faith to be able to act out all of God's gifting in me and all the miracles God intended for me to do, I had to let God transform me, change me, into the holiness God had planned for me! I answered first saying,

____

____

____

____

This time, it took awhile for everyone to finish answering Jesus's questions. After we finished policing (cleaning up) the area, we were ready to depart again. But before we started the next leg of our journey, Jesus said to us, **"Before we get on the road again, take a seat just one more time, because I have a couple more questions I want you to answer before we leave. As you are allowing God to make positive changes in your character, what are some of the changes you have made for yourself, your family, your job, and your church, since you have been on this journey with me to the center of your soul?**

I answered first as I addressed each of the following areas, saying,

SELF: ___________________________________
FAMILY: _________________________________
JOB: ____________________________________
CHURCH: ________________________________

Then Jesus said one last thing to us before we departed and asked us a couple more questions, saying,

Most often it is difficult for you to see the forest for the trees, so to speak. In other words, it can be difficult for you to see the positive changes that God has been orchestrating into your lives because it is your specific lives that are changing. If it was someone else's life that was changing, you would be able to see it easier. So it might help for you to ask for feedback from someone you love and trust like your guide or some of your fellow journeyers. Ask them specifically, have you seen any positive changes in me lately and, if so, what are they? Tell them you need to be encouraged, built up, edified, so you can move on.

Have you been able to realize the personal changes God has already made in you? Were those changes scary and awkward at first? When you realized those positive changes God has made in you, how have you been able to accept and enjoy them?

Someone else answered first saying,

____
____
____
____

As the final person finished answering, we stood up and moved toward the road to the next city that was ahead of us. It was the town where Jesus was from. Just then, I reflected on the verse from James 1:12f (TLB), paraphrased:

> **So get rid of all that is wrong in your life—all the hurts, bad habits, hang-ups, bad addictions, secrets, struggles, and feelings of failure, both inside the mind and spirit, and in your actions and, instead, humbly be joyful for the wonderful message of hope.**
>
> **God, through Jesus Christ, is able to save our souls, our spirits, even our bodies, and take hold of our hearts and our lives and change them, for our good and God's good purpose.**

As I kept my eyes on Jesus, who was leading us to the next city, I remembered the verse in James 4:10 (TLB), and I began to shed tears of gladness for the changes already realized in me, as I recalled, **"Humble yourselves before the Lord, and He will lift you up."**

My Savior and King, Jesus, was leading me, in so many ways, down my personal road to recovery, and I was humbled and tearful yet with a smile on my face and with each step that I made. I was loudly thinking, "Thank you, Jesus. Thank you, Jesus. Thank you, Jesus." Then another Scripture came to mind in Matthew 5:6 and in 1 John 1:9, paraphrased:

> **Happy are those whose greatest desire is to do what God requires, and if we confess our sins, God is faithful and just and will forgive us, our sins, our hurts, bad habits, hang ups and bad addictions and purify us from *all* unrighteousness.**

Wow, "*all* unrighteousness"! All of our hurts, bad habits, hang-ups, and bad addictions! Wow!

We could see the next city in the distance, and as we approached the city entrance, Jesus said to us,

> **With God, there is always victory over your hurts, bad habits, hang-ups, and bad addictions. So I want you to remember how to teach this to others by remembering another acronym of the word VICTORY:**

- **The *V* in the word VICTORY will remind you to teach others to *voluntarily* submit to God and to every change he wants you to make in your lives and humbly ask him to remove all your hurts, bad habits, hang-ups, and bad addictions.**
- **The *I* in the word VICTORY will remind you to teach others to *identify* character defects (hurt, bad habits, hang-ups, bad addictions) and list them in their moral inventories so they, their guide, and God can work with them and loosen their grip on the journeyers.**
- **The *C* in the word VICTORY will remind you to teach others that the work, in this journey, will help them to *change* their minds, which happens when we let go and let God. We change into a brand-new creature, a brand-new person. The old nature will fade as the new nature blossoms.**
- **The *T* in the word VICTORY will remind you to teach others that their right attitude will help them *turn* over their character defects, their hurts, bad habits, hang-ups and bad addictions, to God. It will remind you to teach others that God's nature is not to override the will that God has given them. God wants you to come to him by your free wills. Your humility will manifest by your willingness to be brutally honest, open, and willing to write down, talk over, and turn over all your character defects to God and your guides. Anything**

short of that will only keep hurting yourself and eventually those around you again.

- **The *O* in the word VICTORY will remind you to teach others that their journey to recovery happens *one* day at a time. Their hurts, bad habits, hang-ups, and bad addictions took a lifetime to create so it makes sense that it will take a while, one step at a time, one day at a time, to recover. Remind them to be patient with themselves. By the yard it's hard, by the inch, it's a synch.**

Just then, I remembered the words in Philippians 1:6f (TLB), paraphrased:

> **And I am sure that God who began a good work within you, from the time of your beginning and at the time of your salvation, will keep right on helping you by his power and grace as you continue to journey with God, until his work within you is finally finished.**

- **The *R* in the word VICTORY will remind you to teach others that *recovery* is a process that takes time. Remind them not to look for a "quick fix" or perfection, just enjoy the process; the process is the journey along the way to recovery, and it's in the process that we find recovery.**
- **The *Y* in the word VICTORY will remind you to teach others that this is a matter of *your* will. Ridding themselves of hurt, bad habits, hang-ups, and bad addictions depends on the power of God, but it also depends on *you* willfully choosing (your will) to change. Teach others that without their willingness to change and their steadfast belief that God can help them change, God will not minister (serve) his power to help you change. God's nature is to always honor *your* free will. After all, he gave you your free will, why would he**

override something he intended for you to have and to exercise freely?

As we were now entering the city of Capernaum near the Sea of Galilee, where Jesus once lived. Jesus asked us to think back on this word *victory* and what the acronym helps us to remember.

At the entrance to the city, many people met us there along with some men who quickly brought to Jesus a friend of theirs that was a paralytic lying on a mat. Jesus smiled at them as he must have realized their belief, their faith, that Jesus could physically heal their friend on the mat. So Jesus said to the paralytic, as it is written in Matthew 9:2f (NIV), paraphrased, **"Take heart, my son, your sins are forgiven. Get up now, take your mat and go home."**

The man rose and went home! As this crippled man was immediately healed, another miracle was occurring, we overheard the disgruntled mumbling of the so-called teachers of the law. We could overhear them saying that Jesus was blaspheming. It's ironic that these so-called teachers of the law were not so much concerned with the miraculous healing that occurred, but instead, they were only concerned with who facilitated it (it was not one of them) and what Jesus actually said, instead of what he did.

Jesus, knowing what these teachers of the law had said, had a frown on his face as he confronted these teachers, saying to them, **"Why do you think evil in your hearts? For which is easier, to say, 'Your sins are forgiven,' or to say, 'Rise and walk'? But that you may know that the Son of Man has authority on earth to forgive sins"—I said to the paralytic— "Rise, pick up your bed and go home."**

While that teachers of the law were angered at what Jesus said and did, the crowd was in awe over the miracle and was busy praising God for the authority God had given to Jesus. The crowd had responded more appropriately than the teachers. Imagine that. Do you think this still happens today?

Jesus walked us away from this area of town, and in another area of town, Jesus spotted a tax collector who, we found out later, was named Matthew. Jesus called Matthew away from his work, and it was as if Matthew had been waiting all his life for this call from Jesus because Matthew immediately dropped everything he had, abandoned his collected taxes and his tax booth, and joined our ranks. Then, Matthew invited Jesus to have dinner in his home and Jesus accepted. We were glad Jesus accepted the invitation because we were all rather hungry.

Matthew had a huge home, and while we were having dinner, there was a mixed crowd of people like us, broken and searching, who suddenly joined us. The Pharisees were even there, although not eating, they nevertheless asked us all, "Why does your teacher, a rabbi, eat with the likes of you all?" I realized, that was something none of the Pharisees would do because they didn't want to catch our cooties (sin). Jesus, overhearing the Pharisees, shook his head and having a look of disappointment on his face, confronted the Pharisees by saying something I recalled reading in Matthew 9:12, paraphrased:

> **It is not the healthy who need a doctor, but the sick—those with hurts, bad habits, hang-ups, bad addictions, and more; however, those who are really sick don't know they are sick (i.e. Pharisees, teachers of the law, all in our churches, etc.). After all, if anyone, even the churched or the ordained, says they are not a sinner, that they do not have one or more of these problems, they are liars.**
>
> **The ones who finally come to me for help are those who have come out of denial and finally realize they need to be physically, mentally, and spiritually healed, delivered— from hurts, bad habits, hang-ups, and bad addictions that have plagued them for years. I will be there for them and deliver them.**

So go and learn what this means, he told the Pharisees. I desire mercy, not sacrifice, for I have not come to call those who think themselves righteous; they are just fooling themselves are still in denial over their own personal hurts, bad habits, hang-ups, and bad addictions.

Rather, I've come for those who really are righteous but think they are not. They are the humble, the persecuted, the peace makers, the poor in spirit. I've come for those who need physical and spiritual healing and deliverance, who are in need of recovery from their hurts, bad habits, hang-ups, and bad addictions, so that they can be set free, be unshackled, and find their calling, their mission as I equip them for ministry." I've come for you!

When Jesus said "I've come for you," he repeated those words over and over as he looked directly and intently at us and the rest of the crowd.

Then, as we continued to eat, I remembered what our pastor preached to us last Sunday while asking, "How many are trained for ministries of all kinds but are still emotionally and spiritually damaged and hurt, so you don't feel like you should use your training? How many of you feel so damaged and hurt that you won't even seek training? We know that hurt people hurt others, and we know you don't want to be one of those people in a church position to hurt people. How many of you feel like that?"

Only a few people felt compelled to raise their hands, I was one of them, but I know there are many more that were identifying with what the pastor was saying.

The pastor continued, "Without facing and dealing with our personal hurts, bad habits, hang-ups, and bad addictions, we are not ready to minister very well, so dealing with those things is part of our equipping. We often do more damage than good, if we don't, and we usually blame everyone else but ourselves—Adam and Eve's genetic curse—this is the nature of humanity because of the curse. The curse is that we don't tend to take personal responsibility for our actions and, instead, prefer to blame others."

Jesus continues His ministry. After Jesus addressed the Pharisees, he addressed some of the journeyers of John the Baptist, who asked Him about fasting.

Then, as Jesus was just finishing, a ruler, who obviously knew of the resurrecting power of God working through Jesus, came and humbled himself by kneeling at the feet of Jesus. The ruler had the faith to ask Jesus to resurrect his daughter from the dead.

As the ruler led Jesus to his home, we followed. On the way, we encountered a woman who touched Jesus's cloak. She had faith to believe that if she could just touch the cloak of Jesus, it would heal her systemic bleeding problem. Jesus, aware of the woman's faith, stopped, turned, and told her that her faith alone had just healed her. And in fact, she was immediately healed!

From this encounter with the miraculous, I learned that when our faith resonates (i.e., vibrates in matching rhythm), believes exactly with the truth, the miraculous happens! Believing is merely believing in the truth. The truth is permeated throughout God's written (Bible) Words and his Rema (Spoken) Words to us! That truth for that woman, and for all of us, was that Jesus can heal her and wants to heal her; her strong belief was in that truth. She believed that truth and the very natural happened. For God, it's natural. She was miraculously healed! Jesus confirmed her healing, sealing the healing within her when he said, **"Your faith has healed you."** Do I have that kind of faith in the truth? Do you?

I answered first, saying,

____

____

____

____

We finally arrived at the ruler's home, the ruler who had asked Jesus to resurrect his daughter from the dead. The crowd was noisy, and you could tell, from what the crowd was saying, that many had already heard that Jesus was asked to resurrect the ruler's daughter.

We and Jesus walked through a disbelieving crowd. You could hear those mumbling negative comments. Jesus entered the home and went into the dead girl's room. Jesus touched her hand, said some words, and the ruler's daughter suddenly came to life! Jesus resurrected her! She got up! This was another amazing miracle, but I could see it was just a matter of fact to Jesus. In any case, the girl's resurrection was amazing news, and it quickly spread throughout the region.

Jesus prayed over the girl and the house. He said some words to the girl's father, then Jesus led us away from the father's home. As we were walking away and were leaving that area of town, Jesus said to us, **"Some of you have already given your total *wills* to God and have submitted to having God help you recover from your hurts, bad habits, hang-ups, and bad addictions. Have you noticed any positive change or a different pattern of thinking?**

As we continued walking, I answered first, saying,

____

____

____

____

Jesus encouraged us to work on our moral inventories so we would know how to teach and help others, while maintaining our emotional and spiritual health.

As we continued to walk to another part of town, Jesus said,

> **Teach others that real personal change, which eventually changes the world around us, results from our willingness to change our own personal minds and our own personal thinking patterns, our wills. Remind others that as they open themselves to changing their own personal thinking patterns, they will need to develop**

an action plan. In their action plans, and yours, it's important to identifying the following.

Action Plan

- **Make a list of personal character defects you are currently aware of.**

____
____
____
____

- **What exactly do you need to stop doing?**

____
____
____
____

- **What exactly do you need to start doing?**

____
____
____
____

- **What specific steps do you plan to take to rely on God's will for your life instead of your own free-will?**

____
____
____
____

As I pondered how scary it can be to turn over my will to the control of God because I don't know what mission(s) he may delegate to me, I knew I had to put this personal fear into perspective. What helped me was remembering the words in Matthew 26: 42f (NIV), paraphrased, how Jesus put his money where his mouth was and modeled following the will of the Father regardless of the immediate results, his death. It's the end result I have to keep my eye on. Jesus said, while in the Garden of Gethsemane and knowing that he would be nailed to the cross having to physically die and endure our hurts, bad habits, hang-ups, and bad addictions, our sins;

> **My Father, I know that if I take this cup, this mission that we both planned, I will suffer. I will bear everyone's hurts, bad habits, hang-ups, and bad addictions, all their sins, and my physical body will die. I know I have to do this in order for humanity to have a chance to recover, to be redeemed back into your arms, and to enjoy life on earth with us now and forever.**
>
> **This, our redemption plan, was our will for humanity, and now, as the end of this mission nears, I am afraid. And yet, I know it is your will for me to finish what we planned, and you are concerned about my individual will. Do not be concerned, Father, not my will but yours, your will shall materialize as we had both planned from the very beginning, and our mission will succeed for our creations' sake. The end result is now in perspective Father. Thank You, I'm ready now.**

As we continued to walk to the other side of town, Jesus asked us a couple of questions, **"What do the terms 'one day at a time' and 'it's a process, not perfection' mean for your personal recovery journey? Do you think your recovery process will be over when our journey ends?"**

Someone else went first, saying,

____

____

____

____

Then Jesus asked us a couple more questions, **"What does the word *humility* mean to you? How does being humble allow you to change your mind, your personal thinking patterns, and facilitate your recovery?"**

As we walked, I answered first, saying,

____

____

____

____

As the group finished, I mentally recalled the following Scriptures as they applied to our teachings and experiences on our Journey, to the center of my soul, with Jesus:

> **If we confess our sins, our hurts, bad habits, hang-ups, and bad addictions and hold ourselves accountable for those people we owe amends to, God (Jesus) will forgive our sins. As we continue to journey with him, all we have to do is confess and he will purify us from all unrighteousness.** (1 John 1:9, paraphrased)

> **Don't copy the behavior that you have developed in your past while caught up in a lifetime of hurts, bad habits, hang-ups, and bad addictions; this is the custom of the world. Instead, hand your will over to God, and he will help you become a new and different person, a new creature. He will provide a fresh newness in what you believe, in the way you think** (i.e. paradigms, **thinking patterns), and in your behavior patterns. Then, and only then, can you appreciate your transformation and how his ways, his will, his truth, is satisfying and fruitful and will set us free.** (Romans 12:2, TLB, paraphrased)

> **If you want to know what God wants you to do, ask him and he will *gladly* share that with you. God is always ready to give you a bountiful supply of his wisdom and will do this for you and *all* who ask him, without resentment or prejudice.** (James 1:5, paraphrased)

As we journeyed across town and came close to another home we were headed for, two blind men who had just begun to follow us, began yelling, "Have mercy on us, Son of David." "Son of David" was another name for Jesus.

As we entered the next home, these two blind men came over to Jesus, and Jesus asked them, "Do you have faith that I can help you?" They quickly responded "Yes!" Then Jesus touched their eyes and said, **"According to your faith, it will be done to you."**

Why did Jesus always seem to mention that a person's "faith" was an integral part of a miracle? I'm not sure, but I think it's because our minds, our belief system, needs just as much healing, restoration, as our bodies. I think Jesus was concerned with the "whole" of who we are, our body, minds, and spirits, not just our bodies. I've been meaning to ask Jesus about this every time we camp, but I keep forgetting. What would you like to ask Jesus next time we camp?

At this point, I also wondered if the two men had lacked faith, would they not have been healed? Would Jesus or God been unable to heal them, or does God's healing depend on our faith? Or is it that God's will does not override our faith to heal us because it is not in God's nature to override our will? What do you think?

In any case, as I was pondering my questions about faith, while those that had confronted Jesus and asked for their eyes to be healed were immediately healed and they were restored! Then, for some reason, Jesus warned them not to let others know about their healing. I wondered how they were going to keep this miracle a secret. I don't know about you, but I would want to blab my miraculous healing to anyone and everyone and shout it out, as I gave glory to Jesus and to God! How about you?

The words and actions of Jesus caused many mixed feelings and questions to stir within me, which I wanted to ask him at a later time.

In the courtyard of this other home, our host put out some food and drink for us. We took a break, began to snack, and Jesus began talking about forgiveness. Jesus said,

> **When you get a chance to evaluate your relationships, as you complete your moral inventories, I want you to think about how you will apply forgiveness (make amends) to those who have hurt you in the past, or how would you apply forgiveness to yourselves or, for some of you, to God?**
>
> **On the same note, how would you ask for forgiveness (make amends) from those you have hurt in your past, including yourselves or, for some of you, how would you ask for forgiveness from God?**
>
> **Someone else from the group of journeyers answered first saying,**
>
> ____
> ____
> ____
> ____
>
> **For some of you, forgiveness could be quite difficult, so I want you to review your moral inventories with your guides and answer these last two questions with your guides.**
>
> **You may remember earlier when I taught the crowd how to pray and I recited, "Our Father." Remember I said, "Forgive us our debts—our bad habits, hang-ups, bad addictions—*as* we**

forgive others. I pray that you'll want to be highly motivated to forgive, that's why the *as* is part of the prayer, so you can be reminded that we are asking God to forgive us our sins *as* we forgive the sins of others. For some of you, this will be a self-curse until you learn to forgive.

To further explain, there are two sides to the coin of forgiveness. On the one side of the forgiveness coin, it's to ask for forgiveness by making amends, compensation, replacement, to repent (turning 180 degrees the other way). It's more than just saying you're sorry. It's willing to compensate or replace, without repeating the same damage. For some of you, not repeating the offense may be initially difficult due to personal circumstances. But let me assure you of your success, over time, and this does take time. Just always remember, with the power of God, nothing is impossible.

On the other side of the forgiveness coin is the forgiveness we are (giving to somene). However, both sides of the forgiveness coin have a symbiotic relationship with each other. One side of the forgiveness coin is mirrored and dependent upon the other side. Forgive us our sins *as* we forgive the sins of others.

This all amounts to another supernatural law of God's, a law of attraction—what we sow, we reap, to come to bear, to be worked out, in our lives with God and with each other.

The words of Jesus reminded me of words from Matthew 5: 7 & 9 as well as Luke 6:31, **"Happy are the merciful and happy are the peacemakers. Do unto others as you would have them do unto you."**

Jesus then said to us,

> **This is important for those whom you teach and for your own personal recovery. I want you to teach others to think hard about and pray hard about what I am about to teach. Making your amends (compensation, replacement) is the beginning of combating the isolation you have from others and from God.**
>
> **Making amends is also important for your and their personal recovery to work. As you and others admit and recognize the hurt you all feel, and the harm you all have done, you all will face the hurts, bad habits, hang-ups, and bad addictions including resentments, bitterness, and other wrongs you have personally practiced and have also endured from others. It's in the coming face-to-face with these things (talking to your guide and others) that you will be able to access God's power to overcome them and you will break free. You may even hear the chains pop off, as in the words of Jeremiah 40: 4 "Now, behold, I release you today from the chains on your hands."**
>
> **Holding on to hurts, bad habits, hang-ups, and bad addictions, including resentments and bitterness, will only block God's forgiveness and damage your relationship with your spouse and others as well as damage your recovery and the recovery of those you are**

> **teaching. So instead of holding on, just let go and let God.**
>
> **Let go of those hurts, bad habits, hang-ups, and bad addictions, and let God take them, including resentments and bitterness, as you continue on this life-long journey with me and as you continue your recovery and let go and let God. Let God, your guide, and maybe some others help you on your journey to recovery, your journey to the center of your soul.**

I was beginning to realize that much of what is in the New Testament is only a peak of the full revelation of what Jesus was teaching. I was reminded of the words in Luke 6:37 (GNB), paraphrased: **"Do not judge others for their hurts, bad habits, hang ups, and bad addictions, and God will not judge you. Do not condemn others, and God will not condemn you. Forgive others, and God will forgive you."**

Just then, a man who was possessed by a demon had an evil spirit or critter, as I call them, attached to him and was brought to Jesus. Jesus immediately expelled, cast out, the demon. He just ordered the demon to get out, and the demon obeyed. Besides this immediate exorcism, the other immediate miracle was that the man began to speak, once freed of the demon. Obviously, the demon had kept this man silent.

Most of the crowed was amazed and gave God glory for such miracles, except for the Pharisees, the religious, of course. It reminded me of this Pharisee-tical critical spirit, is the yeast of the Pharisees that Jesus often talked to his journeyers about. The Pharisees, then and today, don't wish to share the glory or the power of God with anyone else. I see this kind of yeast, this kind of greed, repeatedly in different churches. I believe it's a spiritually genetic curse, fueled by pride and greed, and just like yeast, it moves through each generation, wherever it can find a home (a person) that would let themselves be tempted and overcome by power and greed.

We left the area with, Jesus and as we walked through the town, Jesus would stop from time to time and he would teach us many things and answer our individual questions.

Jesus then said to us,

> **I will teach you another acronym of the word AMENDS to help you teach others how to make amends (compensation, replacement). Along with your Moral Inventory; it is the beginning of admitting the hurt, anger, resentment, jealously you feel, and the harm you have done because of those feelings. You will face the hurts, bad habits, hang-ups, and bad addictions, and other wrongs you have endured from others, while also facing the wrongs you have done too others.**

And so Jesus asked us to memorize the following acronym:

> **The A in the word AMENDS will remind you to teach others to *admit* the hurt and the harm they have done or are feeling. Remind them to face the hurts, resentments, and wrongs they have experienced from others, and face the wrongs they have done too others as well. Remind them also that not letting go of their hurts, resentments, and wro*ngs not* only blocks their personal recovery but blocks God's forgiveness in their own lives. Let go and let God.**

Again, I was reminded of the words in Luke 6:37 (GNB), paraphrased: "Do not judge others for their hurts, bad habits, hang ups, and bad addictions, and God will not judge you. Do not condemn others, and God will not condemn you. Forgive others, and God will forgive you."

Jesus continued to teach us, saying,

- **The *M* in the word AMENDS will remind you to teach others that their *Moral Inventory list* will allow them to review, to refer to from time to time and add to the list, those individuals they need to forgive or those persons whom they seek forgiveness from. Teach them when requesting forgiveness, it will not always happen, they will not always be ready to forgive you, and that's okay. The most important part is in the asking, especially how you ask, without justifying what you did. See your guides for more help with how and when to ask for forgiveness and what to do if it is not given.**

I remembered the words in Luke 6:31 (TLB): **"Treat others as you want them to treat you."**

Jesus continued to teach.

- **The E in the word AMENDS will remind you to teach others that *encouraging* one another is crucial. Before you make amends, to face the hurts, resentments, and wrongs you have experienced from others, and face the wrongs you have done too others, you need to meet with your guide. Your guide will encourage you and provide you with some valuable objective opinions while helping you to make sure your motives stay on track when asking for or giving forgiveness. Your recovery should never be at the expense of someone else's peace.**

When Jesus said this, I was reminded of the words in Hebrews 10:24, paraphrased: **"And let us consider how we may spur—give incentive, encourage, motivate—one another on toward love and good deeds."**

Then Jesus said,

- **The *N* in the word AMENDS will remind you to teach others that making amends, facing the hurts, resentments, and wrongs you have felt from others, and facing the wrongs you have done too others is *not for them.* It's for your recovery, it's only for you; you're working on, not theirs. Remind them to willfully approach those to whom they are offering forgiveness or amends to or those they are asking forgiveness from with humility and sincerity. Remind them to not give excuses or justify their actions while making amends. Focus only on their part, without expecting anything back from the ones they are making amends to.**

Jesus emphasized that "not justifying or giving excuses" was key to having a *humble* and *sincere* attitude, thereby essential to our amends and our personal recovery. Expecting nothing back is especially significant for the persons we are making amends too, ascertaining amends should never be at the expense of the one we are making amends too.

This teaching reminded me of Luke 6:35 (GNB), paraphrased: **"Instead, love those whom you think are your enemies and do good to them, pray for them, lend [offer them amends] and expect nothing back."**

Then Jesus said to us,

- **The *D* in the word AMENDS will remind you to teach others, *don't procrastinate.* Instead, as you muster up the courage and good judgment that's required to make your amends, it will include a careful sense of timing, to not cause additional damage. Seek help from your guide as you pursue your amends.**

I suddenly remembered the words from Philippians 2:4 and Romans 12:18 and was able to put it in this context. Wow! Thank you, Jesus!

> **Each of you should look not to your own selfish interests, but instead to the interests of others. If possible, as far as it depends on you, give it (your amends) away and live at peace with everyone.**

Then Jesus said,

- **The *S* in the word AMENDS will remind you to teach others to *start* living the promises of their recovery as they are recovering and they will discover these promises: Promise One, the*y* will begin to find the peace and serenity that they, and you, have lo*ng been* seeking. Promise Two, all of yo*u* will prepare to embrace God's purpose for your lives. These are *God's* promise to you, "I will repay you for the years the locusts have eaten."**

What a promise! Then, as Jesus rose to lead us out, I silently prayed a quick prayer as follows:

> God, please give me a very willing heart, a willingness to boldly and fearlessly evaluate all my past and current relationships. Please show me the people whom I have hurt and help me become willing, with care, to offer my amends to them.
>
> God, I also pray for you to give me strength to become more willing to offer forgiveness to those who have hurt me, no matter what they did, because that's the same kind of forgiveness you offer me. Please give me the timing that you have set aside for me to do these things. I ask this all in

> the name of your Son and my Savior Jesus, whom I am following and will continue to follow for the rest of my life, as I enjoy God's promises for me, and as I continue this journey to the center of my soul and I recover, with your help, oh God.

As we walked with Jesus, he led us through a few more towns and villages, showing us how to preach in the synagogues (Jewish churches and community centers) and how to heal people who are afflicted with various diseases and illnesses. When he saw the crowds, he felt such compassion for them because they were like sheep without a shepherd and thereby, harassed by the enemy of our souls and they were helpless.

Then Jesus said to us, **"The harvest is large and ready but the workers are few"** and explained there are too few who have journeyed with him as we have and have not been saved, recovered, healed, delivered, and made ready to teach and to shepherd others, as we have been.

And so we ended up at the outskirts of another town, near a steam, and some trees and decided to make camp. As we approached our new camp area, Jesus told us,

> **Before you make camp, I want you to set all you packs down, pull out your Moral Inventory lists and go off separately and meet with your guides and review or finish your first run at your moral inventories. You can always add to your moral inventories later, but it's time to get started. As you finish, I want you to do the following:**

- **In "The Person" part of your Moral Inventory, list the object or person of your resentment or fear. This is where you list those individuals who have hurt you and whom you need to forgive. In addition, you will list those you have hurt and seek to make amends (ask for forgiveness).**

- **In "The Cause" part of your Moral Inventory, specifically list what was done to you or you did to someone else.**
- **In "The Effect" part of your Moral Inventory, describe how you felt when "The Cause" was done to you or the effect you experienced when you did something to someone else.**
- **In "The Damage" part of your Moral Inventory, list the specific damage (resentment, anger, bitterness, fear, etc.) any hurts, habits, or hang-ups that resulted.**
- **In the "My Part" part of your Moral Inventory, list the actions you must take now. Should you forgive or ask for forgiveness (make amends)?**

As you keep this Moral Inventory close to you, and maybe add to it from time to time, going over your additions with your guides, notice how God has helped you to spiritually mature and to grow in wisdom over the next thirty to ninety days. Ask for feedback from your guides regarding your spiritual growth. Your guide will be able to see what you cannot see.

We dropped our gear in the campsite, as Jesus asked, and left to meet with our guides to continue working on our moral inventories.

When we returned to the campsite, Jesus had the fire going for us so we selected our camp sleeping areas and spread our bedding as we cleaned ourselves up and began to help prepare dinner. Jesus commented, **"Remember, our group is a safe place. What is said here, stays here; Hear, hear?"**

We all shouted; "Hear, here!" Then, as we began to serve each other what we had prepared, Jesus asked me to give thanks and say a blessing. At first, I was stunned! I thought, *You want me to say a blessing in the presence of my Master? I'm sure I'll mess it up!* Then a feeling of empowerment came over me, and in an instant, I understood that Jesus came to make journeyers of us and show us how to make journeyers of others, not just to show us *how* to "*do the stuff*" (i.e., heal, pray, deliver, do miracles, etc.) but to empower us to *do it ourselves.*

My friend and the late Pastor John Wimber, Vineyard Church, used to call this "*doing the stuff*".

So I prayed in front of everyone, including Jesus! I raised my hands toward the sky and gave thanks to God, The Father, first and foremost for his Son and my Savior Jesus Christ and for God's Holy Spirit. I thanked him for this journey to the core of my soul, with Jesus and others, for the opportunity to learn, to share, to be healed, to learn to heal, to love, and to let myself be loved. I thanked God for his angelic hosts who help us, for my health, for family, friends, Church, things he has let me have, and so, so much more.

Then I reached down and picked up a piece of bread and a cup and gave thanks for what is available for us to eat and drink, and I thanked God again for the very special leader we have in Jesus Christ to help us learn to *see* and to *know* the *way* of God. Then I blessed everyone in the group, including Jesus himself, with the fullness and greatness of God, with protection and power, and with God's love and my love for them, forever and ever, amen.

Jesus looked at me with one of those penetrating smiles of his, thanked me for giving thanks and then said, **"I want you to keep everything you are about to hear from another journeyer a secret as we continue to share. If you are comfortable sharing with the whole group answer the following question: Whom would you like to identify, that you listed on your Moral Inventory, that you had to make amends to, one of the persons you needed to forgive?"**

I don't know if I really felt comfortable sharing with the whole group, but I couldn't help but share! My thoughts were bubbling up within me, and I just had to speak out, so I said,

Jesus continued to ask, **"Who have you developed a relationship with on this journey that has encouraged you to offer forgiveness to others and make amends to others? Has it been your**

guide? Has it been one of the other journeyers or more than one person? Was it a past or present incident that has encouraged you to offer forgiveness to others and make amends to others?

Someone else began to answer first, saying,

By this time, we were all were eating. Then Jesus said to us, **"You journeyers probably remember the acronym AMENDS. Remember the *N* meant *not for them*? This N (not for them). This will remind you to teach others not to expect anything back from those they are making amends to? What does that mean to you?"**

My Guide and I worked on this one for a while, so I couldn't wait to respond to Jesus's question, so I said,

As we continued to eat, Jesus said, "**As you ask those you've hurt, for forgiveness as you make amends to those you have hurt, remember that *timing* is crucial. That's why you should go over the timing with your guide first. Create a list of those who you have injured, how you have injured them, and when you will be asking for forgiveness and making amends and share this written amends with your guide.**

Jesus asked if anyone would like to share. I had someone in mind, so I spoke first, saying,

As we finished eating and began cleaning up, Jesus said, **"In the acronym AMENDS, I'm sure you remember the *S* meant to *start living the promises*. Remember the promises were that you would begin finding peace and serenity while preparing to embrace God's purpose for your lives. Remember God's promise to you? His promise is 'I will repay you for the years the locusts have eaten.' Are you aware of what God is doing in your life? If you can, share with us some of the promises of God, in recovery, that you are starting to realize are materializing in your life."**

Someone else immediately spoke out first, saying,

____

____

____

____

We were still cleaning up and getting our sleeping packs ready for us to slide into and cover up later, when Jesus said to us,

> **Do you know that there are three primary areas for making amends and forgiveness for you and others to process?**
>
> **To be completely free from your resentments, anger, fears, shame, and guilt, you need to make amends and both give and receive forgiveness in three primary areas of your lives. Pay special attention that if you do not forgive and make amends in all three areas of your lives, your recovery will be stalled and incomplete. One of the three areas of our lives where we need to make forgiveness is:**
>
> **God's forgiveness. Have you accepted God's forgiveness? God's forgiveness is a free gift. That means there is nothing you can do or give that will qualify you to deserve God's forgive-**

> **ness. God just offers forgiveness, for free, to all who simply "just ask for God's son to come into your life, confess your sins to God and, as God's son comes to you, forgiveness for all your sins is freely given, it's free!; that's why it's called God's grace.**

I was reminded that another description of God's grace is his willingness to let his Son, Jesus, become the perfect, blameless, once-and-for-all sacrifice for our sins by dying and shedding his blood as payment for our sins. I don't currently understand this particular "law" of God, but I do know that, for some divine and supernatural reason, God requires that blood has to be shed, as payment, for the sins of human beings, God's creation.

God's law then erases any trace of that sin from our body, minds and spirits, and we are "like new" as if we have never sinned before. When we believe this, we can *see* it, and we can also understand and feel the freedom of being set free. We can also understand this version of God's grace.

This reminded me of the words in Romans 3:22–25 (GNB), paraphrased,

> **But by the free gift of God's grace (you) are all put right with (God) through Jesus Christ, who set (you) free. God offered (Jesus Christ) so that by his sacrificial death (on the cross), Jesus would become the means by which (your) sins, your hurts, bad habits, hang-ups, bad addictions are forgiven through (your) faith in him (Jesus the Christ).**

Then Jesus asked us something I found very interesting. He asked; **"Do some of you need to forgive God? Do you need to make amends to God for not forgiving him for something you hold against him? Some of you may need to list this area of amends with God also in your moral inventories and work on this with**

your guides so that you can make your amends with God. Ask God to forgive you for your anger toward him because of what you think God let happen. Remember that God did not abandon you. The harm that others did to you, or you did to yourself, was from humanity's free will, not from God's will. Your guides will explain further.

Then Jesus described another primary area of our lives where we need to make forgiveness and amends:

1. **Forgiving others. Have you forgiven others who have hurt you? You must let go. Let go and let God. Let go of the hurts or the past harm and abuse caused by others. Until you are able to let go and let God and forgive others, you will be held captive by your own unforgiveness, like a prisoner, and in so doing, you will be the cause of your own pain, hurts and maybe even physical disease.**

   Now listen carefully. If you have been the victim of sexual abuse, physical abuse, childhood emotional abuse or neglect, I am truly sorry for the hurts you had to endure. I hurt with you. I can rid you of any demons (critters) that have attached to you because of this and because you would not let go and let God. But you will not find the peace and freedom from your perpetrator until you are able to forgive that person just as God has forgiven you.

   Remember, forgiving the other person, the perpetrator, *in no way excuses the harm they did to you.* They are guilty and need to make their own amends and ask for their own forgiveness. But your forgiveness of them, thereby giving your anger and hate over to God, will release you from the power that perpetrator had over you by virtue of your own anger, rage, bitterness, and maybe visions of revenge.

All these ill feelings have manifested physical, psychological, and mental damage to you over time. All these ill feelings are like poison that you have been consuming while thinking of getting even with your perpetrator. Doesn't make sense, does it? You only hurt yourself by hating others. That's why you need to forgive seventy times seven. It's for your good, not theirs.

On the other hand; If you need to make amends to others, then list your amends on your Moral Inventory, what you think you have done to offend someone, and talk to God about it, review it with your guide, and, with your Guide's help, meet, if possible, with the person you need to make amends to and say you're sorry. You may or may not get the forgiveness you're asking for, and that's okay. Just making the amend, just asking for forgiveness, will set you free.

Then Jesus explained the last of three primary areas of our lives where we need to make amends and forgiveness:

2. **Forgive yourself. This can be the most difficult area for you to make amends and forgiveness. One of the reasons for this difficulty could be if you have been the victim of sexual abuse, physical abuse, or childhood emotional abuse or neglect. Some people blame themselves for their own abuse, thinking it was their fault. It was not your fault, so forgiving yourself in this and even other areas is vital.**

   You may feel the guilt and shame of other areas of your past which you think are just too much to bare or forgive. You think you have done the unforgivable, and that just isn't true. Forgiving yourself is exactly what God wants you to do with the burden and darkness of the pain of your past, no matter what you did.

> **God wants you to talk it over with him at some point with your guide and maybe with others at some later date. No matter how painful and deep something in your past may seem to you, God can remove the hurts, the pain, and the burden of the something in your past and release you from the burden and weight of the offense, so you can start over. All you have to do is trust God and let him help you. Just let go and let God.**

Jesus was quoting Isaiah 1:18f (TLB), paraphrased, when he said, **"Come now, let us reason together, says the Lord: though your sins, your hurts, bad habits, hang ups, bad addictions are like scarlet, they shall be as white as snow; though they are red like crimson, they shall become like wool."**

As Jesus said this, I also remembered the words in Romans 8:11: **"Therefore, there is now no condemnation for those who are in Christ Jesus."**

Then Jesus said, "**Before we pray and sleep tonight, let me ask you something. As you remember the three kinds of forgiveness and amends, which one of those areas do you think will be the easiest for you to discuss with your guide, and which areas do you think will be the hardest to discuss with your guide? Explain why please."**

I answered first, saying,

____

____

____

____

We all finished answering the last question, and then Jesus asked us to get ready for bed and that he had a few more things to ask of us before he prayed us to sleep. Jesus said,

> **I want you to write down what I am about to tell you so before you have breakfast tomorrow morning, you can work on these privately with your guides.**

- **Take the names of the individuals you listed in your Moral Inventory as those you need to make amends or offer forgiveness to and highlight the ones you can take care of immediately.**
- **Review that list with your guides to ensure that making your amends or offering your forgiveness will not emotionally or spiritually injure those you are offering amends and/or forgiveness to.**
- **Pray with your guide and by yourself with God and ask them to show you the right time and place to make your amends and/or offer your forgiveness with the right motives.**
- **Develop a plan and go over that plan with your guide. For those whom you cannot make immediate amends or forgiveness to, discuss what to do with your guide. If someone on your list has died or you cannot locate them, your guide will show how you can make amends or forgiveness in a letter and what you can do with that letter. Your guide might recommend that you burn the letter, share the letter, or otherwise choose what you would like to do with the letter.**

I thought I would tie my letter to a helium balloon, sign it anonymous, and send it into the ozone. Someone else said they were going to do the same thing except stuff theirs in a bottle and toss it into the ocean.

Summary of the Eighth Day
What We Learned

At the end of the eighth day, we learned how important it is to make and maintain a current and personal Moral Inventory list. That means we need to keep adding to it as time passes. We are also reminded to, as prompt as possible, make amends and forgive others and keep our Moral Inventory list current so we do not fall back into our bondage of hurts, bad habits, hang-ups, or bad addictions.

We also learned about the term "easy does it" and what it means about renewing our minds and making changes. We were assured that God can deliver us, and we learned about VICTORY. We experienced another miracle and encountered the yeast of the Pharisees again that Jesus warned us about. We learned about grace and reflected on the sermon on the mount in the context of recovery. We learned the "Serenity Prayer" and witnessed another deliverance. We understood that recovery is *a process, not perfection*, a deeper understanding of AMENDS, and the three main areas of amends. We learned of promises made to us, that our group is a "safe place" (anonymity), a deeper understanding of forgiveness and especially in the context of sexual abuse. We processed much more stuff, and we talked about balloons!

I was reminded of the verse in Luke 6:31 (OTB), paraphrased, **"Do you have a bad attitude toward others? Or do you speak to and treat others as you would have others have an attitude toward, speak to, and treat, you?"**

Having a right attitude toward someone else (others) is key to being able speak to and treat another person well. If someone has a yeast infection, the yeast of the Pharisees (i.e., race or economic prejudice, jealousy, anger, hatred, bitterness, etc.), they have a bad attitude against a particular person or persons, and they will not be able to speak to them or of them well or treat them well. They will not be able to follow one of Jesus's greatest laws of love. Without *love* all other gifts are meaningless. Therefore, you may have to ask your guide and God to rid you of any yeast infection so you can have a good attitude toward others and be able to speak to and treat others as you would have others treat you?

Jesus overheard us summarizing and talking about our future plans to make amends and smiled. We finished writing things down, and then Jesus prayed over us saying,

> **Thank you, Father God, for taking these journeyers this far in their personal recoveries and thereby teaching them to help others on their forthcoming journeys. I pray they continue asking you to help them to be ready to have their hurts, bad habits, hang-ups, and bad addictions healed and changed.**
>
> **Father, please continue giving them the courage and insight to see and turn over all their hurts, bad habits, hang-ups, and bad addictions over to you. Father, please give them strength to help them deal with all they turn over to you. Help them to be the fearless, glorious, gift-filled, strong persons you want them to be.**
>
> **We've had a long day, Father. We have seen your power at work as your kingdom is at hand, as it always has been, helping the lives of others, and have covered a lot of teaching this day. As you know, we covered surrendering, readiness, humility, VICTORY, action plans, faith, AMENDS, moral inventories, GRACE, forgiveness, and much more. We had a busy day.**
>
> **Please continue to protect them, Father, even in their sleep, even in their dreams, and continue replenishing them with the fullness of**

> **your Holy Spirit, teaching them how to love themselves and each other. I pray this for you, as you sleep, with God's and my protection, and with God's and my love for you, forever and ever, amen.**

We slept well that night.

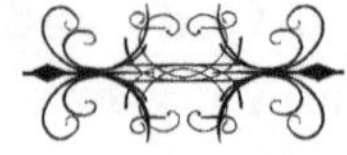

CHAPTER 9

The Ninth Day with Jesus

This was a Sabbath day, and when we awakened, we noticed Jesus in the distance praying. Jesus noticed us waking, and he began to walk toward us. He always seemed to be glowing and smiling when he returned from His prayer time with God, and yet one day, I know Jesus will not be smiling or happy, just obedient (i.e., Luke 22:42: "Not my will, but yours).

The fire was ready, and we assumed Jesus had started the campfire before he left for his prayer time. We cleaned up and circled around the campfire and around Jesus. Some started preparing breakfast as Jesus asked us, **"Did you sleep well again?"**

We all smiled back at Jesus and, almost in unison, answered, "Yes." Jesus said, "Good" and asked us the following, as we maneuvered into our seating areas and prepared our breakfast: **"How have you let God use your weaknesses by turning those weaknesses into strengths?"**

I had something in mind, so I spoke up first:

____

____

____

____

Then Jesus asked us, **"How do you receive God's gift of grace?"**

I noticed someone drop their head and squirm. Quickly, someone else spoke up, saying,

____

____

____

____

By this time, most of us were eating when Jesus asked, **"How can you model God's gift of grace when making your amends or asking for forgiveness?"**

Someone else spoke up first again, saying,

____

____

____

____

As we ate, Jesus asked us, **"How have you experienced God's grace during this journey with me?"**

I spoke up first, saying,

____

____

____

____

Then Jesus said, **"Remember, when you make amends or ask forgiveness, review your motives with yourself and then with your guide. Sometimes, you may say the right words but your body language communicates the wrong motives. Remember, you are not trying to get even, but to just get right with yourself and with God. Speaking the truth in love is having honorable, edifying motives as you speak to someone else. What does speaking the truth in love mean to you when you have spoken what you consider to be the truth, yet with the wrong motives at heart?"**

This question caught many of us off guard because no one wanted to answer. A few bowed their heads and looked down to the ground. In the midst of the long silence, Jesus turned his head and looked directly at me. I was taken back. It was as if he could see right through me, and I couldn't help but speak up, saying,

____
____
____
____

By the time I was done answering and a few others answered, some of us had finished eating and were beginning to clean the campsite and take a seat as Jesus asked us another question, saying, **"When making amends or asking for forgiveness, it's not important what the other person says in response to you. They may not forgive you, or they may lash out at you, and that's okay. Why do you think it is important for you to focus only on your part, in making amends and asking forgiveness or giving forgiveness?**

Someone else spoke up first, saying,

____
____
____
____

Then Jesus told us to finish cleaning and to pack our belongings as we answered this question, **"Share with us what God has revealed to you about amends, forgiveness, and grace."**

I spoke up first, saying,

____
____
____
____

As we prepared to depart from our campsite, Scriptures passed through my mind from 1 John 4:20 paraphrased, Matthew 5:43–44 (TLB) paraphrased, and Romans 12:17–18 (TLB) paraphrased:

> **If anyone says, I love God but is continuously jealous or resentful of his brother or sister,**

they are a liar. If they don't love their brother or sister who is directly in front of them, how can they love God whom they have never seen? There is a saying 'love your friends and hate your enemies,' but I say love your enemies and pray for those who persecute you! Never pay back evil with evil. Conduct your actions so everyone can see you are honest, clear and thorough. Don't quarrel with anyone and remain at peace with everyone, as much as possible.

We all finished answering the last question, Jesus asked us, and soon, we approached another town. Then we were surprised, as Jesus began to meet with the twelve journeyers whom we have studied about in the Bible. They seem to have come out of the blue as if something unseen had called them to meet with Jesus, and we witnessed it!

On that day, he met with Peter and Matthew, who Jesus had met with earlier. And also met with Peter's brother, Andrew, as well as James (the son of Zebedee) and his brother John. Then came Philip and Bartholomew, Thomas and Mathew (the tax collector), James, Thaddeus, Simon, (the Zealot, devotee, advocate, etc.), and Judas (who later betrayed Jesus).

We, the new journeyers, greeted and shook hands with the actual twelve journeyers, disciples, from the Bible! It was great! I also shook hands with Judas! He didn't seem like a bad guy. He seemed quite friendly, like the others.

I don't know why I was so amazed that all those he called to be his journeyers were ordinary-looking and ordinary-acting people, just like us; and, just like us, had no special outstanding physical or verbal features. They were just ordinary people like you and me! Maybe I expected something different. How about you? Would you have expected the journeyers or Jesus to look more than ordinary, to look or to talk in a special way? If so, why?

I spoke up first, saying,

____
____
____
____

Jesus told these twelve journeyers, disciples as Jesus called them, that they wouldn't be able to follow those of us who have been on this particular journey to the center of the soul with him. Jesus further explained that our journey was almost over. Jesus told the twelve journeyers, disciples, that later, he would be taking those who were interested, on a similar journey, to help them recover, and further prepare them for ministry.

It's interesting that he said "those who were interested." He was, as God's nature is, respecting the personal will of his journeyers. My guess is, not all of them will want to do this, many are called but few are chosen. It seems the only time we (humanity) seek recovery or personal growth is when we fall, and sometimes we must fall hard. What are your thoughts about this? Have you taken a bad fall lately?

____
____
____
____

It's interesting that he asked the twelve to take some time to do ministry before their particular recovery journey would begin with Jesus himself. I would not have expected that before more healing and equipping, Jesus would instruct his twelve journeyers to go out and do ministry first. But then again, it continually seems as if the Lord doesn't call the fit but fits whom he calls. In other words, while someone is doing ministry, the Lord equips them.

Apparently, one doesn't need to be fit before one is sent to do ministry; Just called. It appears as if Jesus has set a protocol for fitting someone while they are in the process of doing ministry as well as fitting them through the kind of classroom experience, on the road and in the campsites, and even while doing field work. We also sensed we were getting "fit" as we had ministry experience including when we encountered people around and in the towns, as well as being fit (made ready for ministry), while we are on a personal journey to the core of the soul with Jesus.

Having people do ministry without any training or healing at all doesn't make sense to me. However, God's ways are not my ways, and the world can be thankful for that because I can do some stupid things sometimes. I'm only human and prone to error and sin. On that note, it's interesting and ironic that God called me into ministry and only now, years after I retired from ministry and pastoring a church, am I going through recovery. Go figure?

After the twelve journeyers, disciples, and we said our goodbyes to each other, Jesus said to the twelve journeyers,

> **Go to the lost sheep of Israel… Preach this message: the kingdom of heaven is near. Heal the sick, raise the dead, cleanse those who have leprosy, drive out demons. Freely you have received, freely give, so take nothing for this service… Let your presence rest and your ministry provided only in a guest's home that is worthy. If anyone will not listen to you, then dust off your feet and leave that home or town. Be shrewd as snakes and innocent as doves. What I've told you in the dark, when we were alone, speak out loud now in the daylight. What God whispers in your ear, shout from the house tops. Do not be afraid. He who receives you receives me, and they will be blessed.**

Jesus told them so much more, and we heard it all! It was amazing! It reminded me of the words in the book of Matthew 10.

Jesus sent the twelve journeyers, we know of in the Bible, away. He hugged and kissed them, and after they left, Jesus led us out of town. He led us down a road and said we were headed to a stream on the way to the next set of towns. He knew of a nice shaded clearing where we could set up camp.

As we continued to walk, Jesus asked us, **"What hurts from past relationships are you still holding on to, and how do you think you will be able to specifically let go of such hurts?"**

I had someone in mind, so I spoke up first, saying,

____

____

____

____

Then Jesus asked us, what I considered to be a very tough question, saying, **"Do any of you owe God an amends? When do you expect to make it? Have you been blaming God for the harmful actions that others took against you?"**

I just had to speak up first. I felt Jesus was talking directly to me. You remember, like when the preacher is preaching, from the pulpit, and you believe she or he is speaking directly to you. So I said,

____

____

____

____

Apparently, I wasn't the only one who owed God amends as many other disclosed as well. As we continued to walk, Jesus said we were getting closer to our next destination.

Then he asked us, **"Have you forgiven yourself for any past actions that caused you to feel guilt or shame? You'll want to also list these past actions in your moral inventories, but for now, who would like to share?"**

All of us eventually shared but, in this case, someone else answered first, saying,

____

____

____

____

As the last person finished sharing, Jesus pointed in the distance where we would take a break and a nap. It was then that I recalled certain scriptures from Colossians 3:13 (TLB) and part of the "Lord's Prayer" in Matthew 6:12, paraphrased, **"Be gentle and ready to forgive. Never hold grudges. Remember, the Lord forgave you, so you must forgive others... and forgive us our sins and our trespasses, just as we have forgiven those who have sinned and trespassed against us."**

We made it to a beautiful open area near a stream. The open area was surrounded by palms, which were full of ripe dates. As we proceeded to set down our packs and take a break, we also walked around and picked some dates.

Jesus suggested we take some time to work further on our moral inventories before we take a break, to go to a secluded area and continue working with our guides. He said we could meet with our guides for any other reason as well as to work on our moral inventories. So we all ended up leaving for a short time to work with our guides again.

When we returned to the break area, we noticed Jesus was sitting on a stump. Jesus said to us, **"Before you lay down for a nap to rest, I want you to think about what God's grace means to you."**

I immediately thought of the words in 2 Corinthians 12:9–10 (NCV), paraphrased,

> **My grace is sufficient (enough) for you. When you humble yourself and show (disclose, give testimony of) your weaknesses, people see and feel (God's) glory and power and how it is being made perfect in you.**
>
> **So be happy, brag about and give testimony about your weaknesses because people will see and feel the power of Jesus Christ (and God) living and working in you. Be joyful that you have weaknesses, hard times, sufferings and that people may insult you because you are**

> **giving testimony for Christ's sake by showing others that you are weak and then because of God's power and glory manifesting in you, you will be truly (showing) how strong (God is).**

Then Jesus said, "**I have another acronym using the word GRACE for you to memorize and teach others.**" As we began to eat those juicy dates and prepare for a nap, Jesus began to teach us again, saying,

- **The *G* in the word GRACE will remind you to teach others that the *G* is *God's free gift*, a gift that cannot be purchased or earned. Grace is a free gift from God to you and others when you ask for it.**

  Likewise, it is when you offer your amends and forgiveness to others that you end up giving this gift of grace to yourselves as well.

  Even though amends and forgiveness (grace) is offered to another, *grace* is when you do not expect anything in return because *forgiveness* is not dependent on what you are given back by others. In other words, whether or not they forgive you, it's only dependent on you freely giving away your amends and forgiveness (grace) alone. Amends and forgiveness (grace) is a significant part of your recovery.

- **The *R* in the word GRACE will remind you to teach others that the *R* stands for *receiving God by faith* and faith alone.**

  Faith is not believing in what you see; faith is seeing because you believe. It is only by professing that I am Jesus, your savior, that you will be able to see and expe-

rience God's own grace and the promises of eternal life with God.

Remind them, that it is only by this profession, spoken words, of faith in me (Jesus) as their Savior that they will also find the strength, courage, and wisdom needed for them to make amends and offer forgiveness to God, to self as well as to others.

Suddenly, I was reminded of the words of Ephesians 2:8–9 and Romans 5:2, both paraphrased:

For it is by grace you have been saved, through faith and not from yourselves or your own understanding, logic, reason, or any particular ministry or calling; otherwise, you would boast and try to take personal credit. Instead, you were saved only because you asked and because *salvation* is the free gift from God.

Through faith in Jesus, we have gained access into this grace (salvation) in which we now stand. This is God's glory, and we rejoice in the hope that God's glory gives us.

Then Jesus continued to teach us, saying,

- **The *A* in the word GRACE will remind you to teach others that *all are accepted by God.* Teach them God has the kind of powerful love that accepts you even while you sin. This kind of love is also God's grace that continues to give to the unlovely and the unlovable, regardless of the degree of sin. There is no sin greater than the love of God or his willingness to forgive.**

  With God's model of acceptance, and in the same manner, we are encouraged to love others by accepting

them, regardless of themselves, in the same way. We have the power to love that way, the way that God loves and accepts us because God first loved us and continues to love us in this manner. You can also forgive that way because God forgave you and continues to forgive you regardless. Freely, love and forgive because it was freely given to you, so freely give it to others, mimicking the Father as good and faithful children of God.

- **The C in the word GRACE will remind you to teach others the *C* is for *Christ*!**

I am an essential part of God's grace. It is my mission to pay the price for all your sins and the sins of others, so that God will forgive your sins. My mission is to pay the price and sacrifice myself for you so that, if you ask for our—God's and my—salvation, the forgiveness of all your sins will be freely given to you but first you have to ask.

Teach others that some may need to plow through their own pride and selfishness to get there, to ask, but I can even help them break through their pride and give them the ability to ask for my help and the help of others.

In love, remind those you teach that the grace of God, including God's salvation, is not attained by working or volunteering in a church or giving away money. God's grace is not attained by following religious laws like some of the Pharisees as well as modern day religious people (modern Pharisees) do. If God's grace could be attained in those ways (through works), it would not be attainable for many people and it would make my mission meaningless.

What Jesus said reminded me of the words in Galatians 2:21 and Ephesians 1:7 (NIV), both paraphrased:

> **I do not set aside or forget my understanding of the grace of God, for if righteousness could be gained through the law (religious rules, ministry or money, then), Christ died for nothing.**
>
> **In Christ, we are set free by the blood of his death and so we have forgiveness of sins. How rich is God's grace (and it is by this grace alone, and by nothing else, that we are forgiven and saved).**

Jesus continued to teach us saying,

- **The *E* in the word GRACE will remind you to teach others that the *E* stands for the *everlasting* gift. God's free gift of grace is everlasting. Tell them that once they have accepted me as the only begotten Son of God and their personal Lord and Savior, that God's free gift of grace, the forgiveness of their past, present, and future sins can never be taken from them and that it is everlasting. Once my grace is given to you, it is everlasting and can never be lost or returned.**

I remembered the words in Philippians 1:6 (TLB), paraphrased:

> **I am sure that God, who began the good work within you at the time of your Salvation, will continue helping you grow in his grace until his task within you, his ministry, worked through you, is finally finished.**

We, eventually, all fell asleep for a short nap and a deserved rest.

When we awoke, we hiked back to the road to continue our journey to a nearby town. While on the road, some people who identified themselves as journeyers of John the Baptist said to Jesus, "Our teacher, John, who has baptized us and many others, sent us to find out if you Jesus are the one, the Messiah whom we have been waiting for, or are we to expect another?"

Jesus replied to them saying, **"Who do you think I am? Go back and tell John what you have seen and heard. The blind have received sight, the lame now walk, those who have leprosy are cured, the deaf hear, the dead are alive and have ascended, journeyers have been taught, and good news is preached to the poor."**

Then as John's journeyers turned to leave and while the journeyers of John were leaving, Jesus began to edify John the Baptist out loud to the crowd. Jesus called him a messenger sent from God and a prophet, the greatest of all men who were born. But Jesus put the kingdom of God in perspective when he said that even the least of those in the kingdom of heaven were greater than John the Baptist. Wow! The kingdom of heaven must be an awesome place that can make the least of us be in such high character and strength, that we would be considered as even greater than the greatest of all men, in reference to John the Baptist.

Then Jesus warned the crowd, he called this generation and warned the cities that were thinking and speaking evil of God's messengers. He praised God for revealing spiritual information to his children, hidden from the so-called wise, and then he again beckoned the weary to come to him to find rest and comfort.

Then, we departed the city and walked through a grain field on our way to a resting place. We picked some heads of grain and ate them and packed some heads of grain to eat later at our resting place. At the end of the grain field, there was a clearing with trees and a well. We set up a resting place in the shade of the trees, drank from an available well, and filled our skins and canteens with water.

As we circled around Jesus to hear him teach again, the Pharisees from town had followed us and finally caught up with us. The Pharisees stood near as they addressed Jesus, as they pointed to us, accusing us of breaking the law of the Sabbath because we worked on the Sabbath by picking heads of grain. Jesus corrected them by saying they did not really understand the Sabbath. I think the Pharisees became even more bitter and resentful of Jesus as their obvious jealousy grew. After they left, Jesus commented, **"This jealousy, bitterness, and resentment that you've seen and heard demonstrated against you and me, I call the yeast of the Pharisees. Do you know anyone who has mimicked the yeast of the Pharisees, or have you ever mimicked these same attitudes of the Pharisees with someone else—jealousy, bitterness, resentment—because they had something or had an understanding you did not have? Have you ever seen this in the church?**

I couldn't wait to answer. I think I had an "axe to grind," so I started out saying,

____

____

____

____

Jesus said,

> **I want to teach you another acronym for you to teach others. It's with the word RECOVERY. Teach them this:**

- **The *R* in the word RECOVERY will help them to *remember* that they, and you, are not God. Realizing you, and they are unable to control tendencies, to do wrong without God's help to stop you, is a sign of spiritual maturity and the beginning of developing spiritual strength.**
- **The *E* in the word RECOVERY will help them remember to *earnestly believe that God exists*, that you will always matter to him, and that only He (God) has the will and the power to help you recover, when nothing and no one else can! There is no greater higher power than God.**
- **The *C* in the word RECOVERY will help them remember to *consciously commit* their entire will and life to**

God's care and control. Let go and let God. You have to first let go.

- **The *O* in the word RECOVERY will help them remember to *openly examine and confess* their faults to God, to yourself, and to your guide and/or a trusted friend or advisor and then ask them to guide you and especially pray for you.**

This reminded me of the words in James 5:16, "Therefore, confess your sins to one another and pray for one another, that you may be healed." This is one of my favorite Scripture verses. God knows I've done a lot of confessing and have needed, and still need a lot of prayer.

- **The *V* in the word RECOVERY will help them remember to *voluntarily submit* to every change God wants to make in their lives and yours and humbly ask God to remove all character defects. This will take time, but it starts with taking the first step, the asking.**
- **The second *E* in the word RECOVERY will help them remember to *evaluate all relationships*, offering amends and forgiveness with good and honorable motives, ask your guides about this, so as not to hurt anyone. Remind them to always check with their guides first before they offer amends or forgiveness to anyone. The guides will help them understand how not to use the word *you*, how to not back someone in a corner, and how to not expect anything in return.**
- **The *R* in the word RECOVERY will help them remember to *reserve daily time with God* to focus on listening to what God has to say, for self-examination, and to read God's written word. Encourage them to do this in order to develop a friendship with God, to learn to recognize God's voice, over time, and to understand God's will and mission for their life. Remind them that spending time with God will also result in spiritual**

maturity, understanding, and the power to do God's will, just as I do.

- **The *Y* in the word RECOVERY will help them remember to *yield themselves totally to God* and God, then, can use them to bring the good news to others, that the kingdom of God is at hand. As you are all now in recovery on a journey with me, you are better able to be a good example of God's power and better able to express love by the words you use, by volunteering your time, and by how you treat yourselves.**

After Jesus spoke about recovery and as some of us began to take a nap again, before we continued, I remembered the words in Matthew 5: 1f (OTB), and those words took on new meaning for me in the context of my recovery with Jesus. When Jesus was on the mountainside teaching the crowds, he said what we later call the Beatitudes, and we also later added eight corresponding principles of recovery.

Jesus said, **"Memorize the eight principles of recovery in the acronym of the word RECOVERY and how those eight principles of recovery relate to the words in, what you call, the Beatitudes of Jesus Christ in the book of Matthew. Remember what this acronym means to you.**

THE BEATITUDE

Blessed are the poor in spirit, for theirs is the kingdom of heaven. (Matthew 5:3)

The First Principle
In the Acronym RECOVERY

***R* in the acronym for the word RECOVERY will help you *realize that they, and you, are not God*—that means you realize you and others are spiritually poor compared to God and that you and they do not have the power to do what only God can do.**

On the first day of my journey to come closer to God, I now understand, and I admit that I am powerless to control my tendency to do the wrong thing and that my life is unmanageable without God. I guess I finally had to admit I am not God and stop trying to fix this, in secret, by myself. My first step on my journey with Jesus was admitting that I am spiritually poor without God. Now I'm a happy camper and the kingdom of heaven is at hand!

This reminded me of the Scripture in the OTB, Romans 18f (paraphrased): **"For I know that nothing good dwells in me, that is, in my flesh my old spirit. For I have the desire to do what is right, but not the ability to carry it out. For I do not do the good I want, but the evil I do not want is what I keep on doing."**

Like all of humanity, I am spiritually poor, so I cry out to God (willing to do his will not mine anymore), and I delight that God, the power greater than myself, can deliver me, change me, and strengthen my spirit.

Then Jesus said,

THE BEATITUDE

Blessed are those who mourn, for they shall be comforted. (Matthew 5:4)
The Second Principle
In the Acronym RECOVERY

***E* in the acronym for the word RECOVERY will help you to *earnestly believe that God does exist*, that you matter to him, and that he, and only he, has the only power to help you fully and permanently recover. Happy are those who have experienced the feelings of morning, for they have experienced being comforted by God and others.**

I had been in mourning before, when my father died, when my dog died, or when I went through a divorce, but it was on the second day of my journey with Jesus that I remembered I was in a lot of pain and in mourning for what I did to my family, friends, work, and even myself when I finally realized and admitted (came out of denial) that

I was weak and I had a drinking problem. I was in deep spiritual and physical pain and sorrowful mourning.

I knew I couldn't help myself break the drinking habit or I would have broken my own habit already. So I had to rely on something/someone greater than myself to help me break this bad habit and help me recover. I already knew, believed without a doubt, that the only one that had that kind of power is God and I finally admitted it and cried out to God while in jail.

In the midst of my mourning and while I was still in tears, I reached out to God, told him how much I believed in him and needed him, told him I was willing to submit to his will instead of doing my will, and I asked God to forgive me for my past stubborn, self-serving willfulness, and then I asked God to break the shackles of my addiction for me, heal me, help me recover, and comfort me so my pain and mourning could stop.

Now, with all my heart, I earnestly believe, and always will, that God exists, that I matter to him and that he has the power to help me recover as he comforts me and he did! In the deepest part of my pain, sorrow, and mourning over what I did to myself, God met me there and comforted me. I felt blessed and became happy again. Indeed, "Happy and blessed are those who mourn, for they shall be comforted."

This reminded me of the Scripture in Philippians 2:13 (OTB), paraphrased:

> **"Therefore, not only as in my presence but much more in my absence, even when you think I'm not watching, work out your own salvation with fear and trembling because now you know what your sin nature can do to you. For now, it is God who works in you, both to shape your will and to guide what you do and say as well as all your works, including ministry, for his good pleasure and your own salvation and recovery."**

Then Jesus said,

THE BEATITUDE

Blessed are the meek—submissive, obedient—for they shall inherit the earth. (Matthew 5:5).

The Third Principle
In the Acronym RECOVERY

C in the acronym for the word RECOVERY will help you to *consciously submit to God*, to turn over my will to God so he can mold me and shape me, like clay, into the vessel he intended for me to be. I will choose to commit all my life and especially my will (my submissiveness, obedience), over to God and Christ's care and control.

We need to remember that Jesus modeled leadership and obedience to God as he was being *meek*, not *weak*. Jesus modeled submissiveness in his life and even his death (sacrifice) for us. The dictionary defines *meekness* as *submissiveness* and *submissiveness* as *obedience*. Jesus, who was with God when the earth itself was created by God (Father, Son, and Holy Ghost) expressed and modeled what *submissiveness and meekness* sounds and looks like. Jesus said, "**Take my yoke upon you, and learn from me, for I am meek—submissive, obedient—and lowly—humble, modest, meek—in heart.**"

Jesus also taught his journeyers what meekness and submissiveness looks like by his simple deeds, as he insisted on washing their feet. Jesus said to his journeyers then and now, if you want to be the head of all. Whether in the home, work, or church, it means you have to be meek and submissive. In other words, the *servant* of all you are head over.

Jesus expressed the ultimate in submissiveness and meekness when he agreed with God the Father to give up his (Jesus's) life as a substitute, a sacrifice, for all our sins. Jesus agreed to conform to God's will, their combined original plan of rescue, to be beaten up and hung on a cross and continued to bleed and feel pain until his body died. Jesus then willfully became our sacrifice, our righteousness, and our defense. The modern-day Psalmist Matt Maher in the song "Lord I Need You" sings "I need you, oh I need you. Every hour I need you, my one defense, my righteousness. Oh God how I need you."

On the third day of my Journey with Jesus, I realized I could consciously choose to commit and submit all my life and will to Christ's care and control because Jesus did that for me, and thereby I can be happy, content in my display of personal meekness, and submissiveness to God and God's will for me. Happy and blessed are the meek (submissive, gentle, tender, free from pride) for they shall inherit the earth.

As far as "shall inherit the earth," we read in Revelations that we "will inherit all things," and I don't know fully what that means, but I have a feeling that when God restores all of humanity, probably in what we call the end times, that the earth, which seems to be symbiotically connected to us, will be restored as well from all of humanity's digging, polluting, and drawing out earth's resources, and the meek, those that submit their wills to God, will inherit this restored earth as well, as all things.

The meek shall inherit all things, not the rich, not the powerful, not the physically strong, not just the pretty, or just one particular race, or just the intelligent, but the meek—those that have learned submissiveness, obedience to God our creator, our friend. It is they, the meek, not the weak, that shall inherit the earth.

Then Jesus said,

THE BEATITUDE

Happy are the pure in heart. (Matthew 5:8)

The Fourth Principle
In the Acronym RECOVERY

O **in the acronym for the word RECOVERY will help you to remember to *openly examine* and confess your past hurts, bad habits, hang-ups, and bad addictions to God and to your guide or someone else you trust who can pray for you. Openly exam-**

ining and confessing your past hurts, bad habits, hang-ups, and addictions is good for the soul. It is good for both your soul, and the soul of the one who you are confessing to and receiving prayer from.

I remembered what I learned on the fourth day on my journey with Jesus. I realized how important openly (candid, honest, truthful, unbridled) confessing of my hurts, bad habits, hang-ups, and addictions was good and healing for my soul.

Openly confessing was the instrument that God uses to purify my soul, to make my heart pure again and my soul happy. And it is not only in the open confession to myself (breaking out of denial), but it's in the open confession to God and, ironically enough, especially in the open confession to a brother (if you are a man) or to a sister (if you are a woman) that purifies the heart and is good and healing for the soul. I'm reminded of one of my favorite Scriptures, **"Therefore, openly confess your sins, your hurts, your bad habits, hang-ups, and bad addictions to one another and pray for one another, so that you may be healed"** (James 5:16, OTB, paraphrased).

It was on these days of my journey with Jesus that I really learned the importance of and how to use a Moral Inventory sheet and then what to do with it. In the process, I openly confessed all of the things on my Moral Inventory sheet to my guide, and as a result, I was healed as he prayed for me! The memories were still there, but they have *lost their sting*! Yeah, God! My heart was pure again, and I could feel it, and I couldn't help but rejoice with tears in my eyes. I still feel that way, in remembrance, every time I worship God now.

I am so grateful that my heart is pure again, like when I was a child! And then I remembered what Jesus said in **Mark 9:36 (OTB): "Unless you are like a one of these children, you shall not enter the kingdom of heaven."**

With confession, I felt like a child again. I felt pure in heart! Indeed, **"Happy and blessed are the pure in heart, for they shall see God"** (Matthew 5:8, OTB, paraphrased)

Then Jesus said,

THE BEATITUDE
Happy are those whose greatest desire is to do what God requires. (Matthew 5:6).

The Fifth Recovery Principle
In the Acronym RECOVERY

***V* in the acronym for the word RECOVERY will help you remember to *voluntarily submit* to every change God wants to make in your life and humbly ask God to remove your character defects.**

Voluntarily submit your wills to God. God gave you a free will and, because of that (God's gift) you have freedom; however, you therefore have the ability to accept or reject God. That's the way God intended for our free wills to work but God did not wish or intend for us to use our free wills to reject him even though he gave us an ability (freedom) to choose.

God always hopes that you would choose to accept him, yet he is willing to take the risk of rejection because he wants you to freely come to him. Therefore God does not ever override your free will. Instead God honors the free will he gave you and patiently waits for you to decide how you will use your free wills.

By voluntarily submitting your free wills to God, he will be able to make changes in your lives; However, It is only by voluntarily submitting your free wills, that God will remove your character defects.

I remembered what I learned on the fifth day on my journey with Jesus, when Jesus congratulated us for making it that far in our journey. Jesus recognized that we had experienced a great deal and learned a tremendous amount of information, and he was proud of us.

He reminded us that we learned from the acronym of the word DENIAL, as we faced issues we had been denying for some time. We learned from the acronym of the word POWERLESS to admit that we are powerless on your own, and we learned to manage our hurts, hang-ups, bad habits, and bad addictions, while realizing the importance of relying on God's power to help us manage these things. Jesus congratulated us, and I remembered how awesome it felt. It still does!

I remembered how the words in Romans 7:18 (OTB), paraphrased, meant so much to me at the time: **"I know that nothing good lives in me, because of my sinful nature, for I have the desire to do what is good, but I do not have the power to carry it out."**

Jesus reminded us how we learned from the acronyms of the words HOPE and SANITY and how we found hope in Jesus and in God to restore us to sanity (healthy, right thinking). We discovered that God and Jesus have the power to assist us, and we realized nothing else has been able to help us in the past.

I remembered it was on or about days five and six that I finally realized that in order to practice real submissiveness and meekness and be truly happy, like a child again, I had to humbly ask God to mold me and make me into the kind of person he wanted me to be. I had to humbly ask God to make any and all changes he would like to make in my old character, which was filled with character defects from a hard life and my own bad choices, and God had mercy on me and still is helping me change. It was then that I realized my happiness was also at hand. Happy are those whose greatest desire is to do what God requires of them.

Then I recalled the words in Philippians 2:13 (OTB), paraphrased: "**For God is at work within you, helping you want to obey him, and then giving you the power to help understand and do what he wants.**"

We also learned that using the acronym of the word TURN. We could remember how to turn our lives over to Jesus and to God's care and direction. Then we learned, through the acronym of the word ACTION, how to take significant action and make the decision to turn your lives over to Jesus and God. We were congratulated by Jesus, it felt great, and he reminded us he had much more to share with us.

Then Jesus said,

THE BEATITUDE
Happy are the merciful. Happy are the peacemakers. (Matthew 5: 7, 9).

The Sixth Recovery Principle
In the Acronym RECOVERY

The second *E* in the acronym for the word RECOVERY will help you remember to *evaluate all your relationships.* Offer forgiveness to those who have hurt you and make amends for harm you've done to others, *except* when to do so would harm them or others.

The *E* in the word RECOVERY will help you remember that you have taught them that they have been led by God and guided by your journey tools (i.e., moral inventories, journaling, etc.) and your guides to make amends (compensate, return, make restitution) to those you have harmed in the past.

Your guide will help you understand how to write it down first (needed in some cases) and run it by your guide so you can make sure you are not expecting forgiveness, not justifying or especially, not blaming. You're just there to humbly explain that you know what you did and that you are truly sorry.

Making amends is a merciful act and will move you into the reality of peacemaker as you feel the load (physical and spiritual tension and division) lift from you and maybe the person you are making amends to.

"Happy are the merciful. Happy are the peacemakers for they shall receive mercy and be called children of the most high God."

THE BEATITUDE
Happy are those who are persecuted for righteousness' sake, because they do what God

requires; for theirs is the kingdom of heaven. (Matthew 5:10).

Blessed are you when others revile you, persecute you, and utter all kinds of evil against you falsely, whether on my account or yours. Rejoice and be glad, for your reward is great in heaven, for they (the religious, prejudice, jealous, willful and murderous) also persecuted the prophets who were before you. (Matthew 5:11–12, paraphrased).

The Seventh and Eighth Recovery Principle
In the Acronym RECOVERY

The second *R* in the acronym for the word RECOVERY will help you remember *reserve a daily time with God* for reading your Bible, praying (talking and listening to God), journaling, and self-examination, in order to really understand and know God, his will for your life, and to gain his power to be able to follow his will for you.

The *Y* in the acronym for the word RECOVERY will help you remember to *yield yourself to God* so you can be a good example to be used to bring the good news of the Bible, your journey to the center of your soul with Jesus, and your personal recovery, showing the genuineness of all this by your words and deeds.

My personal time with God, to read the Bible, to journalize, to listen and talk to God, to sing to God is very early in the morning, when life's usual noise level is diminished and I have no interruptions.

Often, especially in my journal, I review the previous day and how I might have said and done things differently. This is how I do most of my self-examination as well. Sometimes I take my personal journal entries to my guide and ask him what he thinks. I may even add these entries into my Moral Inventory sheet, if there is work I need to do.

I will take my new additions to my Moral Inventory sheet and sometimes my new journal entries to my guide at a coffee meeting and go over them to see if I need to make amends or just do something different next time. Then I ask for prayer.

As Jesus finished the eight principles of recovery and what we call the beatitudes, in the book of Matthew of the Bible, I thought, *Wow! Jesus's sermon on that mount took on an entirely new meaning for me in this new context of the acronym of the word RECOVERY.* Then, as I was reflecting on that, I fell asleep, taking a nap.

I awoke a little startled and confused. It was still daylight! Then, I remembered I was only taking a nap, and I felt a little stupid. Jesus looked at me with a smile, and immediately, I knew all was well.

Jesus wanted to speak to us as we refreshed and prepared to leave. He wanted us to write and memorize what He was about to tell us so we could teach it to others. We grabbed our writing tablets and anxiously waited to write. Jesus seemed to keep implying that we should prepare ourselves to teach, just as we were always prepared and ready to learn.

Then Jesus said, **"As we approach the end of our Journey together, I want you to think about this entire journey with me, and when we conclude, my question for you is: when you get tempted to return to your old bad habits and old thinking, what ways or means have you developed to be able to escape from such a return?"**

I felt a little sad thinking this journey with Jesus would inevitably end soon, but I answered first:

____

____

____

____

When we finished answering, Jesus said,

> **Remember to practice the things I did on this journey and to seek through prayer and meditation to improve your relationship with God.**

> **Relationships, with anyone, cannot develop unless you spend time with each other. So build a relationship with God by listening more than speaking, and asking God for knowledge of his will for you and for his power to implement. As always, let my words dwell, reside, live, and abide in you richly.**
>
> **Remember this journey was given to you freely, so freely give back. Recalling the things you have learned to teach, are to be continually practiced and taught to others so they may recover and discover peace and their mission from God.**

With this last item to memorize, I was also remembering the words in Galatians 6:1–7, (OTB), paraphrased:

> **Sisters and brothers, if anyone of you or others are chained up and caught, in any hurt, bad habit, hang-ups, or addictions and if anyone comes to you for help, you who are born again in Christ, and have taken this journey with me, should be prepared to restore them gently and kindly with compassion and humility because you were once in their shoes and God restored you. Keep an eye on yourself, lest you too be tempted to take on the yeast of the Pharisees and be prideful, jealous, or resentful as it leads to murder of some kind. Instead, bear one another's burdens and fulfill the law of Christ. For if anyone thinks they are something, when they are nothing, they only deceive themselves.**
>
> **But let each one test their personal recovery, and then their reason to boast will be only in**

> **their individual effort and not in their neighbor's work. Remember, your neighbor's work is none of your business. Every individual will accept his/her responsibility for achieving recovery.**
>
> **Let the one who is taught the things of recovery on their journey with God, in turn, share and thereby sow all things into the ones who seek to learn. Do not be deceived: God is not to be teased or mocked, for whatever one sows, they will reap.**

And then Jesus said, "Before we move on, I want to teach you this 'Prayer of Serenity, Calmness, and Quietness.' Repeat it with me, then memorize it as follows:

> **Father God, grant me the serenity, calmness, and quietness to accept the things I cannot change, the courage to change the things I can, and the wisdom to know the difference. Living one day at a time and enjoying one moment at a time; accepting my hardships and the world's hardships, as a pathway to peace; taking, as Jesus does, this sinful world as it is—not as I would have it—trusting that you, oh God, will make all things right, only if I surrender to your will so that I may be reasonably happy in this life and supremely happy with you and Jesus forever in the next life. Amen.**

As we finished writing, we synched up our packs and walked with Jesus down the path again. This time, Jesus moved forward about ten yards and was looking in the sky and occasionally raising his hands as if he was praying and talking with someone.

When we caught up with Jesus, we entered the next town and Jesus walked into a Jewish church, a synagogue, where we noticed a man with a shriveled hand. The religious, whom you can find in any modern church, in this case, are called Pharisees. The religious knew who Jesus was, and we realized later they were trying to trap Jesus by asking him, "Is it lawful to heal on the Sabbath?" as they looked at both Jesus and the man with the shriveled hand.

Jesus replied, "Which one of you who has a sheep, if it falls into a pit on the Sabbath, will not rescue it? Of how much more value is a man than a sheep? So it is lawful to do good on the Sabbath."

In today's vernacular, we would say, "Duh!"

We temporarily stopped our Journey atop a plateau clearing, surrounded by trees and a fresh water well nearby. The crowd brought Jesus their sick and crippled, and Jesus asked us to stand closer to him so we could hear and learn. He healed them all while warning the healed and the rest of the crowd not to tell anyone who he was.

It was then that I recalled the words in Matthew 12:18f (OTB), Paraphrased, regarding the book of Isaiah:

> **Behold, my servant Jesus whom I have chosen,**
> **My beloved Son with whom my soul is well pleased.**
> **I will put my Spirit upon him,**
> **and he will proclaim justice to the Gentiles.**
> **He will not quarrel or cry aloud,**
> **nor will anyone hear his voice in the streets;**
> **a bruised reed he will not break,**
> **and a smoldering wick he will not quench,**
> **until he brings justice to victory;**
> **and in the name of Jesus, all the Gentiles in all the nations**
> **will put their hope.**

As evening drew near, the crowds brought Jesus a demon-possessed man who was blind and mute. Jesus called us over to get close to him again as he spoke to the possessed man along with the mute and blind spirits (critters) within him. Jesus wanted us to hear his words, the tone and confidence of his authority as he ushered in healing for this man and ordered the spirits (critters) to leave this man alone. He said much more and told us journeyers, he would teach us more about this later.

The crowd was amazed and astonished and said, "Could this man Jesus be the son of David?" Of course, the crowd's words made the Pharisees even more jealous and resentful, yeast grows. So the Pharisees said out loud to the crowd this man Jesus is only calling upon the power of Satan to heal and deliver!

Jesus responded to the Pharisees, **"Every kingdom that is divided against itself is easily laid waste, and no city or house divided against itself will stand. And if Satan casts out Satan, he is divided against himself. How then will his kingdom stand? And if I cast out demons by Satan, by whom do your sons cast them out? Therefore, they will be your judges. But if it is by the Spirit of God that I cast out demons, then the kingdom of God is at hand and has come upon you. You brood of vipers, by your word, you will be condemned."**

Again we would say, "Duh!"

I think Jesus was rather disgusted with the Pharisees because He called them a brood of vipers (snakes). I don't blame Him.

Jesus then said something in an interesting way because as he said it to the Pharisees, he turned to us Journeyers and gave us a wink. Later, we understood this was part of what Jesus was going to teach us regarding how to pray for the sick, crippled, and demon-possessed. Jesus winked because he knew, he loved even the Pharisees, the "vipers"; they are just as much a part of the Church as we are and Jesus would be teaching us how not to not get "offended" (see book "The Bait of Satan" by John Bevere) so we can forgive (the power of forgiveness) and pray. Some of Jesus's last words were "forgive them Lord, for they know not what they do (how they have offended)."

Jesus said, **"How can someone enter a strong man's house and plunder his goods, unless he first binds the strong man? Then indeed, he may plunder his house. Whoever is not with me is against me, and whoever does not gather with me scatters. Therefore I tell you, every sin and blasphemy will be forgiven,**

but the blasphemy against the Spirit will not be forgiven. And whoever speaks a word against the Son of Man will be forgiven, but whoever speaks against the Holy Spirit will not be forgiven, either in this age or in the age to come."

Jesus taught us many things on our journey about forgiveness, prayer, healing, and deliverance, but this teaching was specifically pragmatic, detailed, and enlightening. He obviously wanted us to learn so we could teach these things as we were learning how to recover and help others recover.

Then, as evening encroached even closer, Jesus told the crowd to return to their homes. We were going to retire here by the freshwater well. As the crowds slowly dispersed and some stayed and camped around us, we gathered wood, filled our skins with water, cleared out a campsite area, arranged our bedding, built a fire pit, and stacked a pile of wood for the fire. While we were working, Jesus went into the woods to pray alone.

When Jesus returned, evening was beginning to set. He asked us to start the fire and eat so He could teach us a few more things. As we started the fire and cooked, we kept our tablets nearby for writing. He said there is a principle I want you to focus on when you are alone with God.

> **Reserve a time in your calendars each day to have some alone time with God, not only to self-examine yourselves but have long moments of silence for listening to God. Over time, you will better recognize his voice and hear him more clearly, I promise.**

Jesus told us we were probably feeling somewhat recovered by now as we have passed through what he called a crossroads or a personal Portal. He said it was important for us not to stop the work of recovery. It is a lifestyle (rest of our lives) process. Jesus said there are three key parts for us to remember which are associated with the number TEN:

- **The *T* in the acronym for the word TEN will help you remember to teach others to *take scheduled calendar time to do a daily inventory* and identify things on your Moral Inventory list so you can work them out with your guide and make amends and ask forgiveness.**
- **The *E* in the acronym for the word TEN will help you to teach others to *evaluate the good things they thought, said, and did* and the bad things they thought, said, and did. Then, they should list both the good and the bad in their daily inventories. Sometimes your journal (letter to God) also works well for this part.**
- **The *N* in the acronym for the word TEN will help you to teach them that they *need to admit their wrongs as promptly as possible* to not let things fester.**

As Jesus taught us these parts, I was reminded of the words in Lamentations 3:40 (OTB), 1 John 1:8f (OTB), and Matthew 5:23f (OTB), all paraphrased:

> **Let us test and examine our ways, and return to the Lord! If we confess our sins, he is faithful and just to forgive us, our sins and to cleanse us from unrighteousness. If we say we have not sinned, we make God a liar, and his word is not in us.**
>
> **If you are offering your gift at the altar or partaking in the Lord's Supper, Communion, and remember that you have a hurt, bad habit, hang-up, or addiction that has adversely affected your brother or sister, leave and don't partake of the Lord's Supper. You may also depart and leave your gift there before the altar and first go and be reconciled by offering your amends or forgiveness to your brother or sister**

> **and then with an unburdened heart, come and partake of the Lord's Supper or offer your gift to God.**

Then, as we continued to cook and began to eat, Jesus taught us more about how to pray for healing, how to heal the crippled and cast out demon (critters) from those who ask. Wow! Whenever Jesus taught us such things, it blew me away. His teachings were simple, logical, even spiritual when explained! He told us, when God prompts us or when we are asked, we should be ready to teach these things to others, as well.

Summary of the Ninth Day
What We Learned

This was a very long day. At the end of the ninth day, we learned how to make direct amends to people, whenever possible, except when to do so would injure them or others.

We also learned about GRACE, the yeast of the Pharisees, the eight principles of RECOVERY and the related BEATITUDES, the Serenity Prayer, Deliverance, and Three Key Things to remember using the acronym TEN.

END OF SUMMARY

As I thought of amends I reflected on the book of Matthew 5:23–24 OTB (paraphrased): **"So if you are offering your gift [i.e., tithe, offering, your time, ministry, prayers, etc.] at the altar and there remember that your brother or sister has something against you, leave your gift there before the altar and go meet with your brother or sister who may have something against you and make amends. Do this so you can first be reconciled to your brother or sister, and then come back to the altar of God and offer your gift."**

As evening fell quickly upon us, we finished cleaning and prepared for bed, Jesus said he would pray over us before we fell asleep. As we were covered in our bedding, Jesus stood in our midst, raised his hands to God, and prayed:

> **Thank you, Father, lord of heaven and earth, for hiding these things that I am teaching these journeyers, from the wise, religious, and self-righteous. Instead, you've asked me to reveal these things to those you regard as your children, children of God.**
>
> **Father, for such was your gracious Will that all power and things of the Spirit have been**

handed over to me, and no one knows me like you, Father, like me your only begotten Son and now you've handed over to these children of God, these journeyers, to whom you chose to reveal your power and might.

I have taught them to teach others how coming to me and submitting to my Will and yours will give rest to all who labor and are heavy laden. I have yoked with them to ease their burdens, and these children of God will learn from me and how to lead others to me, for I am humble, and submissive at heart, and in us, they will finally find rest for their tender souls.

And now Father in heaven, I continue to pray your protection over them, your warring angles to do battle for them, your ministering angels to serve them, and your spirit to go before them wherever they go so that people will find favor with them as you make way. I pray always your love, your Holy Spirit's love, and my love for them forever and ever as they fall asleep and awake again. Amen.

I had a smile on my face as I fell asleep.

CHAPTER 10

The Tenth Day with Jesus

The campfire was already burning bright and making that distinctive crackling and snapping noise once in a while. The morning sun was a bright, white orange while the sky was a beautiful shade of blue with a few clouds dotting the sky and slowly passing by in unison.

Jesus was in the distance, and it looked as if he was sitting down on a tree stump and praying, this time with his head down. Jesus then looked up as we began to awaken, and I could see he was smiling as he walked towards us.

When Jesus got to us, we were washing up, packing our beddings, and preparing our breakfast. Jesus's bedding was rolled up, as usual, and there was always one of us who wanted to carry it for him. This time, Jesus helped us prepare the meal as he would do on occasion. It seemed odd to have him do so, but we knew he would not only insist on helping, but he seemed happy and quite comfortable serving us.

We began to eat after Jesus thanked God for our food and drink. Then, Jesus sat in our midst and asked, "**Since you have been on this journey with me, have you noticed any changes in your behavior so far? What are they?**"

I quickly swallowed the breakfast morsel in my mouth and answered first, saying,

____

____

____

____

Then Jesus said, **"Since you have been on this journey with me, what specific relationships, including your relationship with God, have you been able to repair, restore, or initiate?"**

Someone else answered,

____

____

____

____

Then Jesus said, **"What are some of the new relationships you have made during your journey with me?"**

Someone quickly answered first, saying,

____

____

____

____

Then Jesus asked, "**When you understand that your continued life journey means you will continue to take personal Moral Inventory, and when you are wrong, you will promptly admit it, make amends and ask for forgiveness. What does that mean to you?**

Again, someone else answered first,

____

____

____

____

Then Jesus said, **"For the next seven days, I want you to create a journal and write a short letter to God every day. Write to God about the good things and the bad, the victories and disappointments, and the areas you seek God's assistance. Do it for the next seven days, respectively."**

We finished eating and began to clean when Jesus said to us, **"As soon as you have cleaned and packed your things, I want you**

to take a moment and sit down. I have something important to share with you."

We sat again and Jesus said, **"You have been working on recovering while on your journey with me. At the same time, I have been leading you to honor the two greatest commandments that God is revealing to you. They are the following:**

1. **You shall love the Lord your God with all your heart, with all your soul, and your mind. This is the great and first commandment.**
2. **You shall love your neighbor as yourself; These two commandments depend on and summarize all the laws and the prophets.**

The first and second commandments are symbiotic, they are dependent on each other. One cannot exist without the other. You cannot say you love God when you hate, are jealous, bitter, resentful, or have acted out in anger toward any other human being, and you cannot say you love a human being when you hate God. Either way, you are breaking both commandments and are unable to recover when you hold on to such hate, jealousy, bitterness, anger or resentment.

That is one reason I have asked you to love even your enemies, even those who have abused you and violated you, instead pray for them. As you pray for your enemies, you will be healed, and your relationship with God will amend itself. Some of those you teach may need to start with forgiving God and asking for forgiveness for hating God. Let them know God is always ready to forgive them.

When you follow these two commandments of God, you are not just "hearers" of God's Word, but you are "doers" of God's Word and living examples of my

way, the way of Christ and the way God had designed humanity to live. Your walk will line up with your talk and your recovery will wonderfully overwhelm you.

As we continue on our journey to the center of the soul, I want you to think about a few things. Remember to teach others that your journey of recovery, although uniquely different, will have some things in common. For example, your journey to the center of the soul will be as follows:

- Ongoing—When you check-in each day, either by journaling, praying, or both, remember to teach others to make amends or give forgiveness as soon as possible, making sure to check with your guide first and making sure you do not hurt someone in the process. Don't let the incident fester. Time does not heal all wounds.

Teach others their journey to the center of the soul will also be as follows:

- Pragmatic—Make sure your meeting times with your guide and others is in your calendar, as priorities, like a doctor's appointment. Write as well as pray to God and ask him to help you search where you might have acted out in fear or anger against someone in the past or present.

Finally, their journey to the center of the soul should also be as follows:

- Retreatable—You will need to teach them the necessity of taking regularly scheduled mini-retreats to write in your journals and pray to God to remind you of your changes, your victories, the

things you still need to work on as you continue to ask God for help.

Then, teach others to keep these things in mind for helping others on their journey of recovery and to help others in ministry and service. Keep these things in mind as you continue to observe my ministry and mission.

The words of Jesus reminded me of the words in Proverbs 16:23, Ephesians 4:29, and Proverbs 16:21 (OTB), all paraphrased:

> **The heart of the wise makes his speech cautious and thoughtful. It is wise to think a while before you speak, thereby more likely to persuade another. Always be quick to listen and slow to speak.**
>
> **Let no corrupting talk, no rumors, no words against another, no foul or swear words come out of your mouths. Speak just the right amount for building and edifying others, even your enemies—that it may give grace and benefit the spiritual growth of those who hear you. It will take time to learn to do this consistently, but assure them, God will assist when he is asked.**
>
> **Finally, those who develop spiritual maturity are wise. They will develop discernment, good judgment, sensitivity and shrewdness and, as a result, their speech will be sweet and persuasive to the ears."**

As we prepared to journey out, I recalled the words in 1 Corinthians 13:1f (OTB), paraphrased, about the greatest gift from God.

> **If I speak in the tongues of men and of angels, without love, I am a noisy gong or a clanging cymbal. If I have prophetic powers, understand all mysteries and knowledge, and if I have staunch faith, so as to remove mountains, but I lack love, I am nothing. If I give away all I have, and if I deliver up my body to be burned, without love, I gain nothing.**
>
> **Love is patient and kind; love does not envy or boast. It is not arrogant or rude. It does not insist on its own way, it is not irritable or resentful, it does not rejoice at wrongdoing, but rejoices with the truth.**
>
> **Love bears all things, believes all things, hopes all things and endures all things. Love never ends. As for prophecies, they will pass, tongues will cease and knowledge will pass. So now faith, hope, and love abide, and the greatest of these is love.**

I prayed the following as I walked:

> God please give me this gift of love as I recover. I want to learn to love myself and love others even more and I'm learning to let go and let you teach me your ways. I realize Lord that increasing my time with you, working through my Moral Inventory, making amends and forgiving are paramount to me learning about your gift of love and how it works. Thank you, God.

As we walked with Jesus again, I remembered how easily I could backslide. I recalled the words from Mark 14:38 (OTB), paraphrased, as a personal warning: **"Watch and pray that you may not enter temptation. The spirit indeed is willing, but the flesh is weak."**

I'm fortunate to be developing some new tools (i.e., journaling, new recovery friends, Moral Inventory, having a guide, having private prayer time and letters to God, etc.) to help me stay on track.

The next town was close by, and within the hour, we entered the home of a host that knew Jesus. But quickly, some Pharisees and teachers of the law came to the home to speak to Jesus. They didn't seem to ask very respectfully when they asked Jesus to show a miraculous sign. Even I could tell they were bating Jesus.

I couldn't help but smile when Jesus referred to those who ask for signs as wicked, adulterous, and evil. Jesus went on to talk to the Pharisees and teachers of the law about Jonah, The Son of Man (Him), Nineveh, and the Queen of the South. Then, Jesus turned to us Journeyers and taught us about spiritual matters. He said,

> **When the unclean spirit has been eradicated, delivered from a person, it passes through waterless places seeking rest, but finds none. Then this unclean spirit says, "I will return to my house—this person—from which I came," because the house, the person, has not sought out the Spirit of God and God's will. When this evil spirit arrives, it finds this person, empty, swept clean from the previous deliverance, and put in order but without the Spirit of God filling their house, spirit.**
>
> **Because this person has not pursued their own salvation and recovery, by hearing and doing God's Words and recovering from a life of hurts, bad habits, hang-ups, or evil addictions by taking this or a similar journey to the core**

> **of the soul, then this evil spirit brings with it seven other evil spirits more evil than itself.**
>
> **Such evil spirits enter and dwell in the same home, in the same person, where they had been, and now this condition of the person is worse than the last state of condition of the same person.**

Then Jesus turned and addressed the Pharisees, the teachers of the law and the rest of us to inform us about who his real mother, brother, and sisters really were. He said his real brothers and sisters happened to be people like us journeyers, his journeyers, and his followers who believed in him and followed him. Thereby, his brothers and sisters were not necessarily his biological family but his spiritual family!

As Jesus walked out from the courtyard of the house through the village's larger open area and toward the nearby lake, a large crowd was waiting for him. The crowd was so large Jesus decided to go into an anchored boat near the shoreline and stand up in the boat to speak.

I couldn't tell if he did that to get some distance from the crowd or so that the crowd could just hear him better as his voice seemed to resonate and amplify off the water and over the crowd. In any case, he spoke in parables about a sewer of seeds, weeds, mustard seeds, and the yeast as he described the kingdom of heaven.

Then he came back to shore, left the crowd and walked back through the house courtyard and back into the house, where we would be staying that night. As we entered, we realized the host had already prepared our meal and drink. It was spread nicely on a large table with short legs and pillows all around it. It was grand.

Then Jesus said to us, "**Before I give thanks to God for our host, the food and drink they have prepared for us, I'm going to answer a question that was just asked of me by one of you. I was asked why I spoke to the crowds in parables instead of plain explanations. I do this because the knowledge of the secrets of the**

kingdom of heaven is for you and the rest of my journeyers, not for just anybody."

Then, Jesus explained to us that many prophets, Pharisees, and teachers of the law, even righteous men long to see and hear what I have been showing you and teaching you. But it is only for you that the secrets of the kingdom of heaven are revealed. He told us to guard these secrets, in your heart, and share them only with those who are saved, who follow me and my way, the way of God. He warned us to be wise with those secrets, lest they be snatched away by the evil one. I remember the parable of the seeds. Most of the seeds were snatched away or just died on unfertile ground (those still in denial).

Then Jesus explained to us, in detail, the complete meaning of all the parables he had previously just shared with the crowds, so we could understand their full meaning.

Then Jesus, in prayer, gave thanks to our host for the room and board and thanks to God for the food, the day's activities and a special thanks for us journeyers, and the recovery that is happening in our lives. When he was finished, we all said amen and served Jesus a portion of the food and drink, but he waited until we were served before he began to eat anything. As we were serving the food and drink, Jesus asked us,

You now understand how the inventories and tools, help you discover the root causes, some would say, the rest of the iceberg, of your hurts, bad habits, hang-ups, and bad addictions and you especially learned how the tools will help you to stay on track. The recovery tools are the following:

- **your regular meetings with your fellow journeyers**
- **your Moral Inventory**
- **your ongoing daily inventory**
- **your periodic quarterly, annual retreat.**
- **your continued service to others.**

What advantages do such inventories and tools offer? How can they help you stay on track?

Someone else answered first, saying,

____
____
____
____

Jesus then explained to us the parable of the hidden treasure, a pearl, and the fishing net.

As we continued to eat and drink Jesus said, "**I want you to give me some feedback on the following phrases and answer the question about what you think is the greatest of all the gifts and why.**

- **Wisdom—From a wise person comes cautious and influential speech.**
- **Service—Don't use foul language, instead bless people using helpful and edifying language. Find different ways to be of service to others.**
- **Love. Love one another, as I have loved you.**
- **Teaching—A wise person is known by their common sense and pleasant teaching.**
- **Calmness—Anxiety sits heavy on someone but encouragement uplifts them.**
- **Strong spirit—The spirit is willing but the body is weak.**

What is the greatest of all the gifts and why do you think so?

There were many answers one could provide. I began saying,

____
____
____
____

While we still continued with our meal, Jesus asked, "**When you have completed your journey of recovery with me, describe**

your specific plan of action for continuing to take personal Moral Inventory and describe your plan for promptly making amends and forgiving others?

I had some things in mind so I promptly spoke first, saying,

____

____

____

____

As we continued to eat and drink, Jesus asked us, **"What are the recurring events or issues that can continually require you to make amends or ask forgiveness, and how do you plan to work them out and make amends? Consider the following:**

- **biological family issues?**
- **church family issues?**
- **issues between friends?**
- **issues between work mates?**
- **issues with those you are in recovery with?**

I had finished eating so I spoke first, saying,

____

____

____

____

As we finished eating and helped the host of the house to clean up, Jesus led us out to the home's courtyard. There was a fire pit toward the corner of the courtyard, and the host had started a nice fire for us. We had our bedding against the courtyard walls, close to the fire pit where we had planned to sleep.

A slight hint of evening began to set over the area. Jesus began to teach us again, saying,

> **Do not judge others. Instead, it is important for you to take time to self-examine and**

> **self-evaluate (take a look at the beam in your own eye) to do a Moral Inventory of your behavior and the things you say to yourself and to others. Here is an example of a prayer you can offer to God:**
>
> **"Help me to test and self-examine myself, oh God, for I have tried to walk in the integrity you have shown me, and I have trusted in you, oh Lord, as I try not to waver. Prove me, O Lord, and try me. Help me to see through any denial I might have and to test my heart and my mind. For your steadfast love is before my eyes. Help me to walk in your faithfulness."**

His words reminded me of the words in Romans 12:3 (OTB) and 1 Timothy 1:19 (OTB), both paraphrased:

> **I give each of you God's warning. As you do your moral inventories and work with your guides and others you are accountable to; be honest in your self-examination and not think of yourselves better than someone else, more highly than you ought to think. Instead consider your thoughts, words, and actions, with sober judgment, and with measuring your own words, deeds, and actions according to the measure of faith that God has assigned you and the things you are learning in your journey to the center of the soul.**
>
> **Hold tightly your faith in God and keep a clean conscience doing what you know God approves. Always remember, by rejecting this teaching, some have made a shipwreck of their faith.**

Then Jesus said,

> **We can justify things we say and do but God is fully aware of our motives, so we should also examine our motives. Remember that a sensible person will "play it forward," so to speak, and as they "play it forward," they will analyze and anticipate problems. If barriers occur, they will use the tools discovered in their journey to the center of the soul—journal, Moral Inventory, making amends, forgiveness, recovery buddies call list, calling guide, prayer time with God, etc.—to absolve any issues and keep from making a mistake as they play in forward.**

This teaching Jesus just provided reminded me of the words of 1 Timothy 4:16 (OTB), 1 Corinthians 10:12 (OTB), Matthew 5:25 (OTB), Proverbs 14:30 (OTB), and James 1:2–3 (OTB), all paraphrased:

> **Keep a close watch on all you think, say and do and on the teaching of the way of Christ, and God will bless you. Persist in this to bless yourself, your family, and others close to you.**
>
> **Therefore, let anyone who is prideful (the yeast of the Pharisees) because they are in recovery and feel superior to others, take heed lest they fall.**

And as Jesus continued to speak, I could see this also was the way of Christ.

> **Make amends and forgive quickly your enemy who lies, falsely accuses you behind your back, infesting themselves with disease and demons.**

They may even become imprisoned through their own thoughts, words, and deeds. Nevertheless, forgive them quickly and let go and let God.

Remember that having a right attitude, ready to make amends, and a loving and forgiving heart will lengthen and strengthen your life. On the other hand, jealousy, resentment, pride, etc. (the yeast of the Pharisees), will rot you away and destroy you along with those around you.

Know this: your trials, your hurts, bad habits, hang-ups, bad addictions, and your hardships are a pathway to wisdom as you work through them, as you have learned in your journey to the center of the soul. You will find peace as you learn to take this sinful world as it is, not as you would have it. Let go and let God.

Learn to see it as joy, your hurts, bad habits, hang-ups, bad addictions, all your hardships and trials of various kinds, for you know that this is the testing and refining of your faith which produces wisdom, peace, and unwavering resoluteness.

Let wisdom, peace, and unwavering resoluteness permeate your mind, body, and spirit so that you may be perfected and complete over time, lacking in nothing that God wants you to learn.

As evening was now fully upon us, Jesus told us to arrange our bedding and come back to the fireside as he had more to teach. We did exactly as he asked.

Jesus said,

> **I want you to memorize another acronym so that you can teach others. This acronym is made of the word RELAPSE. It will help you and other journeyers keep these things I've taught you hidden deep within your heart so that in times of trouble and when your faith weakens, you have something to refer to:**

- **The *R* in the word RELAPSE will help you teach others to *reserve a daily quite time with God* for reading God's word, listening to God and self-examination. This prayer time with God will help you to know God's will for you and be filled with his power to carry out God's will.**
- **The *E* in the word RELAPSE will help you teach others to consistently *evaluate their HEART health*. In other words, are you**

    - **hurting?**
    - **exhausted?**
    - **angry?**
    - **resentful?**
    - **tense?**

- **The *L* in the word RELAPSE will help you remember to teach others to *listen to God*, your guide, and those you have made yourself accountable to! Take a time out, at home, at a park, at a retreat, and just listen to God. Call your guide or accountability partner and check in until you truly understand how you are coping.**

When Jesus taught us this, it reminded me of the words in Isaiah 1:10 (OTB) and Galatians 6:4 (OTB), both paraphrased:

> **Hear the words of the Lord... and give ear to the teaching of our God.**
>
> **But let each one test their personal recovery, and only theirs, and then they can only boast in God helping them with their efforts alone and not be concerned with their neighbor's efforts. For each of you is responsible for bearing your own load.**

Jesus continued to teach,

- **The *A* in the word RELAPSE will help you to teach others to develop their *alone time with God.* Cherish this alone time as I modeled for you my time with God when I would go away to be alone and pray (listen mostly) to God.**
  Be still and know that he is God and he wants you to listen to him. Set a daily appointment time to be alone with God and do more listening than speaking. You'll get better at recognizing and hearing clearly his voice over time.
- **The *P* in the word RELAPSE will help you remember to teach others to *pray* and *plug* into God without ceasing. This allows you to know his will for you and receive God's power to carry out his will in your life.**
- **The *S* in the word RELAPSE will help you remember to teach others to *slow down* long enough to hear God's answer. Your generation is always in a hurry and wants prayers answered immediately. Remind your generation that there is a God and it's not them. Remind them that God's timing is always perfect.**

What Jesus said, about slowing down and listening, reminded me of the words in Job 33:31–33 (OTB) and Philippians 4:6–7 (OTB), both paraphrased:

> **Pay attention and listen, O Job, listen to me. Be silent, and I will speak. Listen to me. Be silent, and I will teach you wisdom."**

That's exactly what Jesus has been teaching us! Be silent and listen, and God will teach us!

> **Do not be anxious about or want for anything, simply pray with thanksgiving in your heart for what you already have, for you already have more than you realize, and we often take what we already have for granted. Do this, and more will be given to you. Communicate (pray) any requests you might have to God. Then listen, and the peace and wisdom of God will surpass your expectations and your understanding.**

Jesus continued teaching,

- **The last *E* in the word RELAPSE will help you remember to teach others to *enjoy* their growth. Celebrate even the smallest success during your recovery. Teach others to remember they are on a *life journey* as essential as eating and breathing every day. Remind them also that when they keep an "attitude of gratitude" for all things, even for their enemies, their hardships, and their trials, they will find the peace and power of God and enjoy spiritual growth. They will learn to trust that God makes all things right, if they completely surrender to his will.**

  Remind them to share their smallest victories with their guides and others in recovery so that their growth will give others hope.

This reminded me of the words in 1 Thessalonians 5:16–18 (OTB), paraphrased:

> **Rejoice always, pray without ceasing, give thanks in *all* circumstances, blessings, as well as all hardships and trials, for this is the will of God, that you learn and grow from all these things, and take heart, feel confident, for your life is in union with Christ Jesus himself, our redeemer and our defense.**

Summary of the Tenth Day
What We Learned

At the end of the tenth day, we learned to continue to take personal inventory (Moral Inventory) of ourselves and, when we discover our errors, where we were wrong, that we promptly admitted it to ourselves, our God, and our guide.

We also learned that we need to always be ready and have a right attitude to make amends again and again. We learned to journalize, how to love, about being sick as our secrets, and more things about deliverance. We learned about the way of Christ and the importance of taking retreats. We also learned about the acronyms RELAPSE and HEART, and we learned about how important it is to always have an attitude of gratitude.

Constantly taking a personal inventory (Moral Inventory) on a regular basis keeps us from getting prideful (arrogant, overconfident, feeling better than others) as we mature in our personal recovery. Guarding ourselves from pride, reminds me of the meaning behind the words in 1 Corinthians 10:12 (OTB), paraphrased: **"Let anyone who thinks that they got it now, or that they can stand on their own two feet without any help now, or that because they are a guide and therefore smarter than the one they are guiding, take heed of a pride [Phariseetical yeast] that can develop, lest you fall."**

Remember, pride always comes before the fall.

Jesus said, **"Before I pray over you, I want you to write in your journals your HEART check. Then identify the tools you will use when your everyday journey is disturbed by life's hardships and trials and your faith becomes weak. In other words, what do you do when you're hurt, exhausted, angry, resentful, or tense?"**

As Jesus prayed over us, he walked around and placed his hand on each one of our heads and blessed us as he was thanking God for us and for our recovery. When he touched me, I began to cry tears of relief and joy as I felt God's peace. I felt healed, comforted, and supported. I struggled to stay awake to conclude journaling, but I managed to finish and fell into deep asleep.

CHAPTER 11

The Eleventh Day with Jesus

A rooster crowing was our morning alarm. As I awoke and lifted myself slowly out of my bedding, I noticed the fire had a gentle crackle, and everyone was beginning to clean up. The host appeared with Jesus and told us breakfast was being prepared and would be ready within the hour.

We packed for the day's journey. Jesus asked us to meet him in the dining area around the table. As we sat or lay around the dining area on pillows, the host and his servants brought us beverages, fresh fruits, and nuts. We joined Jesus in giving thanks for our host, his home, everyone present, and the food we were about to eat. At that time, Jesus asked us some questions: **"I shared with you yesterday about the importance of developing listening skills. What are some of the ways you think you can improve your listening skills with God, yourself and others?"**

I had just listed in my journal some things that came to mind, so I was ready to share first.

____

____

____

____

Then Jesus asked, **"How could you improve your prayer time? When and where do you pray, and what does *quiet time* mean to you?"**

Our host and the assistants began to serve us a magnificent breakfast spread of figs, humus, fresh hot bread, more nuts, and cheese. Wow! They also brought more flowers to put on the table. As they placed everything in front of us, one of the others answered the questions Jesus had just asked,

____

____

____

____

We began to eat and drink as Jesus asked, "**After you speak to God, do you pause, slow down, and listen for God to respond? What, specifically, has God advised you regarding your personal journey of recovery?**"

Someone else spoke first, saying,

____

____

____

____

Then Jesus asked, "**What tools have you developed to keep you from being prideful, getting discouraged, or falling back?**"

I spoke up first, saying,

____

____

____

____

Then, as we finished eating, Jesus asked, "**What do you plan on doing to celebrate even the smallest victories of your recovery?**"

Someone else said they had already celebrated during our journey so they shared, saying,

____

____

____

____

Then Jesus said, "**As we continue on our journey today, a continued journey to the center of your soul, I want you to think about and meditate on developing a strong "attitude of gratitude." As you talk to God and listen to Him while we are walking down this road of recovery, focus on letting God know how grateful you are for Him, for your family, yourself and all others, even your perceived enemies.**

I was reminded of the words in Colossians 3:15–17 (OTB) and Psalms 100:4 (OTB), paraphrased:

> **And let the peace of Christ rule in your hearts, to which indeed you were called in one body. Be thankful. Let the word of Christ dwell in you richly, with thankfulness in your hearts to God. Do everything… giving thanks to God the Father through him.**
>
> **Enter God's gates with thanksgiving, and his courts with praise! Give thanks to God and bless his name!**

As Jesus thanked our host and their assistants, he prayed over them and then led us out of the home's courtyard and onto the road. This time, Jesus informed us that we were headed for Nazareth, his hometown. Jesus had a strange smile on his face when he revealed our next destination.

About half way to Nazareth, we stopped for a rest at an oasis next to a river stream right off the road. As usual, we knew to gather around Jesus, who was leaning with his back against a palm tree and his foot up on the side of a fallen palm. As we sat in the shade of the other palms for rest and refreshment, Jesus moved to a tree stump in the midst of us, where he sat and said, "**Always be thankful to God for his unfailing love, his magnificent creations and wonderful things he has done for all of humanity, especially you, his creation. You were fearfully and wonderfully made in the image and likeness of God the Father and me! Why do you think it's import-**

ant for you and those you teach, to always have an attitude of gratitude? What are three areas of your lives that God has helped you to make positive changes which you are grateful for?

Someone else in the group answered first saying;

____

____

____

____

Jesus then asked, **"Name three people, not including me, which God has placed in your recovery, since we have been on this journey to the center of your soul and why you are grateful for them."**

I spoke up first, saying,

____

____

____

____

Then Jesus asked, "**What are some other areas of your family life, church life, work, or activities which you are grateful for and why?**

____

____

____

____

Then Jesus continued, **"Now that you have created your first gratitude list, at first chance, do not use your phones unless you have to, I want you to make the time to personally thank all those you are grateful for because they have been part of your journey to the center of your soul as well. Then, meet with your guides and inform them how you feel about those listed on your gratitude list and how it felt to personally thank them.**"

Jesus told us to get some rest, before continuing on our journey. Before I took a quick nap, I remembered what Jesus was teaching us as it reminded me of some biblical verses in Job 37:14 (OTB), Ephesians 4:23 (OTB), 1 Peter 1:13–14 (OTB), Colossians 3:10 (OTB), and James 1:5 (OTB), all paraphrased:

> **Listen to this, O Job. Stop and consider the wondrous works of God. Let your attitudes and minds be renewed, and put on your new self, created after the likeness and image of God. Now, with a sober and rational mind you can be, obedient children of God, without conforming to the passions and actions of your former attitude and mind-set.**
>
> **With your hurts, bad habits, hang-ups, and bad attitudes and the mind-sets that set in, you once walked in them, when you were believing and living in them. But now you must put those old attitudes and mindsets, the yeast of the Pharisees, behind you and far away: jealousy, resentment, bitterness, unforgiveness, anger, wrath, malice, slander, and obscene talk from your mouth and in your minds. Do not lie to one another but speak the truth in love, thereby showing that you have put off the old self with its practices and have put on the new self, which is being renewed in knowledge from God and the infilling of the gift of love as you work your personal recovery program, a journey to the center of your soul.**
>
> **Here, in Christ, there are no white, brown, black, yellow people. There is not Christian and non-Christian. There is not male and female. There is not a blue collar and white**

> **collar or financially rich and poor. There is not Republican or Democrat. And there is certainly *no* religion or denominational bent, but in Christ, we are all one, and we are all the same to God and therefore should be to each other. We are all sinners, in the same boat, and in need of God's grace, Jesus, and, very much, need each other.**

I remembered the words of Ecclesiastes 4:9–10 (OTB), paraphrased, as I thought about the importance of regularly attending group meetings and working this program:

> **Two are better than one… for if one falls, one will lift up his sister or brother, but woe to those who are alone when they fall and have not another to lift them up!**

We rested and when we awoke from our naps, Jesus was sitting in the same spot. I think he prayed over us the entire time we slept. As we got ready to continue, Jesus said,

> **Congratulations! I know many, if not all of you, have had a deep spiritual experience on your journey to the center of your soul, as a result of your journey with me, so far. I know most of you have already gone through a "spiritual portal" so to speak, and are not the same anymore. I also know you can't wait to teach others as you continue your personal journey and transfer your experiences to others. I applaud your willingness to give back. Let me ask you this…**

As Jesus spoke, I reflected on the words in Matthew 10:8 (OTB), paraphrased: **"You received without paying anything; now give it away without being paid anything."**

Jesus continued, **"What does the word *give* mean to you and what can you possibly give to God?"**

As we arose to follow Jesus, someone else in the group answered first, saying,

____

____

____

____

We continued walking to our next destination, Jesus's hometown, and Jesus commented,

> **During the journey and teaching, I want you to continually focus on, and teach, the greatest of all my commandments. There are only two, but they both summarize the law and what every prophet has said:**
>
> **Always love the Lord your God with all your heart, your soul, and your mind. This is the greatest and first of the two commandments. The second great commandment is like the first. In fact, it's symbiotic. You can't have one without the other. It will not suffice.**
>
> **You must love your neighbor, which is everyone, as yourself. Of all my commandments, these two are the greatest and summarize all of the law and the prophets.**
>
> **Teach others that God will never waste a hurt. In other words, he will give you the opportunity to share that hurt with others, to share your victories, and how you and God achieved this with assistance from others. This produces hope.**

I was reminded of the words in 2 Corinthians 1:3–5 (OTB), paraphrased,

> **Blessed be the God and Father of our Lord Jesus Christ, the Father of all mercies and help, and the God of all comfort, who comforts and is always ready to help us recover from all our hurts, bad habits, hang-ups, and bad addictions. As a result, we are able to comfort and help those with hurts, bad habits, hang-ups, and bad addictions in turn, with the comfort and help with which we ourselves are comforted and helped by God… We share abundantly in Christ's comfort and help. This is giving it away. Freely give what you have been freely given.**

As we continued to walk with Jesus on this journey, Jesus said,

> **I want you to teach others to be doers of the word of God, to not just hearers and memorizers of the Word of God. Even Satan has God's words memorized.**
>
> **Be doers. Don't be like some Sunday service Christians who are clickish or see yourself as separate from the whole body of God. Instead, become real children of God, where your love for everyone is not just in words but how you express your attitude toward them, how you treat them and lift them up, without tearing anyone down by speaking ill of them.**
>
> **Godly true love manifests itself in actions not just words. Be doers of God's word. Let this light of love shine so others can find their way.**

Do not hide or keep anything from others. Instead, communicate openly without becoming a click, another sign of a Phariseetical yeast infection.

We walked into the town of Nazareth. Most of the people were amazed with Jesus as he taught and performed a few miracles in and around their synagogue churches, but as usual, there were skeptics. It seemed odd because there were more skeptics and hostility than usual. It was odd that people who knew Jesus, since he was a child and knew his family, were the most skeptical. Clearly, familiarity breeds contempt, and Jesus said he did not do many miracles there because of their lack of faith and belief. Then he explained, **"Only in his or town and in his house is a prophet not treated with the honor—respect admiration, esteem, reverence, etc.—due them."**

Now I realize why most of us have such difficulty exercising our ministries in our own personal churches. In order for our spiritual maturity to be recognized or to be treated respectfully, we usually participate in another church or travel to a different town where they don't know us.

Indeed, if even his friends and acquaintances rejected Jesus, then surely our friends and acquaintances, our own churches, would reject us as well.

As we left the last synagogue church, some of the journeyers and students of John the Baptist approached Jesus with sad faces. Jesus pulled them and us both to one side and listened as they informed him that Herod had just ordered John the Baptist's head to be severed. Jesus raised his arms to the sky and then later placed his arms around the journeyers of John the Baptist and prayed for a lengthy time. He spoke highly of John the Baptist to God and honored John's ministry.

Then, Jesus walked to a nearby seashore, the Sea of Galilee, and many of us followed. Jesus told us he had to leave for a bit and be alone in prayer but that we should wait for him here at the shoreline. He went into a nearby boat, rowed away around a curve in the shoreline, and was soon out of sight. For some reason, I was frightened.

As nightfall approached, we gathered wood for a pit fire near the shoreline. A couple of hours later, we saw Jesus rowing the boat back to our shore, so we started the fire and waited for him.

By this time, a large crowd had joined us; and when Jesus arrived, he looked at the large crowd and told us to give them something to eat. Some of us said, "Lord, we don't have much to eat, and there are now thousands of people."

Jesus smiled and shook his head. He directed us to tell the crowd to come to him and sit. They came, and Jesus put what small amount of food we had into a couple of baskets. Then, he lifted the baskets up to God, gave thanks, and served us, and we served the crowd.

We immediately noticed the increasing noise level from the crowd as the food baskets passed from person to person. The crowd shouted with joy, and some sang praises to God. It was electrifying as we realized Jesus had conducted another miracle, which we were eating! Not only was there ample amount of food, but there were baskets of leftovers. Now we knew why Jesus smiled at us and shook his head when we told him there was a lack of food. We realized again what Jesus already knew and was trying to teach us. With God, nothing is impossible!

Jesus spoke to the crowd about many things, and then, as nightfall quickly descended, he told the crowd we would be retiring, and they were welcome to stay if they wished. Many left, but hundreds stayed and made camp around us.

As soon as we placed our bedding near the fire, Jesus told us to circle up as he asked more questions before he prayed us to sleep. Jesus asked, **"During this journey of recovery, you have been developing a closer relationship with God. How has this closeness affected your understanding of the word *give*?"**

I was the first one to answer that question, saying,

____

____

____

____

Then Jesus asked, **"You know to teach others that two are better than one, and why. Describe some specific examples since you have been on this journey with me where you have seen or experienced *two are better than one*?"**

Someone else answered first, saying,

____

____

____

____

Then Jesus asked us to share some recent victories. Someone else answered first again, saying,

____

____

____

____

Jesus continued, **"Please share how you have expressed being a doer of God's Word, with God, your journey recovery group, your family, your friends, work associates, and neighbors?"**

I spoke up first, saying,

____

____

____

____

Summary of the Eleventh Day
What We Learned

At the end of the eleventh day, we learned to seek through prayer and meditation to improve our personal relationship with God. Praying only for knowledge of his will for me and the power for me to do his will.

We also learned about listening skills as we talk and especially listen to God. We learned about recovery tools, the importance of giving thank you(s), group importance, giving it back, the two greatest commandments, being a doer, and how no one is a prophet (receives honor, respect) in his own church or hometown.

All this reminded me of the words in Colossians 3:14–16 (OTB), paraphrased:

> **And above all these put on the attitude of Love for absolutely everyone without prejudice, even your enemies and this kind of love will bind everything together in perfect harmony. Love lets the peace of Christ rule in your hearts, to which indeed you were all called. And always be thankful to God, in all things, so as to let the Words and the way of Christ dwell in you richly, in addition, always teach and hold one another wisely accountable in all things.**

Jesus then prayed over us, thanking God for us and blessing us. I think I fell asleep while he was still praying. I remember just the sound of his comforting voice. I slept like a baby as I'm sure the others did as well.

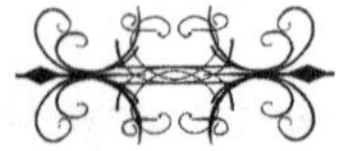

CHAPTER 12

The Twelfth Day with Jesus

The morning sun dawned over the rolling hillside and twinkled over the sea. Once again, Jesus had started a morning fire. This time, fish were stacked on a rock next to the campfire and loaves of bread were in a basket next to the campfire as well. No one asked how the fresh fish and baked bread got there because we now knew that with God, all things are possible.

We arose, cleaned up and cooked the fish for breakfast as Jesus began to teach.

As you teach others to yield themselves to the will of God so they may deliver the good news of my teachings to others, remind them to communicate this good news by deeds, not just by words.

You have now had many spiritual experiences as a result of this journey to the center of your soul with me. Describe this journey to all who will listen and, for those interested, teach them these things as you continue to practice daily.

Remember to teach them how fragile they are and easily tempted to get off track. Remind them this is why they need God every day. They need to learn how to use the tools I have given you on this journey and teach them how much they need each other for support and guidance.

As they yield themselves to God, show them what a wonderful experience it is to volunteer service to their churches, communities, and to their family and friends. Show them how to make their walk match their talk through service. They can serve as

a guide to someone in need. I came to serve and conducted my ministry as a servant to all and so can they. They will feel gratified and be rewarded in heaven as well.

Explain to them they will produce a great capacity to love—a love that issues from a pure heart and a good conscience, which comes from a journey with God and confessing your sins to one another for healing. They will develop a sincere and strong faith as they work though hurts, bad habits, hang-ups, and addictions.

When Jesus said all this, I was reminded of the words in 1 John 3:18 and in John 13: 14–15 (OTB), both paraphrased:

> **Children of God, let us not love, just in word or talk, but in our deeds and in truth (honesty) as well. If I, your Lord and Teacher, have washed your feet, you also ought to wash one another's feet. For I have given you an example of servant leadership that you also should do to others just as I have done to you.**

Jesus then served us breakfast with assistance from two other journeyers. Jesus asked us, "**If you knew that you couldn't fail because God was on your side, how would you provide service to others? How else will you practice what you have learned on this journey with me?**"

Since I was not one who helped Jesus serve breakfast, I was determined to help clean up. I got it! I understood what he was saying about service, but sometimes, I can be a little slow.

As I was eating, I spoke up first answering his questions, saying,

____

____

____

____

Then Jesus asked, "**When I tell you, 'You can't keep your recovery growing unless you give your recovery away,' what does that mean to you? If you understand this, then what is your action**

plan to give it away? In other words, what service opportunities are you going to explore?"

Someone else spoke up first, saying,

____
____
____
____

I couldn't help but think of the words in 2 Corinthians 1:3–4, Deuteronomy 4:9, Ephesians 4:1, Hebrews 10:24, and Romans 12:9, 13 (OTB), all paraphrased:

> **Blessed be God, the Father of our Lord Jesus Christ, the Father of all mercies and the God of all comfort, who comforts us, and inspires others to comfort us, with all our hurts, bad habits, hang-ups, and bad addictions so that we are then able, in turn, to comfort those who are struggling with the same kind of afflictions (hurts, bad habits, hang-ups, and bad addictions).** In other words, when we've been there, it helps others to know that we have been there before.
>
> **Take care and use the tools you have learned and remember the journey, from your very beginning, lest you forget the things that your eyes have seen, the deep experiences you have had, and they depart from your heart… In your testimony, make those special moments known to all children of God and their children's children. I urge you to walk in the way of Christ in a manner worthy of your recovery and the calling to which you have been called to rightly live and to teach and serve others.**
>
> **Look for ways to encourage and stir up one another to Love each other and do good works. Remember to not neglect to meet together. This is critical to your recov-**

> **ery and the recovery of others, so remember always to meet and encourage one another.**
>
> **Let your love for each other be genuine. Detest and be repulsed by clicks, gossip, jealousy, and all evil things that separate you from others and, as a result, from God. Instead, hold fast to what is good. Love one another with holy affection. Outdo one another by showing your honor and respect for each other.**
>
> **Do not be lazy about exercising your new skills. Instead, be fervent in spirit and in serving others for the Lord's sake. Rejoice in hope, be patient in tribulation, be consistent with prayer, work the tools of recovery, contribute to the needs of others, seek to show and teach what you have learned. Seek to give it away.**

Then Jesus said,

> **I need to cover a couple of other things with you before the crowd comes, and we continue the last leg of our Journey. I am also congratulating you for working hard on your personal recoveries, for being great students, and learning how to teach others to do the same! I am very proud of all of you, good and faithful servants, saints, and ambassadors of God!**

I had mixed feelings about what Jesus just said about this being the last leg. I was sad our journey was ending but excited at what I had learned and was ready to teach and serve, as the others were as well.

Jesus said,

> **I want you to teach others the reasons people slow down or stop from fully recovering. To avoid this dilemma, teach them to continue to**

- ***Take their time.*** **Proceed through recovery at a sure and steady pace. Remind them this journey is a process that will take some time. Remind them that it took a long time to develop deep hurts, bad habits, hang-ups, and bad addictions; so it will take some time to heal.**
- ***Completely surrender.*** **Remind them to completely surrender to God and to me, as you have on this journey. Remind them to trust me in the small things as well as the bigger things. I will never fail them and neither will God.**
- ***The cross.*** **I know you are aware of the price I will soon pay for your salvation, your forgiveness and your freedom. Remind them to honor me and the price I will pay. They must forgive themselves as well as others and bring them back to the importance and reality of the cross and a relationship with God the Father.**

At this time, I remembered the words of Ephesians 1:7 (OTB), paraphrased:

> **In Jesus, we have redemption through his wounds and his shed blood on the cross, the healing of our deepest hurts and the forgiveness of our bad habits, hang-ups, and bad addictions, according to God's grace, which he lavished upon us, in all wisdom and insight, making known to us the mystery of his will. According to their purpose—Father, Son and Holy Ghost—which they set forth in Jesus Christ as the fulfillment of the plan over the fullness of time, so that all things will be united in Jesus, all things in heaven and all things on earth.**

Then Jesus said, "**Tell them to remember**

- **Let go and let God. Remind them they need to fully let go of the hurts of the past harm, abuse, bad habit, or**

bad addiction. Remind them until they are ready to let go of it all and release it all, to forgive themselves and others, the past will continue to hold them captive.

- **Paralysis. Remind them that fear of what they think will happen or fear of failure will only paralyze them. Fear of intimacy, rejection, and repeated hurt is common. God will help them break through those feelings of fear, so their personal recovery will continue.**

It was then I remembered the words in 1 Peter 5:10-11, Isaiah 41:10, and Hebrews 13:6 (OTB), all paraphrased:

> **God, who has called you to his eternal glory in Christ, will himself restore, confirm, strengthen, and establish you through your recovery and your continued salvation in Christ Jesus. For God tells us to "Fear not, for I am with you. Be not dismayed, for I am your God. I will strengthen you. I will help you, I will uphold you with my righteous right hand, so you can confidently say, 'The Lord is my helper. I will not fear.' What can a person really do to me since God is my helper?"**
>
> **Remind them to fight for, tenaciously hold on to, and prioritize their recovery. Their personal recovery is the best thing they can do for themselves or anyone else they love.**

Then Jesus provided a couple more reasons why some may slow down or stop from fully recovering. He told us to not forget to do the following:

- ***Be responsible.*** **Teach others to quit blaming someone or something else for past hurts, bad habits, hang-ups, and bad addictions. If someone or something else was at fault, teach them to forgive and let it go. If they were**

at fault, they need to also forgive themselves, make amends, and let it go.

- ***Use your support team.*** **Teach them that no one does it alone. Remind them to build an effective support team of persons they can call and meet with from time to time, including their guide.**

I was reminded of the words in Galatians 6:2, James 5:16, Proverbs 13:20, and Galatians 5:13 (OTB), all paraphrased:

> **Bear one another's hurts, bad habits, hang-ups, and bad addictions, and so fulfill the law of Christ. Confess your hurts, bad habits, hang-ups, and bad addictions to one another and pray for one another to heal each other.**
>
> **Remember, whoever walks with the wise becomes wise, but whoever walks with fools, those who try to live with their hurts, bad habits, hang-ups, and bad addictions will become foolish, but you have found freedom in recovery, your journey to the center of your soul. Now use your freedom as an opportunity to love and serve one another. Give it away.**

Then Jesus said,

Lastly, I want you to teach them about the eight principles you have experienced on this journey to the center of the soul with me. These principles are in the last acronym I have for you to memorize, so you can teach others. The acronym is in the word RECOVERY:

- **The *R* in the word RECOVERY will remind you to teach them to remember to *realize* there is a God, and**

it's not you or them. Remind them the key to their recovery is realizing they are powerless to control their tendency to do wrong and that their lives are unmanageable and that's why they are participating on this journey with me.

What Jesus just said, reminded me of the words in Matthew 5:3 (OTB), paraphrased: **"Blessed are those who know they are spiritually poor [hurt, broken, depressed] and therefore, in need of God, for they will enter the kingdom of heaven."**

Then Jesus continued,

- **The *E* in the word RECOVERY will remind you to teach them to *earnestly* believe that God exists. Remember, seeing is not believing. Rather, believing is seeing. Remind them they matter to God and that God has the power to help them fully recover.**

This reminded me of the words in Matthew 5:8 (OTB), paraphrased: **"Blessed are the pure in heart, those that have confessed and reached out to God and others, for they shall see God."**

Jesus continued,

- **The *C* in the word RECOVERY will remind you to teach them they need to *consciously choose* to commit their wills (this is key) and the rest of their lives to the care of God and to me, his only begotten Son, Jesus Christ.**

This reminded me of the words in Matthew 5:5 (OTB), paraphrased: **"Blessed are those who do the will of God, the meek like Jesus, not the weak, and blessed are those who have learned to give it away for they shall inherit the earth."**

Jesus continued,

- **The *O* in the word RECOVERY will remind you to teach them to always *openly self-examine and especially confess.* Confession keeps them accountable, to God, to themselves, and to their guide and/or someone they have made themselves accountable to.**

This reminded me of the words in Matthew 5:4 and James 5:16 (OTB), both paraphrased:

> **Blessed are those who mourn, for they shall be comforted and recovered. Confess your hurts, bad habits, hang-ups, and bad addictions to one another and pray for one another, and you will be healed.**

Jesus continued,

- **The *V* in the word RECOVERY will remind you to teach them to *voluntarily submit* to every change that God wants to make in their lives as they continue to humbly ask God to remove their character defects.**

This reminded me of the words in Matthew 5: 6 (OTB), paraphrased: **"Blessed are those who hunger and thirst to follow God's will instead of their own will and who hunger and thirst to reflect God's character, for they shall be satisfied."**

Then Jesus continued,

- **This second *E* in the word RECOVERY will remind you to teach them to *evaluate their relationships in their moral inventories.* Remind them to mercifully offer forgiveness, as I have forgiven them, to those who have hurt them.**

> **Remind them also to make peace by making amends to those they have harmed, except when to do so would harm them or others in the process. They can check with their guides first to rehearse their amends.**

This reminded me of the words in Matthew 5:7 and 5:9 (OTB), paraphrased: **"Blessed are those who understand mercy, because they have received the mercy [salvation, forgiveness, grace] of God and now, in understanding what mercy feels like, they can offer mercy to others; they will continue to receive mercy. Blessed are those that have received the peace of God, his salvation in Christ Jesus because they are more able to be the peacemakers of God, making amends and peace with others. They shall be called the children of God."**

Jesus continued,

- **The second *R* in the word RECOVERY will remind you to teach them to *reserve* a daily time to be with God, communicate in prayer and especially listen to God, always asking God to examine you and lead you in his ways of righteousness. Ask God specifically to show you his will for your life and to give you his power to follow his will.**

This reminded me of the words in Matthew 5:12 (OTB), paraphrased: **"Rejoice and be glad, for your reward for following God is great in heaven. Remember, they persecuted the prophets and Jesus who came before you, for their obedience to God, and they [the church and its leaders included] as in current times, will persecute you as well. Nevertheless, rejoice, pray for them and forgive them, for great is your reward in heaven, rejoice and be glad!"**

Then Jesus said,

- **The *Y* in the word RECOVERY will remind you to teach them to *yield* themselves to God by describing this journey of recovery to others, either by words,**

> **volunteer service, life examples or by leading them through their personal journey to the center of their souls as well.**

This reminded me of the words in Matthew 5:13–16 (OTB), paraphrased: **"You are the salt of the earth… You are the light of the world. A light set on a hill cannot be hidden. Nor do people light a lamp and put it under a basket, but on a stand, and it gives light to all in the house therefore, give your light, knowledge of this journey of recovery, your words and your volunteer service. In the same way, let your light shine before others, so they may see your good deeds, service, recovery, your testimonies, be a guide to others and thereby glorify your Father who is in heaven."**

Then Jesus said he knew he had taken most of the morning to teach us these things, as the noonday sun was already shining.

We were already at the shoreline where we had camped, so as the crowd appeared again, Jesus asked us to push the boat offshore and climb in, then sail the boat to the other side of the Sea of Galilee, and wait for Him. When we climbed into the boat and Jesus pushed us off, he turned to the crowd to talk for a moment and then dismissed them. As we sailed away, we saw Jesus walking up the hillside, probably to be alone and pray, as he often modeled for us throughout this journey.

When evening finally came, Jesus was on the shoreline alone. Our boat, by this time was a long way from the land and a storm was rising. The waves were starting to slam against our boat. Then came another astounding, breath taking miracle of God.

In the fourth watch of the night, just before dawn the next morning, Jesus walked on the seawater! When we first saw him walking on the sea, as we thought what we saw was a ghost! Many of us cried in fear. But immediately, Jesus spoke to us, saying, **"Fear not, take heart. It is I, Jesus.** Do not be afraid."

One of us answered, "Lord, if it is you, command me to come to you on the water and I will follow you!"

He said, **"Come!"**

The journeyer got out of the boat and walked on the water and went over toward Jesus. But when the journeyer saw the wind and the rushing waves beating against him, he was afraid, and he began to cry out, "Lord, please save me!" When he cried out for Jesus to help him, Jesus immediately reached his hand and took hold of him, saying to him, "**O you of little faith, why did you doubt you could walk on water as I am?"**

Throughout this journey, Jesus tried to teach us to have faith, that we could do everything he did, and even more, if we would just keep our faith by keeping our eyes on him and not the waves (our hurts, bad habits, hang-ups, and addictions). When Jesus and the journeyers got into the boat, the wind ceased, and all of us in the boat fell to our knees and worshiped Jesus, saying, "Truly, you are the Son of God."

Jesus said to us, "**Be alert! We will soon be landing at the town of Gennesaret. When this boat docks there, most of you will depart and return to your homes. It is now, that I will continue my journey with other** journeyers."

Summary of the Twelfth Day
What We Learned

At the end of the twelfth day, we learned that because we have had a spiritual experience as a result of our journey with Jesus himself, we will

1. carry the message of this journey and recovery to others and
2. practice the way of Christ, the principles, and practices we learned on this journey to the core of our souls in all our affairs.

We also learned about how we can yield to God, having an ACTION plan, how RECOVERY helps us avoid barriers. We learned how to be servant leaders, how to heal and deliver others, how to walk on water and do even greater things than Jesus did!

This reminded me of the words in Galatians 6:1–6, paraphrased:

> **Brothers and sisters, if anyone is caught in any transgression or infected by the yeast of the Pharisees, you who are spiritual, who have become children of God and have recovered from your hurts, bad habits, hangups, and bad addictions should gently restore him or her. However, be careful and be mindful of your own stink'n' think'n' that was in your past. Therefore, lest you too be tempted, stay close to your guide as you guide others. Do not guide unless you are under the authority of your guide.**
>
> **By going through recovery, (recovery is a process all God's children need to do to facilitate, with God's help, their own transformation), and by volunteering and guiding another journeyer on their journey to the center of their soul. You can bear one another's burdens and so fulfill the law of Christ. This is the way of**

Christ. This is also the way Church was supposed to be and look like.

Remember, if anyone thinks he or she is something more special than anyone else, particularly those they are guiding, then they have caught a yeast infection—a pride that I call the yeast of the Pharisees. Don't forget your past, how humbly you came to recovery. Don't deceive yourself by being prideful as if you didn't need the power of God when everything else you tried didn't work, didn't have enough power. Don't forget, your guide will help your memory.

Remember, we do not take this journey or become a guide to "fix" one another. This is not our way. The fixing is between God and the journeyer alone.

Do not judge anyone else's work or progress just be there to help and guide them if they ask. Instead, let each of you focus and test only your own work and your own "day by day, one day at a time" progress, and then your reason to boast will be in the power of God working in you and in how you finally yielded to him and are following his way. In this way, you will be bearing your own load and burdens and not bearing another's.

Then Jesus said his last words to us, on this particular journey to the center of our souls with him.

Congratulations on finishing your journey to the center of the soul with me! You have done well, and I'm proud of you! Remember to celebrate when you get home and have a celebration party together to summarize and congratulate each other.

> **Carry the knowledge of this journey to the center of the soul on to others. Do not discriminate. Instead, spend time with everyone and love everyone as I have loved you. Do the best you can; you will get better at it in time. Remember, I, God the Father, and God's Holy Spirit will always be with you, good and faithful servants.**

As I teared up thinking that the journey with Jesus himself was over and knowing how much I would miss him, I remembered he said he would be with me always, and I remembered a song by one of our modern-day Psalmist groups called Hillsong. The song is called "Oceans, Where Feet May Fail."

> You call me out upon the waters, the great unknown where feet may fail. And there I find you in the mystery, in oceans deep, my faith will stand.
>
> And I will call upon your name and keep my eyes above the waves, when oceans rise. My soul will rest in your embrace, when I am yours, and you are mine.
>
> Your grace abounds in deepest waters. Your sovereign hand will be my guide. Where feet may fail and fear surrounds me. You've never failed and you won't fail now.
>
> And I will call upon your name and keep my eyes above the waves, when oceans rise. My soul will rest in your embrace, when I am yours and you are mine.
>
> Spirit, lead me where my trust is without borders. Let me walk upon the waters wherever you would call me. Take me deeper than my feet could ever wander, and my faith will be made stronger, in the presence of my Savior.

> I will call upon your Name. Keep my eyes above the waves. My soul will rest in your embrace, for I am yours and you are mine.

Then Jesus lifted his arms up toward heaven and moved his hands over us as he said,

> **To my fellow journeyers, as this part of our journey ends, my prayer for you is this:**
>
> **May God continue to fill you with His Holy Spirit and all the gifting he has planned for you to overflowing so you and others may be built up (edified).**
>
> **As God places his full armor about you each day,**
>
> > **His shoes of peace so you can walk, step by step, in the power of God's peace;**
> >
> > **His belt of truth around your waist to gird you up with God's truth not man's truth;**
> >
> > **His breastplate of righteousness, the righteousness of God and God alone;**
> >
> > **His crown to remind you to keep every thought captive for God;**
> >
> > **His sword, the Word of God in one hand, that divides truth from lies and cuts to the very core of your beings;**
> >
> > **His mighty shield of faith in the other hand that thwarts the flaming lies (arrows) of the evil one and helps you to break through barriers of doubt or fear.**
> >
> > **His teaching you, through me, how to pray at all times and on all occasions without ceasing. In addition,**

> **His bloodstained robes of righteousness—Jesus, always covering you, marking you as children of God.**

May he also place his warring angels about you to do battle for you in every moment of every day, and his ministering angels about you to serve you. May God's Spirit go before you wherever you go so that people will find favor with you at all times.

I bless you with this and more, with God's love and my love for you forever and ever. Amen.

—Dr. G

The Eight Principles Learned
Through the Days of Journeying with Jesus

Principle 1:

- *Realize* there is a God, and it's not you or them; realize you were powerless to control your tendency to do the wrong thing and that your lives were unmanageable.

Matthew 5:3 (OTB), amplified: "Blessed are those who know they are spiritually poor, for theirs is the kingdom of heaven."

Principle 2:

- *Earnestly* believe that God exists, that you matter to God and that God has the power to help you fully recover.

Matthew 5:8 (OTB), amplified: "Blessed are the pure in heart, for they shall see God."

Principle 3:

- *Consciously* choose to commit their wills (this is key) and the rest of their lives over to the care of God and Jesus.

Matthew 5:5 (OTB), amplified: "Blessed are those who do the will of God, the meek like Jesus, not the weak, for they shall inherit the earth."

Principle 4:

- *Openly self-examine* and especially be willing to *confess* your hurts, bad habits, hang ups, and bad addictions to each other because it keeps you accountable, to God, to yourself, and to your guide.

Matthew 5:4 and James 5:16 (OTB), amplified: "Blessed are those who mourn from the joy yet temporary pain of confession, for they shall be comforted and recovered… confess your hurts, bad habits, hang-ups, and addictions to one another and pray for one another, and you will be healed."

Principle 5:

- *Voluntarily submit* to every change God wants to make in your life as you continue to humbly ask God to remove your character defects.

Matthew 5: 6 (OTB), amplified: Blessed are those who hunger and thirst to follow God's Will and reflect His character, for they shall be satisfied."

Principle 6:

- *Evaluate* your relationships in your moral inventories and mercifully offer forgiveness, as Jesus has also forgiven you, to those who have hurt you. Make peace by making amends with those whom you have harmed, except when it may be harmful to you or others.

Matthew 5:7 and 5:9 (OTB), amplified: "Blessed are the merciful, for they shall receive mercy. Blessed are the peacemakers, for they shall be called children of God."

Principle 7:

- *Reserve* a daily time to be with God, for communicating in prayer and especially listening to God, always asking him to examine you and lead you in his ways of righteousness. Ask God specifically to show you his will for your life and to give you his power to follow his will.

Matthew 5:12 (OTB), amplified: "Rejoice and be glad, for your reward for following God is great in heaven, they persecuted the prophets and Jesus, who were before you, for their obedience to God and they, even the church and its leaders, like in these times, will persecute you as well. Nevertheless, rejoice!"

Principle 8:

- *Yield* yourselves to God and communicate good news of a journey of recovery to others. Bring this particular good news by word, by volunteer service, by life example and by leading them through their personal journey.

Matthew 5:13–16 (OTB), amplified: "You are the salt of the earth… You are the light of the world. A light set on a hill cannot be hidden. Nor do people light a lamp and put it under a basket, but on a stand, and it gives light to all in the house therefore, give your light, your knowledge of this journey of recovery, your words, your volunteer service and your personal testimonies. In the same way, let your light shine before others, so they may see your good deeds, service, recovery and your testimonies; glorify your Father who is in heaven."

References

The Thompson Chain-Reference Bible, New International Version, (TCRB)
The Olive Tree Bible (OTB)
The Learning Bible (TLB)
The GNB bible
The NCV Bible
Serenity Prayer by Reinhold Niebuhr
Modern Day Psalmists: HillSong
Note: Alcoholics Anonymous (The Big Blue Book & Material)
Celia Taghdiri was a contributing editor for this book:
Celebrate Recovery 12 Step and other material.

Tools

Moral Inventory Sheet
Negative vs. Positive Balance Sheet (See pg. 29 of book 2 Participants guide).
Participant's Guides (4) by John Baker. Forward/Edited by Rick Warren

Attachments

Group Guidelines
Guide Guidelines
Guide to Moral Inventory and Moral Inventory Sheets

NOTES

It is Very Important that Facilitators and other and all leadership positions are shared (pairs) and always rotated! In that way, new people are always learning how to lead (for growth) and no one person starts feeling like they know it all or they are better at it than someone else (the yeast of the Pharisees).

Journey to the Center of the Soul (JCS) Facilitator Guide

How the Book (JCS) Works

Your initial larger combined (men and women) group time will usually be between thirty to forty-five minutes consisting of a check in, singing (worship), announcements, testimonies (from those who have already made the *Journey to the Center of the Soul*, a lesson plan (from one of the days of the *Journey to the Center of the Soul*, and an offering, etc. The initial larger combined group time can be combined with both men and women. This journey to the center of the soul with Jesus will only work if the groups are separated by gender from each larger small group meeting. The worship and fellowship time can be combined at the beginning, but not during the journey to the center of the soul with Jesus. The separate female/male group's smaller groups will be working through *Journey to the Center of the Soul* with Jesus and a group facilitator/leader(s) of the same group sex.

Since small groups usually meet in a home, the women should go into one room (far enough so the men cannot hear them), and the men into a separate room (also far enough for the women not to hear). Sharing is always deeper and more effective when people are grouped by gender, and the personal bonding should be men-to-men and women-to-women. If the small group is meeting in a church, then different church rooms should work well.

When both groups have reached halfway, maybe the sixth day of their journey with Jesus, they may want to hold a halfway potluck celebration. The women-only and men-only potluck should take place separately so more same-sex bonding can take place.

When both groups have completed the book *Journey to the Center of the Soul* and journey with Jesus, we suggest you celebrate with a combined potluck, worship, and celebrative singing (worship) with the leader(s) speaking, some of the new journeyers speaking, and a testimony or two, including a celebration cake! It will be quite exciting!

Purpose of Recovery

The church (universal) often sends a person on a mission with little or no healing or they focus on training only and teaching only practical things, without concern for their spiritual health or spiritual maturity. After all, we were once in the world, and most, if not all of us, have been damaged and/or have thought stinkin' thinkin' because of the world. Our minds and especially our spirits are in need of recovery. We need to be cleansed and straightened out; we need to recover before we try to function in our world again and try out our new spiritual reality of Christianity.

My prayer is, "heal us, Lord, recover us from ourselves, as you continue to teach us your ways and equip us for ministry as we mature in you."

The fire that once burned bright will relight. I guarantee it. Your family will appreciate your commitment to this journey. Your larger group leader, some refer to her or him as a pastor, will especially appreciate it and will be surprised at your newfound fired-up willingness to give, to serve and to seek out your personal gifting and ministry.

Facilitator's Summary
The Twelve Days and Their Biblical Comparisons

Summary of the First Day

At the end of the first day, we quit denying reality and instead realized we were powerless over our bad habits, hurts, hang-ups, and bad addictions and that our lives had become unmanageable.

We were also encouraged not to fear and about the acronym DENIAL, what our focus is, and that we are not to try and fix anyone but ourselves. We learned about self-examination. We promised each other to keep anonymity (secrecy, concealment, faceless). What's seen here and said here stays here, …here, here!" and we began to bond with each other.

This reminded me of Romans 7:18–21 (OTB) paraphrased: "For I know that I am damaged, like everyone else, and thereby evil can dwell in my flesh. For, as I grow in Christ, I have the desire to do what is good and right, but not always the ability to always carry it out. Instead, there are times when I do not do the good I want, but instead, the evil I do not want is what I keep on doing. I do this evil because of the sin that still dwells within my mind and, with time and without correction, will dwell in my heart; This conundrum is the law of things, my sin nature, that when I want to do right, evil, prompted by my hurts, habits, hang-ups, and bad addictions, lie close at hand within me to try and persuade me to do what is wrong again."

Summary of the Second Day

At the end of the second day, we realized that a power greater than ourselves, God and God alone, could restore us to sanity (as God had intended). We admitted that we are powerless to recover independently, and only God has the power to help us recover from our hurts, bad habits, hang-ups, and bad addictions and restore us to sanity.

We also learned about POWERLESS through the acronym about pride and our past, about resentments and loneliness, and about getting close to God. We learned about the acronym HOPE and SANITY and about the power of prayer (spending time with God).

Then I remembered the words in Philippians 2:12–13 (OTB) paraphrased: "Therefore, my beloved… not only as in my presence but more so in my absence, work out your recovery, with fear and trembling. It's hard, but I will give you the power to do it. It is I who works in you, both to will and to work for my good pleasure."

Summary of the Third Day

At the end of the third day, we realized how important it was for us to always turn our personal wills over to the care and rule of God.

We also learned about our wills, the definition of *sanity*, realistic expectations, our reconciliation, and what it's like to follow Jesus.

This reminded me of the words in Romans 12:1 (OTB), paraphrased: **"I urge you, brothers and sisters, by the mercies of God and for the sake of others and yourselves, to present your bodies, personal wills and spirits as a living sacrifice, holy and acceptable to God, which is your spiritual act of worship."**

Summary of the Fourth Day

At the end of the fourth day, we learned to make a fearless, honest, and soul-baring Moral Inventory of ourselves and that we can revise your Moral Inventory list as often as needed.

We also learned about surrendering our wills to God, and about the importance of repenting, (turning 180 degrees the other way) believing by faith alone. In addition, we learned about the yeast of the Pharisees, a strong BASE from which to work out our recovery, and if we get stuck, getting unstuck is by taking ACTION.

This reminded me of the words in Lamentation 3:40–42 (OTB): "Let us test and examine our ways, and return to the Lord!"

Summary of the Fifth Day

At the end of the fifth day, you learned how important it was to admit to God, to yourselves, to your guides and/or a trusted friend the exact nature of your wrongs. Then you learned to ask for our guide's or friend's guidance and ask them to to pray for you.

We also learned about living one day at a time, about the anointing, our guides and guidelines, our moral inventories, and the be-attitudes.

I remembered one of my most favorite scriptures in James 5:15–16 (OTB), paraphrased: **"And the prayer of faith will help you recover, and the Lord will raise you up. And if you have any hurts, bad habits, hang-ups, or bad addictions, you will be forgiven and set free of these things that you struggle over. Therefore, just confess your hurts, bad habits, hang-ups, and bad addictions to one another and pray for one another so that you may recover, be healed, and be set free."**

Summary of the Sixth Day

At the end of the sixth day, we were reminded to always request from God to remove all of our character defects and be ready to have God remove your hurts, bad habits, hang-ups, and bad addictions.

We also learned about how to complete a Moral Inventory form, being accountable and creating a check-in list, how to be a guide, also four important things to remember with your guides. We also experienced another miracle! We also processed some personal stuff, did some personal goals, processed more personal stuff, and experienced more miracles and deliverances! We processed more personal stuff again and Jesus taught us a prayer to remember.

All this reminded me of the words in James 4:10 (OTB) paraphrased: **"Humble yourselves before the Lord; confess your hurts, hang ups, bad habits, and bad addictions; and receive prayer and the Lord will unshackle you from these things. The Lord will heal you, he will set you free and he will lift you up, and he will get you back on your feet and make you a new person—a different**

more mature, at peace, knowledgeable kind of person than you were before."

Summary of the Seventh Day

At the end of the seventh day, we are reminded to be humble (modest, meek) and always be willing to ask God to help you remove any of your shortcomings (weaknesses, flaws, inadequacies), and any of your future hurts, bad habits, hang-ups, and bad addictions which you will encounter in the future.

It's important for us to remember that God wants us to have good addictions, such as time with him, time in his Word, servant-hood volunteer, and being addicted to the fellowship of his Church (the people of God).

We also learned about our minds, we did more processing, we learned about giving back, and we sailed with Jesus! We also experienced more miracles, processed more stuff, witnessed deliverance and healing, processed more stuff again, learned about CONFESS, and we chose a guide. We faced the truth, stopped the blame, and eased the pain. We learned why we need to confess and that we are already healed, and then we learned to be READY.

I was reminded of the words in 1 John 1:9–10 (OTB), paraphrased: **"If we confess our hurts, bad habits, hang-ups, and bad addictions, God is faithful and just to forgive us, our hurts, bad habits, hang-ups, and bad addictions, and God will cleanse us from all of these things. But remember this, if we say we have no sins, no hurts, bad habits, hang-ups, and bad addictions, we make God a liar for all have sinned and come short of the glory of God, and if we say we have no sins [no hurts, bad habits, hang ups or bad addictions], God's Word is not in us, and we cannot have fellowship with God."**

Summary of the Eighth Day

At the end of the eighth day, we learned how important it is to make and maintain a current and personal Moral Inventory list.

That means we need to keep adding to it as time passes. We are also reminded to, as prompt as possible, make amends and forgive others and keep our Moral Inventory list current so we do not fall back into our bondage of hurts, bad habits, hang-ups, or bad addictions.

We also learned about the term "easy does it" and what it means, about renewing our minds and making changes. We were assured that God can deliver us, and we learned about VICTORY. We experienced another miracle and encountered the yeast of the Pharisees again that Jesus warned us about.

We learned about grace and reflected on the sermon on the mount in the context of recovery. We learned the "Serenity Prayer" and witnessed deliverance. We understood that recovery is a process, not perfection, and we had a deeper understanding of AMENDS and the three main areas of amends. We learned of promises made to us, that our group is a safe place, and we had a deeper understanding of forgiveness, especially in the context of sexual abuse. We processed much more stuff and we talked about balloons!

I was reminded of the verse in Luke 6:31 (OTB) paraphrased: **"Do [have an attitude toward, speak to, and treat] others as you would have others have an attitude toward, speak to and treat you, as well."**

Summary of the Ninth Day

This was a very long day. At the end of the ninth day, we learned how to make direct amends to people, whenever possible, except when to do so would injure them or others.

We also learned about GRACE, the yeast of the Pharisees, the eight principles of RECOVERY and the related BEATITUDES, the "Serenity Prayer," deliverance, and three key things to remember using the acronym TEN.

As I thought of amends I reflected on the book of Matthew 5:23–24 (OTB), paraphrased: "So if you are offering your gift [i.e., tithe, offering, your time, ministry, prayers, etc.] at the altar and there remember that your brother or sister has something against you, leave your gift there before the altar and go meet with your brother or sister who may have something against you and make amends. Do this so you can first be reconciled to your brother or sister, and then come back to the altar of God and offer your gift."

Summary of the Tenth Day

At the end of the tenth day, we learned to continue to take personal inventory (Moral Inventory) of ourselves and when we discover our errors, where we were wrong, that we promptly admitted it to ourselves, our God, and our guide.

We also learned that we need to always be ready and have a right attitude to make amends again and again. We learned to journalize, how to love, about our secrets and how they can make us sick, and more things about deliverance. We learned about the way of Christ and the importance of taking retreats. We also learned about the acronyms RELAPSE and HEART, and we learned about how important it is to always have an attitude of gratitude.

Constantly taking a personal inventory (Moral Inventory) on a regular basis keeps us from getting prideful (arrogant, overconfident, feeling better than someone else) as we mature in our personal recovery. Guarding ourselves from pride reminds me of the meaning behind the words in 1 Corinthians 10:12 (OTB) paraphrased: **"Let anyone who thinks that they got it now, or that they can stand on their own two feet without any help now, or that because they are a guide and therefore smarter than the one they are guiding, take heed or a pride (Phariseetical yeast) that can develop, lest you fall."**

Remember, pride always comes before the fall.

Summary of the Eleventh Day

At the end of the eleventh day, we learned to seek, through prayer and meditation to improve our personal relationship with God, praying only for knowledge of his will for me and the power for me to do his will.

We also learned about listening skills as we talk and especially listen to God. We learned about recovery tools, the importance of giving thank you(s), group importance, giving it back, the two greatest commandments, being a doer, and how no one is a prophet (receives honor, respect) in his own church or hometown.

All this reminded me of the words in Colossians 3:14–16 (OTB), paraphrased: **"And above all these put on the attitude of love for absolutely everyone without prejudice, even your enemies, and this kind of love will bind everything together in perfect harmony. Love lets the peace of Christ rule in your hearts, to which indeed you were all called to. And always be thankful to God, in all things, so as to let the Words and the way of Christ dwell in you richly, in addition, always teach and hold one another wisely accountable in all things."**

Summary of the Twelfth Day

At the end of the twelfth day, we learned that because we have had a spiritual experience as a result of our journey with Jesus himself, we will

1. carry the message of this journey and recovery to others and
2. practice the way of Christ, the principles, and practices we learned on this journey to the center of our souls in all our affairs.

We also learned about how we can yield to God, having an ACTION plan, how RECOVERY helps us avoid barriers, being a servant leader, and how to walk on water and even do greater things as Jesus told us we would do.

This reminded me of the words in Galatians 6:1-6, paraphrased:

> **Brothers and sisters, if anyone is caught in any transgression (infected by the yeast of the Pharisees), you who are spiritual, who have**

become children of God and have recovered from your hurts, bad habits, hang-ups, and bad addictions should gently restore him or her. However, be careful and be mindful of your own stink'n' think'n' that was in your past. Therefore, lest you too be tempted, stay close to your guide as you guide others. Do not guide unless you are under the authority of your guide.

By going through recovery, recovery is a process all God's children need to do to facilitate, with God's help, their own transformation, and by volunteering and guiding another journeyer on their journey to the center of their soul. You can pray for another's burdens and so fulfill the law of Christ. This is the way of Christ. This is also the way Church was supposed to be and look like.

Remember, if anyone thinks he or she is something more special than anyone else, particularly those they are guiding, then they have caught a yeast infection—a pride that I call the yeast of the Pharisees. Don't forget your past, how humbly you came to recovery. Don't deceive yourself by being prideful as if you didn't need the power of God when everything else you tried didn't work, didn't have enough power. Don't forget, your guide will help your memory.

Remember, we do not take this journey or become a guide to "fix" one another. This is not our way. The fixing is between God and the journeyer alone.

Do not judge anyone else's work or progress just be there to help and guide them if they ask. Instead, let each of you focus and test only your own work and your own "day by day, one day at a time" progress, and then your reason to boast will be in the power of God working in you and in how you finally yielded to him and are following his way. In this way, you will be bearing your own load and burdens and not bearing another's.

Forms and Guide to Filling them Out

The Journey to the Center of the Soul Moral Inventory Sheet

Page ____ of ____

COLUMN 1	COLUMN 2	COLUMN 3	COLUMN 4	COLUMN 5
THE PERSON	THE CAUSE	THE EFFECT	THE DAMAGE	MY PART
Who or what is the object of my resentment or fear?	What specific action did that person or entity takes that hurt me?	What effect did that action have on my life?	What damage did the person, cause, effect have on my a) basic social development b) feeling of security c) sexual instincts d) intimacy	What part of the resentment am I responsible for? a) Whom have I hurt? b) How did I hurt them?

Guide to Completing the Journey Moral Inventory Sheet

This *Journey* Moral Inventory sheet will help you to come out of denial and focus on reality, as you ask the Lord to help you recall any repressed events.

Remember, you are not alone. There are others in your group for you to converse with, including your guide because you have all sworn anonymity (secrecy, private, concealment). Working with others, your guide and especially with God, helps you develop a stronger relationship with God and others throughout this journey with Jesus.

As you can see, the *Journey* Moral Inventory sheet (see above) is divided into five sections. Completing each section helps you stay focused on reality while helping you recall events you may have repressed over time.

Note: if you run into a writer's block, please meet with your guide for assistance. It will take you more than one sheet to write or type your *Journey* Moral Inventory. Therefore, make as many copies as you need.

Column 1—The Person

In this column, you will list the person or entity (organization, etc.) that you resent, fear, and have anger toward. Reflect as far back into your past as you can. Remember, resentment is mostly unexpressed anger or fear.

In Ephesians 4:31, (OTB), paraphrased, we read, "Get rid of all bitterness, wrath, resentment, anger, rumors, and slander. Put these thoughts and actions away from you, along with all hatred and jealously. Instead, forgive one another, as God in Christ continues to forgive you."

Column 2—The Cause

It has been said, it is only hurt people that hurt people. Consider that next time you are hurt or you hurt someone else. What and where is the hurt?

In this column, please specify the actions that someone or something did to hurt you. What exactly did this person or entity do to cause you to feel resentment and/or fear (i.e., an alcoholic father who was emotionally unavailable to you as you were growing up, a codependent parent who tried to control and dominate your life)?

Note: completing this column can be emotionally painful so you may have to work on this with your guide. Certainly, your guide will take time to review your Moral Inventory work sheet and may suggest some revisions.

In Isaiah 41:10 (OTB), paraphrased, we read, "Fear not, I love you so I am with you. Do not be frightened or overwhelmed, for I am your God and will strengthen you and help you. I will also support you and defend you with my blameless and compassionate right hand."

Column 3—The Effect

In this column, describe the specific affect (the hurtful action) from someone or something. List the effects it has had on your past and present.

Column 4—The Damage

Which of your basic instincts were damaged or injured?

a) Were your social relationships damaged (i.e., slander, gossip, lies)?
b) Was your security damaged (i.e., physical or verbal abuse, financial loss)?
c) Were you damaged sexually (i.e., rape, other sexually abusive relationship)?

d) Was your ability to have intimacy damaged (verbal or physical abuse)?

Note: No matter how badly you have been hurt, no matter how lost you may feel, God, if you let him, will help you recover. He will restore you and even reinvent you. Just give him a chance.

In Ezekiel 34:16 (OTB), paraphrased, we read, "I will seek out the lost, bring back the strayed, and I will heal, restore and bind up the injured. I will strengthen you while you are weak… I will feed you justice."

Column 5—My Part

This section can be challenging for some of you. Humility can be tough to attain. Someday, when you conduct a deep and fearless Moral Inventory of yourself, you will realize all wrongs, all sins, all mistakes have already been forgiven.

When you're ready, ask yourself how much of the resentment, anger and fear of someone or something is my responsibility? Ask God to show you your part in a broken or damaged marriage, friendship, or other relationship whether it's family or other type of relationship. Ask God to show you your part in a broken or damaged relationship with a child, a parent, other family member, or colleague. Identify the people or organizations you have hurt and how you have hurt them.

Read Psalm 1:39:23–24 (OTB), paraphrased: "Search me, O God, and know my heart! Try me and know my thoughts! And see if there are any dangerous, selfish or awful characteristics in me, and then lead me in the ways that are yours, oh Lord, in the way of everlasting peace, joy and abundance!"

Special Note: If you have been in an abusive relationship, especially as a youngster, you will discover great freedom in this part of the journey with Jesus. We can proclaim justice over you, claiming you had *no part* and *no responsibility* for of this kind of resentment, anger, or fear. In sections four and five, you can write "none" or "not guilty." Let yourself feel the freedom from the misplaced guilt and shame you have carried for many years as you renounce the lie that the abuse was your fault.

Special Note: In your *Journey* Moral Inventory, list both good things and the bad things so you can keep your inventory balanced (i.e., the good person, the good causes, the good effects, your part).

Balancing the Scales

Helplessness	"For it is God who works in you, both to will and to work for his good pleasure."
Dwelling on the past (i.e., PTSD)	"Therefore, if anyone is in Christ, he is a new creation. The old has passed away. Behold, the new has come."
Wanting	"And my God will supply every need of yours according to His riches in glory in Christ Jesus."
Loneliness	"Behold, I am with you always, to the end of the age."
Oppression, Trouble	"The Lord is a stronghold for the oppressed and the abused, a stronghold in times of trouble."
Fear, Doubt	"Be strong and courageous. Do not be frightened, and do not be discouraged, for I am with you wherever you go."
Melancholy, Apathy	Be thankful for the smallest of things. "This is the day that the Lord has made. I will rejoice and be glad in it!"
Worry	"Let God have all your worries and anxieties, because he can handle them and he loves and cares for you like no one else can."

Prayer of Serenity

Dear God,

I am so far from perfect, and I pray this prayer so often. Help me to focus on the special words in it. Words such as *serenity*, *courage*, *wisdom*, *acceptance*, *trusting*, *surrender*, and *happy*!

God, grant me the *serenity* to accept the things I cannot change, the *courage* to change the things I can, and the *wisdom* to know the difference.

Living *one day at a time*, enjoying one moment at a time, accepting hardship as the pathway to peace. Taking this sinful world as it *is*, not as you would have it. Trusting that he will make all things right *if* I surrender to his will, that I may be reasonably happy in this life, and supremely happy, with him, forever in the next. Amen.

By Reinhold Niebuhr

Attachments

Journey to the Center of the Soul
Small Group
Journeyer's Guidelines

The following *Journey* small group guidelines will ensure that your group is a "safe place" to share.

Very Important: Always share these guidelines at the beginning of *every Journey* small group meeting (as a reminder and for new participants).

Strong Suggestion: Close the entry of newcomers to the *Journey* small group once you start the third or fourth day of journey with Jesus so the group can bond. It is up to the facilitator and/or the group when the group closes its doors.

a) Keep your sharing focused on your personal thoughts and feelings.

b) Limit your total sharing to thirty minutes/number of people in the group (i.e., if six people in the group, then 30/6=5 min. ea.). The facilitator must use a timer to stop those who abuse the limitation. There will usually be one or two people who don't understand the selfishness of exceeding their time limit and cutting someone else's allotted time.

b) c) There is *no cross talk* allowed while during group sessions. Cross alk is when two or more individuals engage in conversation, excluding all others. Each pers*on must feel* free to express her/his feelings without interruption or judgment (judgment = praise, rating [whether it's a good or bad rating, it's still judgment] or criticism). Keep your comments to yourself because it may form judgment and divide the group.

c) We are not in group to "fix" one another but to support each other in our individual journeys with Christ. We can let God and each individual alone do the fixing, in their time and their way.

d) Anonymity (secrecy, privacy) and confidentiality (concealment) from even our spouses or significant others are a

> fundamental requirement for the success of the group. It provides a "safe place" and a "way to work" through recovery and to "bond" with one another.

What is shared in the group should always remain in the group. It is often said, "What's done here and said here stays here. Hear, hear?" and the group responds, "Hear, hear!"

The exception is if someone threatens to injure another individual or themselves. At this time, the group facilitator (leader) has a legal obligation to report it to whomever he/she is accountable to and to the authorities.

Swearing or any other kind of offensive language can often trigger the individual sharing, or another individual in the group, to act or speak more in kind or violently. Offensive language has no place in a journey with Christ recovery group.

A Facilitator's Guide to a Marketing Strategy and Guidelines

Days 1–30

1. Pray!
   a) "Pray continually" (1 Thessalonians 5:17).

2. Give the book *Journey to the Center of the Soul* to the pastor and staff to read. Let your pastor know your small groups want to use this book to bond and grow.
3. Ask the individuals who have already been on a twelve-day journey to pray and see if they are being called to be a part of this new ministry.

   "Pray at all times, with all kinds of prayer and appeal. To that end, keep alert and never give up praying" (Ephesians 6:18, OTB, paraphrased).

4. Recruit and interview potential facilitator(s).
5. Select your facilitator(s) before your first month.
6. Have the leaders read *Journey to the Center of the Soul.*
7. Determine meeting date, time, and the possible location(s), for the journey with Jesus.
8. Ask one of your leaders to create an Excel sign-up sheet with name, mobile telephone number, e-mail (for notices), etc. Make copies to be placed later in specific spots.
9. Ask one of your leaders to be in charge of the *Journey* book, *Journey* small group information, and sign-up sheet table.
10. Ask another one of your leaders to oversee working (advertising) with the local media.
11. Ask your leaders if anyone has finished the book *Journey to the Center of the Soul* or have completed a similar type of journey. Ask the leaders who have finished their journey that at some time in the future, if they would be willing

to give a five- to eight-minute testimony of their recovery in a regular church service or organizational meeting. For those who volunteer, ask them, at the end of their testimony, to personally invite others to a *Journey* small group meeting or to register on the sign-up sheet.

I pray; Blessed be the God and Father of our Lord Jesus Christ, the Father of mercies and God of all recovery, who emotionally heals our affliction, so that we may be able to help those who are in need of recovery, with the knowledge we have been taught by Jesus".

As we share abundantly our hurts, bad habits, hang-ups, and bad addictions and how God has helped us to recover, it is for other's comfort in knowing that recovery, as is God's salvation, is at hand. We attest to our recovery, it is for your comfort, which you experience when you patiently endure the same kind of hurts, bad habit, hang-ups, and bad addictions that we suffer. Our hope for you is unshaken, for we know that as you hear our testimonies and identify with any of our hurts, bad habits, hang-ups, and bad addictions, you will also share in our comfort that recovery is at hand as you journey to the center of your soul. (2 Corinthians 1:4, OTB, paraphrased)

12. Spread the word. If you're in a church or any existing small group, it must have a pastor or other organizational leader's support:

    a) Ask the pastor or leader to make pulpit or other similar group announcements of the new book *Journey to the Center of the Soul* for sale online or at the bookstore. Ask your pastor or leader to announce your group's date, time, place, and location of sign-up sheets along with the person's name that is standing at the table/booth.

b) Ask the pastor or organizational leader if you can make bulletin inserts to inform the church or other organizational small groups that a twelve-day journey to the center of the soul is going to begin within the next few months.

13. Read the *Journey*'s "A Guide's/ Leader's Guidelines and the Journey Small Group Participant's Guidelines" so you become knowledgeable and comfortable with the program. This is my prayer for you:

a) your love will grow more and more and
b) you will have knowledge and understanding combined with love (Philippians 1:9)

Order a few of the books *Journey to the Center of the Soul* ahead of time for your new group participants.

Days 31–60

1. Plan for your initial *Journey* groups to be a mixture of different types of people with a variety of hurts, bad habits, hang-ups, or bad addictions. Eventually, you will be able to form *Journey* groups that are more specific to a particular hurt, bad habit, hang-up, or bad addiction (i.e., over eaters, codependents, rage-a-holics, pornography, adultery, rape, various different drug addicts, gamblers, and PTSD victims, just to mention a few.)

2. As you develop and grow, do not start with more than two different kinds of separate groups. For example:

a) men's chemically dependent, women's chemically dependent and
b) men's codependent and women's codependent groups

Days 61–90

1. Meet weekly with your new facilitator's leadership team. Slowly work through the days of the book *Journey to the Center of the Soul* as you also manage the planning, organizing, marketing, and implementing *Journey* groups.
2. Make weekly announcements to the church or groups of the *Journey* small group kick off date, time, place, and location of sign-up sheets.
3. Display the books for sale and other *Journey* small group information, including the sign-up sheets on information tables at church services or at other group meeting sites.
4. Ask for continued pulpit and other leadership announcements to show that leaders are supporting this effort of recovery and approve of this particular journey to the center of the soul small group.

Just as Important: This will substantiate for everyone that your church or organization is a safe place to confront his or her own hurts, hang-ups, bad habits, and bad addictions so they can have a chance to recover and continue their lives.

5. Again, order enough *Journey to the Center of the Soul* books for leaders, facilitators, and *Journey* small group participants, at least three weeks prior to your first meeting.
6. Inform local Christian therapists and use local newspapers, social media (i.e., Facebook, Twitter) to invite the community to purchase the book *Journey to the Center of the Soul.* Also, invite them to sign up and attend any of the church or other organization of *Journey* small groups beginning, including yours (give them address, date, time, specific place, phone numbers, etc.). Make sure they know *they don't have to be a church or organizational attendee to be a part of this journey small group, neither are they obliged to join the church or small group at any time.*

7. Pray! “Pray continually” (1 Thessalonians 5:17).

Journey to the Center of the Soul continues to be a venue for all people, Christian or non-Christian, to work through their personal recovery.

A Facilitator's Guide to the Meaning of the Twelve-Day Journey to the Center of the Soul with Jesus

The twelve days of *Journey to the Center of the Soul* is both a spiritual and a practical journey with Jesus himself. On this journey, you will witness and experience miracles, be given spiritual insights, some practical tools, principles, and values for your personal recovery and the recovery of others. Such miracles, spiritual insights and practical tools have the ability to free people from old habits, hang-ups, bad habits, and bad addictions. Recovery and an end to suffering is at hand.

The guidance provided in this book *Journey to the Center of the Soul* will empower (endow, invest, enable) people from various cultures, races, religions, or no religion. *Journey to the Center of the Soul* will transform the lives of millions of people throughout the world, and has been translated into many different languages.

Why It May Not Work for Some

The barriers against the powerful teachings in this book are

1. a closed mind and personal *will*;
2. an unwillingness to complete the work or share with your guide or other journeyers;
3. an inability to be honest with themselves or others (ego interference), especially a yeast infection (the yeast of the Pharisees was jealously, envy, hatred, anger, selfish ambition).

Very Important: Do not let the words *God*, *Jesus*, *Spirit*, or references to God's words in the Bible deter you or any of the attendees from working through each day of the twelve days of your personal *Journey to the Center of the Soul* book. Recovery will bring back joy and glad tidings. It may save your life and their lives.

The book *Journey to the Center of the Soul* will repeatedly use the words associated with God each day of the journey. Some readers may agree that even the thought of a God is powerful, even if it is only a concept to some. Let's face it, if you were drowning and if someone were to throw out a life vest, you would probably grab it, even if the word *God* was written everywhere on the life vest!

We are asking agnostics, atheists, and those of alternative lifestyles to please complete the book in some type of group setting (just need two or more people) and not to quit. Even without any trust or faith, these individuals will benefit from the *Journey to the Center of the Soul.*

How to Start Each Day

Facilitators (leaders) should introduce themselves and simply state what they are recovering from, then the person next to you should do the same.

Let the attendees know they will experience a spiritual and practical plan of daily action to remove the compulsions associated with suffering from past hurts, bad habits, hang-ups, and bad addictions. In the process, participants will live a life of recovery and experience incredible happiness, peace, clarity of mind, and a probable personal reinvention of yourself by God.

Judging from our experience, this process works best when the attendee and their guide participate in the *Journey* group meetings together. If you don't have a guide or the guide is not attending, ask someone in attendance to work with you as your accountability partner during this journey.

Very Important: Don't let any journeyer try this journey to the center of my soul without a guide or accountability partner.

The leader says,

1. Those in attendance that have already experienced this journey and would like to volunteer as a temporary accountability partner, please raise your hand.
2. Whoever does not have a guide and needs a temporary accountability partner, please stand.
3. Match them either, men with men or women with women.

After this first session, guides and interim accountability partners should telephone and/or visit their specific attendees frequently to see how he/she is doing and offer encouragement and assistance with the work ahead—particularly with daily issues and guidance.

Before you begin, say something like, "Let us have a moment of silence to invite the God of our understanding into our hearts, and ask for an open mind and the willingness to have a new experience."

Follow this by quoting the "Serenity Prayer," then read the book's introduction and the *Journey* small group's guidelines. Next, proceed with the beginning of the book *Journey to the Center of the Soul.*

End each group meeting by standing, holding each other's hands and saying the following prayer:

> Our father, who art in heaven hallowed is Thy name. Thy kingdom come, Thy will be done on earth as it is in heaven. Give us this day our daily bread and forgive us our trespasses as we forgive those who trespass against us. Lead us not into temptation, but deliver us from evil. For thine are the kingdom, the power, and the glory forever and ever. Amen.

Keep coming back. It works if you work it, it won't if you don't. Let's begin our journey every day, one day at a time.

Special Notes to the Facilitator

No words can describe the loneliness and despair I found in the bitter morass of self-pity, shame, and embarrassment. It was like quicksand stretched around me in all directions, and I had met my match. I was surrounded and overwhelmed by my own hurts and/or bad habits, hang-ups, or bad addictions. I had no hope.

Those who are non-Christians, atheists, or agnostics may need to ask themselves the following question: "Do I believe, or am I willing to believe, there is a power greater than myself?"

Participants will experience that as soon as they can say they do believe there is a power greater than themselves, they are on the road to recovery (as the song goes). I have personally experienced that upon this simple foundational belief: "Seeing is not believing; believing is seeing"—a wonderfully effective spiritual and practical miracle of recovery can and will be experienced.

Most will become aware that a power greater than ourselves is the essence of a spiritual and practical experience as we proceed on our twelve days of journey to the center of the soul. The more religious or spiritual journeyers call it God-consciousness.

Inform the journeyers, at some point, if they honestly confront their hurts, bad habits, hang-ups, or bad addictions, recovery will result, provided they do not close their minds to all this book offers. A person can only be defeated by an attitude of intolerance, willfulness, or belligerent denial.

I find that most people will not have difficulty with the spirituality of the book *Journey to the Center of the Soul* because it's not religious. It's only spiritual, thank God. We don't need another religion or to promote an existing religion. Focusing on an individual's recovery of his/her soul and the strengthening of the individual's spirit is *not* religious.

An attendee's willingness, honesty, and open-mindedness are key essentials on this journey with Jesus for completing the work and attaining recovery. But the following are also indispensable:

1) believe or willing to believe that, with help, they will recover, and
2) that they remain steadfast to their personal conception of God, whatever that may be, to help them recover.

What is this *Journey to the Center of the Soul*? It's a tool to invite a miracle of healing called recovery. Yet its God-orchestrated elements and process are simple and practical. Although it can be emotionally difficult at times, it is not impossible to complete.

Circumstances made you, and those willing, to believe there had to be something other than yourselves that could help you. You humbly offered yourself to your Maker, as you conceived your Maker to be. When we grow closer to our Maker, our Maker grows closer to us and reveals their identity!

First, we have to admit, there is a God, and it is not me. ☺ Next, we realize we are better off turning our *will* over to God because we have witnessed what our *will* has done for us or maybe I should say, to us.

Then, at some point, we will realize most good ideas are simple and, along with other simple concepts, comprise the cornerstones to the individual recovery of our souls. If we have the appropriate attitude and complete the assigned tasks, we will experience a spiritual portal at some time on our journey. As a result, we will navigate into a lifetime of freedom and the recovery of our souls.

You and others are launching into a twelve-day journey with Jesus and it will be exciting and vigorous. Let's remember an important factor: our hurts, bad habits, hang-ups, and bad addictions are but symptoms of causes and conditions that are buried deep in the center of our souls. *Journey to the Center of the Soul* will help us identify and solicit healing for the causes and conditions of our hurts, bad habits, hang-ups, and bad addictions.

On or about the Fifth Day with Jesus

On the day of their journey with Jesus, when group attendees begin working on their *Journey* Moral Inventory sheet, inform them it is not as difficult as they may think.

Note: For those of you who downloaded the *Journey* moral inventories and other *Journey* forms into your computer, tablet, or smart phones, just forward all the forms to everyone in your journey groups.

What we experienced, with our personal work on the *Journey* Moral Inventory, was just slightly embarrassing but quickly converted into relief and then joy, as most of us finally lifted the weight of our causes for the hurts, bad habits, hang-ups, and even bad addictions *off our shoulders*!

We witnessed the truth, confessed it, and let someone else pray for us to set us free! "The truth shall set you free." This is the spiritual portal that most will experience.

Leaders and facilitators will want to check-in with all the group's guides at least once a week to make sure all is well with the guides and the new attendees.

Before proceeding to day 6 on the journey, each individual should discuss his or her *Journey* Moral Inventory with their *Journey* guide or whomever they are accountable to in the *Journey* group.

Our goal is to confront, and get off our shoulders, the conditions causing our hurts, bad habits, hang-ups, and even bad addictions so we can stop whatever has been blocking us to grow spiritually and continue with the recovery of our souls.

What are these causes and conditions? There are numerous different words that have the same meaning. For example, mental traumas, abuses, rapes, stress, bigotry, jealousy, anger, or other wrongs directed toward us or we have done to another, usually manifest in hurts, hang-ups, bad habits, and bad addictions as they block our spiritual growth and disconnect us from our Creator and others.

Journey's personal Moral Inventory is much like a business inventory. When a business does not regularly conduct inventory, it usually goes broke. Taking commercial inventory is a fact-finding and a fact-facing process. It is an effort to discover the truth about our stock-in-trade. One method is to disclose damaged or un-sellable goods, to eliminate them promptly and without regret.

Special Note: If the owner of the business is to be successful, he/she cannot fool anyone about what is valuable enough to keep and what is not.

So when we conduct our personal *Journey* Moral Inventory, it is the equivalent of a commercial inventory of our lives. We will discover what has and has not been effective for us (our personal assets or damaged goods). We will learn what has been blocking our spiritual growth.

In our personal *Journey* Moral Inventory we take stock, if you will, of three manifestations of self-will:

1. our resentments, our fears, our conduct
    a. Resentment is the number one offender. It destroys more personal spiritual growth than anything else. From it stems spiritual disease, for we have been not only mentally and physically ill, but also spiritually sick. When the spiritual malady is overcome, we heal mentally and physically.
    b. Resentment basically means to refeel or feel again; it's a persistent feeling of ill will and suppressed anger caused by a sense of an injustice, injury, offense, or wrong done.

When coping with resentments, we identify them in our *Journey* Moral Inventory list. We list people, institutions, or principles with whom we were or still are angry with.

Remember, our self-esteem is how we view ourselves. Our pride is how we think others view us. Our ambitions are our plans for the future and our [emotional] security is our general sense of personal well-being.

We need to pray for the people we resent. Why? It's hard to be resentful of someone whom we are praying for. Also, praying will help us rid ourselves of such resentments. Harboring feelings of resentment inhibit our spiritual growth.

2. our fears
    a. When have we been selfish, dishonest, self-seeking, and frightened? Whom should we blame?
    b. Notice the word *fear* is a short word that somehow touches every aspect of our lives.

Fear can be classified with stealing. It steals our ability to spiritually grow. Fear robs us of our relationship with God, stealing any peace of mind, demobilizing, and causing many hurts, bad habits, hang-ups, and bad addictions.

Evaluate your fears thoroughly. Identify them on your *Journey* Moral Inventory list, even if there are no resentments in connection with them.

c. Ask yourself, why do we have these fears? Was it because self-reliance failed us? Self-reliance was good as far as it went, but it didn't go far enough. Some of us once had great self-confidence, but it didn't fully solve the fear problem or any other. When it made us cocky, it was even worse.

As you experience your twelve days with Jesus and work on your *Journey* Moral Inventory list, you will outgrow your fears.

Notice it's not that your fears disappear from your memory, you simply outgrow your fears. We outgrow fear by praying and relying on God. It's that simple!

3. our conduct

Time after time, newcomers have tried to keep to themselves certain facts about their lives as they try to avoid this humbling experience of making their personal *Journey* Moral Inventory and working through it with their guide.

Sometimes, they try shortcuts or easier methods and fail. They never completed their housecleaning (their personal *Journey* Moral Inventory) or never finished the work required. They sometimes take inventory but hang on to some of the worst items in their personal inventory stock (business inventory) and without transparency and confession; there is no healing of the soul. They cut themselves short of learning humility, fearlessness, and honesty and will fall short of the recovery of their souls.

a. We must be entirely honest with our guide, if we expect to recover our souls and live happily.
b. It's important to select a guide carefully with whom to take this intimate and confidential step of transparency and fearless honesty.

Special Note: It's okay to change guides at any time. Remind yourself that your individual recovery is more important than not trying to hurt a guide's feelings because you think you can work better with someone else. Your personal recovery is priority. Don't let anyone or anything stop you or block your recovery.

c. It is important for our guides to keep a confidence, fully understand and guide us through our recovery work. They should not try to fix us but instead guide us through this journey of recovery. The guide will help us decide if we are ready to give our personal testimony and provide a testimony template to help us construct our testimonies (see continuing pages).
d. Warning: This can be tough on our spouses, partners, or significant others. What we are about to do is renew ourselves at the very core of our souls. We pray they will hold on to us as we renew and recover in this personal life-changing mission, a journey to the center of the soul).

When people explain their journey, in this way, most spouses or significant others will be glad to help. They will be encouraged and, later, inspired by your confidence. Sometimes, however, they cannot adjust to our Journey and it can cause separation. So try to encourage them to go on the journey to the center of the soul with you, if not for any other reason than to understand what you are experiencing. If they choose not to participate, ask them to please hold on to you. Tell them, as Dave said in the movie a *Space Odyssey*, "Something wonderful is about to happen."

As we journey, we set aside our pride and illuminate every twist of character, every dark cranny of our past.

If we have the courage to let the truth set us free and are painstaking about this journey-to-the-center-of-the-soul phase of our personal development, we will be amazed by our spiritual growth before we are half way through.

We are going to discover a new freedom and a new happiness. We will not regret the past nor wish to shut the door on it. We will comprehend the word *serenity* and will know peace. No matter how far down the scale we have gone, we will see how our experience will benefit others. Uselessness and self-pity will disappear.

We will lose interest in selfish things and gain interest in our fellow neighbors. Self-seeking will slip away. Our attitude and outlook upon life will alter. Fear of people and of economic insecurity will leave us.

We will intuitively know how to handle situations that once baffled us. We will suddenly realize that God is doing for us what we could not do for ourselves. Are these extravagant promises? I think not. They are being fulfilled among us, sometimes quickly, sometimes slowly. They will always materialize if we strive at our journey to the center of the soul.

What a message of hope! It is almost beyond comprehension that all of these wonderful events will occur if we just make our amends to those whom we have harmed. But those things will happen—guaranteed!

The Prayer of Saint Francis and Dr. G

Lord, make me an instrument of thy peace. Where there is hatred, I will sow love. Where there is wrong, I may bring a rightness. Where there is discord, I might add harmony. Where there are lies, I may bring truth. Where there is doubt, I may bring hope. Where there is darkness, I may bring light. Where there is sadness, I may bring joy.

Lord, grant that I may seek to comfort others, as I have been comforted by you to give grace, patience; to understand others, as you have given grace and patience to me; to love, as you love me. For it is by the giving away of myself that I am finding myself. It is by my forgiving all others that I understand your forgiveness of me, and I awaken to the understanding of your kingdom being both at hand and eternal. Amen.

The Eight Parts of Myself

1. Self-esteem—how I think of myself.
2. Pride—how I think others view me; how I view myself.
3. Pocketbook—basic desire for money, property, possessions, financial security
4. Emotional security—general sense of personal well-being
5. Ambitions—my plans, wants, desires
6. Personal relations—our relationships with other people
7. Sex relations—basic drive for sexual intimacy
8. Fear inventory instructions

Before the end of your journey to the center of the soul small group meeting and prior to graduation, have your small group do a field study as part of their last day or two with Jesus, of their closest celebrate recovery open meeting at their local church or go to an Alcoholics Anonymous meeting. Have them meet at a coffee clutch, right after, as well as at the next *Journey* small group meeting and have them reflect with each other, their observations, and findings.

How to Write a Testimony

The following is a guide of how to write your journey to the center of the soul recovery testimony.

God's word tells us, "It is a proof of your faith. Many people will praise God because you obey the Good News of Christ—the gospel you believe—and because you freely share with them and with all others" (2 Corinthians 9:13, NCV).

Testimony guidelines:

1. Before you start writing, pray and ask God for help and the words to share.
2. Your testimony needs to be about twelve to fifteen minutes long. It needs to be written.
3. Be sure to include one or two of your favorite scriptures.
4. Be honest.
5. Remember that you are not cured, instead you are on your personal road of recovery.
6. Don't use religious clichés
7. Keep it short and to the point.

Have fun! You are giving your personal testimony of your road to recovery! Even if you are not ready to present your testimony, just putting it to paper will help your recovery process. The four major parts of a good testimony are listed on the following pages.

Answer each section, and you are well on your way to having your testimony written. Who knows, maybe after you have completed this process, you will want to present your testimony at a meeting someday.

Those who are either nervous or not eloquent in their speaking have given some of the most powerful testimonies. God accomplished great things with Paul (a murderer) and Moses (murderer with a speech impediment). Would God do no less with you?

Testimony Format

The Old Me

A. Start out with "Hi my name is ____. I am a believer who struggles with ______."
B. What was the insanity of my life before recovery?
C. How I got into recovery?
D. What are some of the circumstances that others could relate to?
E. How was my relationship with God?
F. How was my attitude with others?
G. What was my bottom (when you hit bottom)?
H. What changes did I experience while working through my journey?
I. What steps did I take to get into recovery?
J. How has my journey with Jesus Christ influenced my recovery?
K. How did completing the program help me? (Be specific.)
L. Did a single day or a particular day with Jesus, touch my heart in a special way?

The New Me

A. What changes has God made in my relationships with others?
B. What areas of my old life are gone and how have they changed?
C. How has my walk with God changed?
D. What are some of the great benefits that I have received from going on this Journey to the Center of the Soul (JCS) journey with Jesus Christ?

Outreach

A. How can I encourage a new potential journeyer?

Give Your Testimony Away Template

Matthew 14: And Jesus said, "Come." And when Peter came out of the ship, he walked on the water, to go to Jesus.

- Introduce yourself
- The old me before the journey to the center of the soul) recovery
- The real work
- Favorite scripture.
- One or more of my hurts, hang-ups, and bad habits, all my resentments, the cause, the person, the effect, the damage, and the all-important my part.
- My transformation
- Favorite scripture
- The continued work of recovery
- The new me
- Words of encouragement to others
- End

Just as important as our *Journey* Moral Inventory is our *Journey* Accomplishments helps us to always attain balance.

JOURNEY (To the Center of My Soul) Accomplishments Table

Age	Accomplishments	The problems or the objectives.	The solutions or method(s) used.	The skills, traits, qualities, special skills, character attributes or other characteristics that contributed to my success.

Notes

- Don't let anything interfere with your recovery.
    - not your guide (you can always switch guides)
    - not your group (bear with them until the journey is over)
    - not your spouse or significant other (sometimes growth will separate you and that's ok, you are both better off; You may end up getting back together, healthier, afterwards.)

- Continue to develop and expand your personal support team.
- Your next journey is to give away what you have received. Give away your journey of recovery by giving your personal testimony to others. Be a guide for others and/or facilitate (like Jesus) on your personal journey with new journeyers. Be of service (volunteer) for your church or other non-profit organization (i.e., veterans, homeless, seniors, pet rescue centers, public television, etc.). Just give it away, and I guarantee you will be blessed continuously.

Summary

The 12 Days On A Journey To The Center Of My Soul, With Jesus

Jesus said,

> Remember these next twelve things for the sake of others and yourselves:
>
> 1. *Humbly admit* to God that you are powerless over your hurts, habits, hang-ups, and addictions as you notice, or someone you love tells you your life is becoming unmanageable.

When Jesus said this, I remembered the words in Romans 7:18 (OTB), paraphrased: "For I know that nothing good dwells in my heart and mind, that is, in my flesh. For I have the desire to do what is right and good, but not the ability to implement, [unless I am in You and You are in me, oh God]. Admit that you are powerless to recover independently and only God has the power to help us recover and restore us to sanity.

Then I remembered the words in Philippians 2:12–13 (OTB), paraphrased: "Therefore, my beloved… not only as in my presence but more so in my absence, work out your recovery, with fear and trembling. It's hard, but I will give you the power to do it. It is I who works in you, both to will and to work for my good pleasure."

Always to turn your wills over to the care and rule of God.

This reminded me of the words in Romans 12:1 (OTB), paraphrased: "I urge you, brothers and sisters, by the mercies of God and for the sake of others and yourselves, to present your bodies, wills, and spirits as a living sacrifice, holy and acceptable to God, which is your spiritual act of worship."

Then Jesus said, "Make a fearless, honest, and soul-baring Moral Inventory of yourselves. Now that you have a form, you can revise your list, as often as needed."

This reminded me of the words in Lamentation 3:40–42 (OTB), paraphrased: "Let us test and examine our ways, and return to the Lord!"

Then Jesus said, "Admit to God, to yourselves, to your guide, and/or a trusted friend, the exact nature of your wrongs. Then ask for their guidance and prayers."

I remembered one of my most favorite scriptures in James 5:15–16 (OTB), paraphrased: "And the prayer of faith will help you recover… and the Lord will raise you up. And if you have any hurts, bad habits, hang-ups, or bad addictions, you will be forgiven and set free of these struggles. Therefore, just confess your hurts, bad habits, hang-ups, and bad addictions to one another and pray for one another, so you may recover, heal, and be set free."

Jesus went on to say, "Always request from God and be ready to have God remove your hurts, bad habits, hang-ups, and bad addictions."

This reminded me of the words in James 4:10 (OTB), paraphrased: "Humble yourselves before the Lord, confess and receive prayer, and he will unshackle you. He will heal you, he will set you free, and he will lift you and make you a new person."

Then Jesus said, "Be humble and always be willing to ask God to help you remove any of your future hurts, bad habits, hang-ups, and bad addictions which you may encounter. Remember God wants you to have good addictions such as, time with him, his Word, servant-hood, and the fellowship of his church."

I was reminded of the words in 1 John 1:9–10 (OTB), paraphrased: "If we confess our hurts, bad habits, hang-ups, and bad addictions, he is faithful and just to forgive us, our hurts, bad habits, hang-ups, and bad addictions, and he will cleanse us from all of these things. But remember this, if we say we have no sins, no hurts, bad habits, hang-ups, and bad addictions, we make God a liar, for all have sinned and come short of the glory of God, and if we say we have no sins, God's Word is not in us, and we cannot have fellowship with God."

Then Jesus said, "Remember to create a Moral Inventory list and to keep it current of all persons you have harmed and how you made amends or those who have harmed you and how you forgave them. Remember, do unto others as you would have them do unto you. Remember, when you are making amends or forgiving someone, which is done best doing face-to-face, that you be careful not to injure their mental or spiritual state. At first, rehearse your amends or forgiveness with your guide and when you make amends or forgive, remember to be kind and humble. Presume a reaction and don't react adversely to one, just do your part and move on.

This reminded me of the words in Colossians 3:12–15 (OTB), paraphrased: "As God's chosen ones, holy and beloved, put on compassionate hearts, kindness, humility, meekness, and patience, bearing with one another, and if one is hurt, angry, jealous, resentful, bitter, and speaks against another, then quickly forgive each other, making amends, as the Lord has forgiven you already, in the same manner you must also forgive. Above all, put on love, which binds everything together in perfect harmony. Let the peace of Christ rule in your hearts, to which indeed you were called into one body."

Then Jesus said, "As said before, remember to make and keep current a personal Moral Inventory list. Promptly as possible, make amends and forgive and keep your list current so you do not fall back."

I was reminded of the verse in 1 Corinthians 10:12 (OTB), paraphrased: "Therefore, let anyone who thinks that they 'got it,' they 'got this thing,' who thinks they are standing firm, or are fully recovered, and who thinks they don't need to keep current a Moral Inventory List or go to meetings—let them remember to take heed lest they fall back into their stink'n' think'n' old wills, ways, and patterns. No temptation has overtaken you that is not common to all of humanity. Someone has always been tempted in the same way. Just keep in mind that God is faithful, and he will not let you be tempted beyond your ability, but instead, with the temptation, God will also provide ways [meetings, recovery tools, people, etc.] of escaping that temptation, that you may be able to endure the temptation and recover."

Congratulations, journeyers!

Now travel throughout the world and give it away as you share the good news!

....

....

"Blessed are the poor in spirit, for theirs is the kingdom of heaven."

I have taken the first step in my journey to come closer to God because now I understand, and I admit that I am powerless to control my tendency to do the wrong thing and that my life is unmanageable without God. I guess I finally admit I am not God.

"NOTE FROM THE AUTHOR"

Part of my cultural DNA is that I'm also a '60s kid, raised with The Beatles, Janis Joplin, Joe Cocker, Jimmy Hendricks, Woody and Arlo Guthrie, Buffy Sainte-Marie, and more from that era.

As a result, I'm accustomed to shaking up the establishment a little with peaceful protest, written words, preaching, teaching, or playing music, whether the establishment is government leaders or religious leaders. I've always been willing to "be a fool for Jesus."

I have a testimony of how a functional drunk lived for over sixty years (since childhood) as an alcoholic and later a prescription drug addict who is now experiencing a fun, lifelong, spirit-powered personal recovery.

God, through others, Christians and non-Christians alike who were already in recovery, helped me journey to the center of my soul and discover my deep soulful pain and the root causes of my personal hurts, bad habits, hang-ups, and bad addictions.

God has also used others to help me take my own twelve days with Jesus, a journey to the center of the soul, similar to the twelve-step journey. Like most journeyers, I needed help to get through it; that's what the guides and others in the group are there for: God using people to help other people recover.

Thereby, I have finally forgiven God and many others; have made amends to many, many, many others; have rediscovered my personal faith in God. And in the process, God has reinvented me and still is reinventing me while in my lifelong recovery (transforming) journey with Jesus.

Why the nom de plume, Dr. G? Some friends call me the twentieth-century renaissance man, while other friends call me ET because I was born the same year that ETs were found at Roswell, New Mexico. But most of my friends just call me Dr. G, since it's shorter and easier to remember than my full name, degrees, and title, The Reverend Dr. G. L. Aldana, PhD (retired). See? ☺

I've been called Dr. G. for years now, so I'm used to Dr. G. It's now my official recovery nick name and nom de plume. My writer name too. ☺

> "I pray you enjoyed this journey to the Center of the Soul with Jesus. I join God in continuing to bless your continued journey of recovery for you and yours forever and ever, Amen.
>
> Your forever friend,
> Forever in His service and for His glory,
>
> Dr. G"

ABOUT THE AUTHOR

Dr. G
A 21st Century Renaissance man
"Carpe Diem"
(Seize the Day)

The (Retired) Rev. Dr. Gregory Leonard Aldana "Dr. G.", AA, BA, MA, MDiv, PhD. His newest degree of higher education is a JAD, which stands for "Just Another Drunk". Dr. G is grateful to be in his "rest of his life" recovery program; clean and sober now for over 3.9 years as of December, 2016.

Dr. G. was born in Sacramento, California and now lives with his wife Carol Aldana, their two dogs Sammy and Sophie (terrier mix and Schnauzer mix) rescue puppies in San Diego County, California. They say the puppies actually rescued them.

Greg's mother, Carolyn (92 years young) also lives in their home and Greg is her full time "care giver". Greg and Carol have two boys (from previous marriages) and four fantastic grandchildren, some from different marriages as well. They are a "Blended Family of Mixed breed", kinda like their rescue puppies.

Dr. G, often called a "21st Century Renaissance Man", while always an academic and usually in some kind of school, Dr. G has been a Rock Band promoter, a short order cook, a life guard, a military parts specialist, a rib iron worker, school bus driver, a Director of a Multi-Service social agency, a substitute teacher, Principal of a school, an Airplane contract specialist, a Top Secret Military Aero-Space support subcontract and contract administrator, a Chaplain, a Presbyterian PC-USA Minister of the Word and Sacrament, a church planter, a Non-Denominational Pastor, always a business owner and now a Writer only because of some power greater than himself, which he calls "The Grace of God".

Dr. G is currently the CEO co-principal of CGA COMMERCE, LLC- a Private Real Estate Investment Group at: www.cgacommerce.com. Dr. G is also a Recovery Ministry Leader, and a Worship Leader (singer/guitarist).